FEMINISMS AND DEVELOPMENT

Disrupting taken-for-granted assumptions, this expert series redefines issues at the heart of today's feminist contestations in a development context. Bringing together a formidable collective of thinkers from the Global South and the North, it explores what it is that can bring about positive changes in women's rights and realities.

These timely and topical collections reposition feminism within development studies, bringing into view substantial commonalities across the countries of the Global South that have so far gone unrecognized.

Series editor

Andrea Cornw

Forthcoming titles

Feminisms, Empowerment and Development:
Changing Women's Lives
Andrea Cornwall and Jenny Edwards

Changing Narratives of Sexuality:
Contestations, Compliance and Women's Empowerment
Charmaine Pereira

Women in Politics:
Gender, Power and Development
Maria Tadros

About the Editors

Sohela Nazneen is a professor of international relations at University of Dhaka and a lead researcher at the BRAC Development Institute, BRAC University, Bangladesh. She has a PhD in development studies from the Institute of Development Studies, University of Sussex. Her research focuses on institutional analysis of gender, particularly in the areas of governance, rural and urban livelihoods, and feminist movements. She is currently leading research on gender and political settlement in selected South Asian and sub-Saharan African countries for the Effective States and Inclusive Development RPC, based at the University of Manchester. Sohela has published many articles and book chapters in her subject areas.

Maheen Sultan is one of the founders of the Centre for Gender and Social Transformation at the BRAC Development Institute, BRAC University, a regional centre on research, teaching and policy related to gender and social transformation. She is a development practitioner with over 25 years' experience working for NGOs, donors, the UN, Grameen Bank and the Bangladeshi government in a range of capacities, from direct programme management to policy formulation. She has worked on issues of social development, poverty, civil society and community participation, and gender equality in various capacities – including a close engagement with government structures in the post-Beijing conference period when her work addressed gender mainstreaming and CEDAW reporting. Maheen is a member of Naripokkho, a Bangladeshi women's activist organization, a board member of Caritas Bangladesh and Utsho Bangladesh, and the chairperson of the ADB External Forum on Gender and Development. She co-edited *Mapping Women's Empowerment: Experiences from Bangladesh, India and Pakistan* (2009).

Voicing Demands

Feminist Activism in Transitional Contexts

edited by
Sohela Nazneen and Maheen Sultan

Zed Books
LONDON & NEW YORK

Voicing Demands: Feminist Activism in Transitional Contexts was first published in 2014 by Zed Books Ltd, 7 Cynthia Street, London N1 9JF, UK and Room 400, 175 Fifth Avenue, New York, NY 10010, USA

www.zedbooks.co.uk

Editorial copyright © Sohela Nazneen and Maheen Sultan 2014
Copyright in this collection © Zed Books 2014

The rights of Sohela Nazneen and Maheen Sultan to be identified as the editors of this work have been asserted by them in accordance with the Copyright, Designs and Patents Act, 1988

Designed and typeset in Monotype Bembo by Kate Kirkwood
Index by John Barker
Cover design: www.alice-marwick.co.uk

A catalogue record for this book is available from the British Library
Library of Congress Cataloging in Publication Data available

ISBN 978 1 78032 968 0 hb
ISBN 978 1 78032 967 3 pb

Contents

Acknowledgements

This book has evolved over three years. We are deeply indebted to our contributors as they stayed with us and engaged with our ideas enthusiastically over this time. Without Andrea Cornwall's initial idea and tireless persistence, the book would not have been written. We arranged a conference on 'feminist voice' at the Rockefeller Center in Bellagio, Italy, where the authors presented their first drafts in November 2009. We are indebted to the Rockefeller Center for hosting us. Our resource persons at this workshop – Sonia Alvarez, Adrian Leftwich and Maitrayee Mukhopadhyay – provided incisive comments and enriched our understanding. We were helped along by a host of brilliant scholars. Deniz Kandiyoti, Rema Hammami, Saba Gul Khattak, Rounaq Jahan, Zakia Salime, Amanda Gouws, Jussara Prá and Adrian Leftwich reviewed our country chapters and provided useful comments. Dzodzi Tsikata, Aurora Vergara Figueroa and Charmaine Pereira participated in the Bellagio conference and enriched our discussions. Initial discussions with John Gaventa, Peter Houtzager and Anne Marie Goetz during Sohela's stint as a visiting fellow at IDS, University of Sussex, pushed us to ask what this book might contribute to the wider political science, social movement and development policy literature. Shanti Mahendra and Jenny Edwards meticulously copy-edited the manuscript. We are grateful to our editor Kim Walker and the publishing team at Zed Books. We thank the University of

Dhaka for granting leave of absence to Sohela to take up her summer fellowship at IDS. We thank the BRAC Development Institute (BDI), BRAC University and the Pathways of Women's Empowerment Research Programme Consortium (funded by the UK Department for International Development, the Norwegian Ministry of Foreign Affairs and Sida) for creating space for this work. Our families – mothers, husbands, children (Maheen), nephews and nieces (Sohela), siblings and in-laws – provided invaluable support and were willing to forego our company at various times. This book is dedicated to our parents: our fathers, Muzaffer Ahmad and Muhammed Sultan, for nurturing our voices even when they were at times in disagreement with what the book has to say; and our mothers, Roushan Jahan and Ruby Sultan, for teaching us the value of having a voice.

Preface

Andrea Cornwall

Voicing Demands makes a unique contribution to a growing literature on women's movements and organizations in the global South. It brings to this literature use of an analytical lens that has been rarely applied to women's political engagement in the global South, that of 'voice'. Challenging assumptions about the positive relationship between voice, constituency building and empowerment, this book explores the political opportunities, strategies and impact of women's and feminist movements in diverse transitional contexts in Africa, Latin America, the Middle East and South Asia. Its approach is rooted in the lived experience of feminist activism; each chapter is the work of authors who have themselves been immersed in the struggle for women's rights, equality and justice in their own countries, many of whom write from perspectives as protagonists as well as participants in their studies. Refreshing in its honesty, the book offers critical self-appraisal and incisive analysis of feminist engagement with social and political change, and provides us with a fresh new perspective on enduring questions in feminist scholarship and activism.

Part of a new series dedicated to feminist engagements with development, Feminisms and Development, *Voicing Demands* arises out of an international research programme, Pathways of Women's Empowerment (www.pathways-of-empowerment. org). Combining multiple methods and disciplinary perspectives,

Pathways researchers in regional hubs in Latin America, the Middle East, South Asia, West Africa and 'Aidland' sought an understanding of what makes change happen in women's lives. Pathways' enquiries were framed by a series of entry points, representing the principal strands of activism and action framed by feminist engagement with the field of gender and development – work, body and voice – and sought to map women's experiences of empowerment. Along with critical studies of the 'motorways' of mainstream development, Pathways' research aimed to seek out and make visible 'hidden pathways' beyond the gaze of conventional development strategies through which significant changes might be taking place.

One of the most vital of these pathways is feminist activism. It has long been evident to feminist activists that one of the most important motors of change in women's lives is mobilization. The most compelling finding to emerge from Pathways' research was just how important feminist and women's movements are in securing advances in women's equality, wellbeing and rights. And yet the vital importance of feminist activism as a force for positive social change is barely reflected in the international development community's efforts to promote women's empowerment and gender equality. The focus on instruments, indicators and institutional reform has sanitized the field of feminist engagement with development from a more overtly political concern with injustice, discrimination and inequality. Strategic framing to match the interests of donors and lenders has tended to produce a politics of compromise in which there is little scope for a genuinely transformative approach that is concerned with tackling the systemic and structural barriers to gender equality. As contributors to this book show, where international development agencies have lent support on their own terms to women's and feminist organizations, the net effect has often been to reorient movements towards an excessive focus on policy, NGOization and a concomitant defusing of political opportunities. We see little of the 'investment' that is so often spoken about in relation to girls and women flow into movement-building.

Many of the settings for the book's chapters are those in which struggles for citizenship, rights and justice have been shaped by a constellation of forms of oppressive governance – military dictatorships in Bangladesh, Brazil, Egypt and Pakistan, apartheid in South Africa and the continuing colonial occupation of Palestine. Contributors highlight the extent to which, in some contexts, reactionary agendas have gained potency and force, mobilizing large numbers of women in their support. They reveal some of the intergenerational tensions that run through feminist movements, and friction and fission that arises in the interplay of these and other dimensions of difference – race, class, religion. And they tell of the challenges of creating credible and legitimate voice, of sustaining that voice through movement-building and the inclusion of diverse constituencies of women and of gaining entry into political arenas marked by their hostility to women's rights. These are tales of disappointments, disillusionment and dissonance, as well as of successful strategic moves that secured significant wins.

Interrogating the concept of voice from vantage points in diverse transitional contexts, the book analyses political opportunity structures for women's voice, dissects dilemmas of representation, examines thorny issues of inclusion and difference, conflict and dissent, and generates much food for thought about women's engagement in societal change. In doing so, it questions the kind of easy assumptions that tend to be made about the positive and progressive nature of women's agency, collective voice and interests. Together, these studies illustrate the complex contours of building movements, creating constituencies, coalition building and the navigation of alliances with actors in bureaucratic and formal political arenas. As such, this book has much to offer – and to inspire – those studying and supporting movement-building, activism and public action.

Voicing Demands

Feminist Activism in Transitional Contexts

Sohela Nazneen and Maheen Sultan

This collection begins with the premise that while there is more and more literature on gender and politics and feminist activism in the Global South, there is little as yet that effectively links voice, feminist activism and transitional contexts. As editors we believe that addressing this gap will help us interrogate our assumptions about the relationships we envisage between voice and agency, constituency building, and the renegotiation of citizenship and rights. There is a pressing need to unpack our assumptions about these relationships for a number of reasons.

First, voice – as a 'metaphor for powerful speech … associated with acts and arguments that influence public decision making' (Goetz and Nyamu-Musembi 2008: 4) – is identified in both liberal discourse and development policy literature as a key pathway towards achieving greater citizenship, rights and empowerment. This is because a group's ability to exercise and organize voice is chiefly associated with political acts such as public engagement, collective action and influence on public decisions. Though feminist writings on women and gender in formal politics have questioned this linear assumption about voice (Htun and Weldon 2010; Childs and Krook 2009; Goetz and Hassim 2003; Phillips 1991), this has been the prescription used by international policy makers, states, and even by women's and feminist organizations in seeking to strengthen women's voice within policy circles and state machinery. In this volume, we depart from this focus on women's public and political engagement in formal institutions. Instead, we seek to analyse the role of feminist activism in building and sustaining constituencies through raising, negotiating and legitimizing feminist voice in transitional contexts (see below) that shape the emergence of women's citizenship.

Second, despite voice's central role, much of the work on voice in feminist and governance literature has addressed the topic in an implicit or an indirect manner. Existing writings on building women's political influence have focused mainly on different mechanisms, such as quotas or institutional changes, and how these amplify women's voice within the formal political or institutional processes (Agarwal 2011; Beaman *et al.* 2008; Chattopadhay and Duflo 2004; Staudt 1990). Other work on women in politics has explored feminist or women's movement building within changing local, regional and international contexts. Researchers have analysed women's role in different social movements, the gendered nature and patterns of women's engagement, different mobilization strategies, how the state is approached, or the impact of transnational linkages on the feminist movement (Basu 2010, 1995; Molyneux 2001; Randall and Waylen 1998; Alvarez 1998). The contributions in this volume aim to give voice a more central role in exploring feminist activism.

The aim here is to explore what has happened to feminist voice in the Global South in the last two decades, as seen by insiders and in a cross-regional perspective. Scholarly works exist on feminisms and feminist activism in specific regions, such as South Asia (Azim *et al.* 2009; Roy 2012), the Middle East (Al-Ali and Pratt 2009), or Latin America (Molyneux 2001). However, cross-regional reflections on the relationships between voice and feminist activism are scarce. We have asked the following questions: What is feminist voice? What strategies or ways of organizing make feminist voice effective and legitimate? What are the challenges and constraints feminists face in exercising voice? Almost all our contributors are either feminist activists or feminist academics based in the South; some are currently based in the North but were a part of the feminist activism and mobilization that they analyse in this book. While contributions to this book are based on insiders' knowledge and experience of participation in feminist movements or state machineries, primary research was conducted for the chapters on Bangladesh, Egypt and Morocco.

One of our objectives is to provide a cross-regional feminist analysis of the influence of global trends, such as the development of transnational linkages; the rise of conservative forces; the NGO-ization of feminist movements; or the increasing power of donors to shape the feminist agenda. These tendencies have created opportunities and challenges for feminist voice and activism in transitional contexts. By 'transitional contexts' we mean countries that have experienced or are now undergoing shifts in political power structure, or renegotiations between political elites regarding the balance of power within the state and society – in other words, a change in existing 'political settlements' (Di John and Putzel 2009).

Existing literature on transitional contexts and feminist engagement focuses on feminist and women's activism in liberation struggles, revolutions, and pro-democracy movements, and on how participation in these creates 'political entitlements' for women (Agarwal 2011). The literature shows how the feminist voice and agenda weakens with the consolidation of nation states, revolutionary forces or democratic transitions. Molyneux's (1985) analysis of Nicaragua's revolution, Waylen's (1997) work on Chile after democratic transition, Goetz and Hassim's (2003) explorations of post-apartheid South Africa, and Tamale's (1999) work on Uganda after the revolution led by the National Resistance Movement all illustrate these points. The present volume expands our understanding of how 'political entitlements' are created and how the agenda accessible to feminists can be constricted with democratization (Fester, Tadros, this volume); but at times our chapters also challenge this analysis (Sardenberg and Costa, Nazneen and Sultan, this volume). We show how 'political opportunity structures' (McAdam *et al.* 2001) – the openness of the political institutions to women's demands, the presence of elite allies in different state and political arenas, and whether or not the state represses women's demands – all have implications for women's effective participation in political processes, and play a key role in creating or constraining space for feminist voice and negotiations.

This introductory chapter is organized in the following manner. The next section provides a brief discussion of conceptual debates on voice and the assumptions that we interrogate from our empirical evidence. This is followed by a discussion of the broader contexts within which feminist activism and voice are organized. This focuses on the various influences at work – the global trends mentioned above – and how these have influenced feminist voice in the selected countries. The section also raises questions about current feminist analysis of these trends.

We then analyse the empirical evidence presented in the chapters on the politics of organizing and channelling feminist voice, and on questions about voice and representation in feminist activism. Finally, we comment on how the empirical evidence challenges assumptions about the relationship between voice, agency and constituency building.

Voice: our initial assumptions and frames of reference

The notion of 'voice' usually refers to the act of articulating opinions, ideas, agendas, or making demands and claims – often through individual writings/speeches or collective mobilizations. These imply that voice is closely linked to expressions of agency – being able to articulate, demand or claim; and making space for these particular acts. But assuming that voice can be identified primarily through these particular expressions of agency is problematic. As our chapters will show, decisions to remain silent or not exercise agency can also be interpreted as a form of collective expression of 'voice' when it comes to feminist negotiations in repressive contexts. In addition, what is publicly voiced may not necessarily represent the underlying agenda of the actor, which implies constrained agency (Tadros, this volume).

Our analysis shows that the act of voicing itself may not be empowering[1] (Fester, this volume), or necessarily lead to positive changes – though this is implied by the way voice is connected to agency in development literature (Kuttab, this volume).

The act of 'voicing' includes two aspects: the performative aspect and the substantive aspect. The performative aspect of voice refers to the characteristics of performed expressions of voice, which include volume, clarity, nuance, or forcefulness – in other words, *how* voice is being exercised. The substantive aspect of voice refers to the content, or *what* is being expressed (Goetz and Nyamu-Musembi 2008). The ways in which these aspects are combined determine the legitimacy and credibility of the claims being made. In feminist literature on topics such as women in politics, leadership, authority, and institutional power, both of these aspects of voice have been studied extensively (Kanter 1980; Jones 1993; Goetz 1997). These analyses have shown how institutional culture and the speaker's identity and interests shape the ability to voice and provide legitimacy. While exploring feminist voice in transitional contexts, the authors have taken cognizance of both these aspects of voice.

The reference to feminist voice in the chapters assumes a 'collective voice';[2] that these are expressions of shared opinions or interests, expressed in specific ways by feminist groups to affect decision making or raise consciousness on issues or policies that affect gender equity and justice. The framing of feminist voice in this particular manner implies the following. First, the goal of collectively voicing opinions and interests assumes the possibility of being *received* and *heard*. As the analysis in the chapters will show, this assumption does not always hold for the groups that feminists target; at times, therefore, there may be 'unintended listeners', which creates difficulties for feminist activism (Nazneen and Sultan, this volume). Second, the creation and sustenance of collective feminist voice requires organizing and activism in different ways and forms. The ways and forms of organizing feminist voice are influenced by which sites and spaces are open to activists; the allies activists have within these spaces or sites

– locally, nationally and internationally; the strength (resources or network capital) of the feminist constituency and their opposition; and the 'political opportunity structures' (Pittman and Naciri, Nazneen and Sultan, Sardenberg and Costa, Zia – all in this volume). These influence the way feminist activists 'name and frame' (Tarrow 1998) or package their demands, how they engage in the performative aspects of voice, and the politics of channelling voice.[3] The theme of channelling refers to the tensions within the feminist movement: the silencing and fragmentation of feminist voices, strategies and compromises for coalition and network building, and so on. All of these are explored in different chapters. Third, feminist activism through collective expression of voice assumes the act of representing the collective interests of a constituency, and the role of voice in constituency building. Representation of collective interests through voice raises many thorny questions, since women are not a homogeneous group and women's interests are hard to define as they intersect with class, caste, religion and ethnic and racial concerns for different categories of women. Power relations and solidarity between different groups of women and feminists play key roles in the representation of collective voice. Contributors explore these issues by investigating the following questions in their own country contexts: Whose voice is heard and whose issues are chosen? How is diversity (of race, class, caste, ethnicity, religion or nationality) accommodated and managed within feminist activism? Whose claims for representation are perceived as legitimate and authentic? How do power and bias come into play in the act of representation?

Transitional contexts and global forces: implications for feminist voice

In this book we explore transitional contexts. The nature of these transitions shaped existing settlements around how the balance of power would be maintained between various political and social elite groups. We focus on organization of and negotiations around feminist voice and activism in selected countries in South Asia, the Middle East, Africa and Latin America that have experienced various types of transitions. The first category includes countries that have gone through long periods of authoritarian or one-party rule, have experienced democratic transition, and have remained democratic for a significant amount of time – South Africa, Brazil and Bangladesh. The second category includes countries that have experienced or remain under repressive rule, are currently experiencing internal ethnic or religious strife, or are occupied by foreign powers – Palestine, Egypt and Pakistan.

These categories are not watertight. 'Repressive regime' should not be interpreted simply as an authoritarian or military regime. Both Pakistan and Egypt have gone through democratic transitions while Chapters 5 and 6 were being drafted. Tadros, in her chapter on Egypt, focuses mainly on the Mubarak period, and Zia, in her chapter on Pakistan, ends her analysis at the beginning of the post-Musharraf democratic transition. However, in both these states, the nature of the ruling powers, the geopolitical interests of the superpowers during the Cold War and post-Cold War eras, and consequent militarization of the state and society have created particular types of impediment for both feminist voice and activism. In Khyber Pakhtunkhwa (formerly the North-West Frontier Province) in Pakistan, for example, despite the country's return to democracy, the threat from religious extremists (Taliban) against gender justice and women's rights has limited the state's ability to protect its citizens, and the province's condition resembles that of a repressive regime. Admittedly, using the nature of political regimes makes it difficult to categorize all case-study countries – for example, Morocco does not fall under either of these two categories as it has a constitutional monarchy.

How the 'woman question' was addressed in nation- and state-building processes (Jayawardana 1986) in each individual country context has influenced the current discourses and mobilizations around feminist voice and activism. Nation-making and national identity construction for colonial countries in South Asia, the

Middle East and Africa were premised on how nationalist elites differentiated national identity from the West. Construction of normative (perhaps middle-class) 'femininity' played a key role in this process. This legacy in the post-colonial states in these regions created a context where feminism and feminist activism are constantly challenged as a Western import. This has particular implications for feminist voice in terms of *what* is voice and *how* agendas and demands are packaged and negotiated for constituency building (by which we mean creating a support base and mobilizing allies). The 'civilizational discourses' of the post-9/11 world have created a complex reality for feminist voice in these post-colonial countries, particularly those with Muslim majorities. For feminist activists, being labelled as 'secular/Western liberals' by their opponents in the post-9/11 world increases the chance of marginalization and threatens survival in repressive contexts. Combined with the process of 'culturalization of women's issues' (Al-Ali 2002: 10), this labelling creates a legitimacy crisis for feminist voice (Tadros, Kuttab, Zia, this volume).

As noted earlier, various global trends in the post-Beijing[4] era have created opportunities and challenges for feminist voice and activism in the Global South. In all of the country chapters, the UN Beijing conference is marked as a watershed moment when large numbers of feminists entered policy spaces and engaged with the state. This gain in access to and presence in policy spaces was a mixed blessing, particularly in countries consolidating the democratization process (Bangladesh or South Africa, for example) and in countries where authoritarian rulers or dominant parties were willing to engage (Pakistan under Musharraf; Egypt under Mubarak). Feminist activists moved from opposing or resisting co-option by the state (Rai 1998) towards creating gender machineries and working with governance structures and tools. Democratization of policy-making and participatory processes through the creation of new spaces, mechanisms for women's and feminist participation in development, increased transnational links, and exchanges between feminist groups at the local, national, or global levels – all created opportunities for channelling feminist voice in different spaces and sites. However, as our contributors show, these new opportunities came at a price as feminist voice became more technical and exclusionary in some instances (Fester, Nazneen and Sultan, this volume).

Globally, the international discourse on gender equity and women's rights has captured much of the space in development policy since the 1990s. In the post-Beijing period the fact that the categories 'woman' and 'gender' gained increased visibility within state and international discourses and state practices is seen as a victory for feminist struggles (Molyneux and Razavi 2005). During this period, as spaces and sites in which feminists voiced their concerns have expanded, feminist practices have been associated increasingly with professionalization, managerialism, bureaucratization and NGO-ization (Roy 2012). The impact of these practices and processes on feminist activism is studied and debated extensively in feminist literature. Feminist voices in the Global South are also shaped by their current struggles in dealing with the rise of conservative forces in their own countries, excessive ethnic or religious nationalisms, and the neo-liberalizing imperatives of state and international development agencies. The forms and natures of feminist struggles and the shape of the terrain within which feminists organize and mobilize their voice are moulded by these forces (Basu 2010).

Thus four broad forces of change can be said to have had an impact on feminist voice and activism in transitional contexts: the development of transnational linkages, the NGO-ization of the feminist movement, the rise of conservative/religious forces, and the increase in donors' powers to shape feminist agenda. We now relate each of these separately to their exposition in the country chapters. Then, in the next section, we will comment on how they influenced the politics of channelling feminist voice and representation.

In all our case study countries, as local and national feminist organizations developed *transnational links and networks* – presenting their agenda in international forums and mobilizing transnational support – they were able to create space, recognition, and legitimacy for their demands. In the Brazilian context, the opportunity for feminists and women to participate in the Beijing conference and the regional consultative processes demonstrated both nationally and regionally that there was a large constituency working on gender equity concerns, and this created legitimacy for the demands made by feminists (Sardenberg and Costa, this volume; Alvarez 2000). Similarly, Nazneen and Sultan show in their chapter on Bangladesh that mobilization for the ratification of the Committee on the Elimination of Discrimination against Women (CEDAW) and women's access to state policy spaces was firmly established during the pre- and post-Beijing process. This was because the Bangladesh state sought assistance from feminists to prepare for and follow up on Beijing, and also for CEDAW reporting, and feminists were able to demonstrate their expertise and legitimize their claims on the state. In Morocco, legal reform of the country's Islamic laws was a part of the regional Campaign to Reform Arab Women's Nationality (the nationality campaign), and was strengthened by the extensive regional networks and coalitions established by the Moroccan feminists.

These transnational feminist networks, whether regional or international, create what is called a 'boomerang pattern' of influence (Keck and Sikkink 1998) for feminist voice. These networks, coalitions and inter-governmental/non-governmental actors are able 'put pressure on more powerful states and IGOs [international governmental organizations] to bring pressure to bear in turn on a particular government which violates rights or resists the desired policy change' (Alvarez 2000: 3). Thus these transnational feminist and women's rights networks have had a clear and far-reaching positive influence on creating space for the feminist agenda and sustaining feminist demands. Yet a number of questions remain – some of which we pursue not now but, as mentioned, in the following section: How inclusive and accessible are these networks, given divergences in expertise and knowledge, including linguistic ability to participate? What of the internal power politics within them? Whose agendas do they promote? And how are they influenced by the broader funding politics and policies of powerful donor states?

The rise of *conservative forces* – ranging from local religious groups that adhere to ideologies and practices that are gender inequitable, to larger national political groups or transnational conservative movements/networks – have created a specific challenge for feminist voice in the last two decades. These conservative forces have gained formal political and public space in popular media in the post-9/11 world, particularly given the shift towards 'civilizational discourses'. In contexts where countries are occupied by foreign powers or where authoritarian rulers had sustained or suppressed religious groups, the rise of these conservative forces as an alternative political force for resisting repressive actors has had adverse implications for feminist voice. Kuttab, in her chapter on Palestine, shows how – in the context of Israeli aggression and the failure of the Palestinian Authority (PA) to deliver peace and basic services – the political views of Hamas (a hardcore Islamist group), along with its restrictive views on women's role and femininity, have gained ground. These views on femininity are strongly linked to the construction of a distinctive Palestinian national identity and are very different from the liberal gender ideology promoted by Palestinian secular feminist activists.

Similarly, in her chapter on Egypt during the Mubarak regime, Tadros highlights how the most successful force on the streets and in neighbourhoods – with a large number of female constituents – was the Muslim Brotherhood. Women mobilized by the Brotherhood tended to voice the party line on various issues, which for the most part was in defence of the Islamist political project. Tadros argues that the voice of these Muslim Brotherhood women activists is highly complex in relation to feminist voice, and in relation to the government and wider society. She shows that the Brotherhood's success in creating a large grassroots constituent base has had wide-ranging impacts, particularly in the post-Mubarak period when transition was being negotiated. The secular Egyptian feminists, while successful in accessing policy spaces and promoting policy changes during the Mubarak regime, found themselves having to struggle when it came to creating a constituency at the local level. This lack of a large, popular feminist constituency in Egypt partly resulted in feminists strategizing for mobilization in a highly repressive context. As Tadros's chapter shows, feminists had to mobilize in a manner that would allow them to divert the attentions of the state security apparatus to avoid harassment. This meant excessive reliance on personal networks within the political elites and engagement in policy circles, leaving popular channels and media open for capture by alternative forces, an outcome we discuss in the next section.

Zia (Chapter 5) shows how, in Pakistan, both military and democratic regimes have tried to appease the Islamist political parties and militant forces in Khyber Pakhtunkhwa (formerly the North-West Frontier Province). The provincial state apparatus is experiencing difficulty in providing security to women (and activists)[5] who are under attack by extremists. At times both the state and the political parties have been willing to bargain away women's rights in their negotiations with the militants. For example, during recent elections in one Khyber Pakhtunkhwa area, all key political parties were pressured by militants into signing a pact that women in that area would not vote in the national elections. They asked male family members to ensure that women did not go to the polls.

The authors of the Palestinian, Egyptian and Pakistani chapters all discuss, against different backgrounds and with different nuances, a strategy employed by secular feminist groups who have tried to create a distance between their situations and what is perceived as 'Western' feminist discourse in order to articulate their demands by using Islamic, culturally specific frames to make their voice appear more 'authentic' and so gain legitimacy. These attempts have to be interpreted in the light of the civilizational debates and the quest for a more 'grounded, pure, authentic' voice (see Zia, Tadros, Kuttab, this volume). This has also given rise to tensions and debates between feminist activists, some arguing that 'there is a common thread between secular feminism and

Islamic feminism that should be explored and used as a stepping stone for collective mobilization and the realization of women's rights' (Kuttab, this volume). However, there are other feminist activists who feel that 'a common ground between Islamism and secularism is not possible ... as the social, class and future vision of the state and society' (*ibid.*) is radically different.

In the case of countries such as Bangladesh, South Africa and Brazil, which have gone through democratic transition and have created and opened up public and policy spaces to women, feminists have found that women belonging to radical conservative movements have entered these spaces and places. In South Africa, while conservative parties such as the Democratic Alliance have not supported the agenda for women's political empowerment, they have taken advantage of these new positions to field women candidates and promote a conservative agenda. In Bangladesh, the rise of Jamaat-E-Islami as an important political ally of the two major political parties in winning elections from the 1990s to 2007 has created difficulties for feminists seeking to voice and negotiate with political parties on issues that bring them into conflict with Shari'a-based religious personal laws. The rise of conservative forces in both repressive and post-democratic transitions have implications for the politics of representation and the channelling voice that will also be explored in the next section.

All our contributors deal with *the NGO-ization of feminist and women's organizations and movements*. The impact and implications of this phenomenon, including the depoliticization and deradicalization of the feminist agenda and voice, are much examined. But this reading of NGO-ization is perhaps too simplistic (Roy 2012). Feminist NGOs are hybrid organizations (Alvarez 1998) and the on-the-ground analysis presented in these chapters shows that NGO-ization is a heterogeneous practice, malleable in the hands of different organizations, entailing different costs and compromises, and creating new modes of organizing, feminist subjectivities, risks and vulnerabilities (Roy 2012).

For some countries, such as Palestine, the process of NGO-ization occurred in the post-Oslo period and had more far-reaching consequences than the professionalization and projectization of the feminist and women's movements. Because NGOs underwent registration based on the requirements of the PA and limited their work to the PA's agenda – so Kuttab argues – the process alienated the women's movement and disrupted the development of grassroots democratic work. Tadros, in her chapter, presents a unique situation featuring quasi-non-governmental organizations (QUANGOs) and government-organized non-governmental organizations (GONGOs). These para-state entities, created during the Mubarak regime, were part of the national women's machinery, the National Council for Women (NCW). They were answerable to the Prime Minister and presided over by the First Lady. These had a specific role in promoting women's rights and were supported by donors, though not recognized as legitimate by the feminist activists. However, feminists lobbying for policy changes and processes were compelled to maintain close relations with these entities as they had the resources, networks and links to push their agendas within the perimeters of the Mubarak regime. However, a close relationship with these entities during the Mubarak period carried a risk of being co-opted (at best, co-option of the feminist agenda; at worst, QUANGOS erased the history of the previous work done by feminists and claimed sole credit); while in the post-Mubarak period, for those who had a close relationship with these QUANGOS, it meant a loss of legitimacy and voice.

In Bangladesh, NGO-ization of the feminist and women's organizations was strategically managed by the national and better-resourced organizations to create institutional structures and processes, and to gain access to the grassroots through funding outreach services (Nazneen and Sultan 2012). Sardenberg and Costa provide similar examples for Brazil. However, both chapters, and also the chapter on South Africa by Fester, demonstrate the impacts of NGO-ization on feminist voice. Forms and modes of feminist activism, and the politics of representation are in some instances dominated by powerful national feminist groups that may silence the voices of smaller, rural, or grassroots organizations within the formal network that links these feminist and women's NGOs.

The epistemic power of donors to shape the feminist agenda and activism, and to influence the state gender agenda, is another force that has influenced feminist voice in the Global South. In fact, a close reading of all the country cases reveals that at the national level feminists in these countries have mobilized and worked on issues at specific periods that were deemed important by the international policy actors and discourse. We do not imply that all local or national feminist agendas are shaped by donors, but certainly a homogenization of the gender equity agenda has taken place. This reflects increased transnational linkages and exchanges between various feminist networks, partly because international development documents and discourses – for example, the millennium development goals (MDGs), or CEDAW – are used by feminists to mobilize and justify their demands; and partly because NGO-ization and donor funding require feminist organizations to work on or link their local agendas to these larger international agendas. The agenda-bending power of donors is bound to increase, given the increased competition among feminist and women's organizations as international funding decreases;[6] the expansion in the number and activities of transnational networks; and the managerialization of feminist and women's organizations and work on women's rights (as reflected in the way reports are written or evaluations conducted, for example). This has implications for feminist voice and organizing, as 'doing gender and development' comes to be seen as a technical project requiring particular skills, expertise and knowledge, and the transformative agenda of feminism is depoliticized.

This is illustrated by Kuttab in her chapter on Palestine. She describes how the imposition of donor discourses and human rights approaches, and the lack of political will on the part of the PA, have separated gender equity both from power-sharing processes between the state and the citizen, and from equality and social justice. In Bangladesh, where the gender and development agenda was largely donor-driven in the 1970s and 1980s, feminists had benefited from donors pushing the international agenda with the state, which has a patriarchal and contradictory attitude towards women's rights. But this benefit came at a cost: the public came to perceive women's rights either as a 'Western import' or as a development issue promoted by the donors (Nazneen and Sultan 2012). Pittman and Naciri, in their chapter on Morocco, show how feminist organizations and networks have to struggle not only against 'local political opposition and contention', but also 'funding challenges … and a donor–NGO relationship built on power imbalances and characterized by parochial relations'. Maintaining these relations required various compromises and struggles against funders, who (intentionally or unintentionally) shaped the forms and structures of feminist organizing and work by requiring processes and structures geared towards delivering outputs rather than movement building.

Feminism and the politics of channelling collective voice and representation

All the chapters in this book highlight the strategies developed by feminist activists to mobilize, organize, and exercise a collective voice. Broad similarities and patterns have emerged as feminists in various regions articulate collective demands and create constituencies. Common strategies include (1) building coalitions within the movement on particular issues; (2) forming alliances with other civil society organizations and the media around these issues; (3) targeting selective parts of the state bureaucracy, including local government, concerned ministries and the national gender machinery, to promote an agenda and advance demands; (4) cultivating allies among women representatives and also male politicians; (5) using international women's rights and human rights discourses to package their demands; (6) establishing and highlighting their expertise and experience on a particular gender equity issue as they mobilize around it.

These points do not present a comprehensive picture of

how feminist activism engages in building and sustaining a collective voice, but they do highlight particular insights. As presented below, these insights show how 'political opportunity structures' strengthen or constrain feminist voice, how power relations within networks and movements shape a particular agenda (content of voice), and how this agenda is articulated (performativity of voice). Through this analysis we highlight some of the contestations that exist within feminist debates on voice, mobilization strategies and constituency building.

Excessive policy focus and state feminism

In the post-Beijing period women have entered policy spaces and engaged with the state through new governance structures (such as participatory policy processes or citizens forums) – whether in countries that are consolidating democratic transition or under repressive regimes. This trend partly reflects gender mainstreaming practices, an increase in donors' epistemic power, and the NGO-ization of movements and organizations. The definition of success and influence has come to be understood in relation to policy gains and reforms. Policy gains are perceived as 'goals' of activism in development discourses. Even though feminist activists have critiqued and countered this understanding, there is pressure on them to deliver on policy, given the overall context within which they operate.

In South Africa, Brazil and Bangladesh, this excessive policy focus has increased the visibility of the gender and development agenda and has led to various policy gains. In the case of Brazil, state feminism has led to stipulations on women's participation at the local level and the establishment of participatory spaces and processes for citizens' engagement. These have managed to capture women's voices. However there are concerns around who (which women) enter these spaces and their perceptions on gender equity. Sardenberg and Costa argue that in Brazil's case state feminism, along with its focus on policies, delivered on women's rights because of the presence of a strong feminist and women's movement.

However, excessive policy focus may depoliticize feminist voice and activism. Over-reliance on the state has proved costly for feminists in a number of ways. For example, Fester in her chapter on South Africa shows how the creation of various national gender machineries, such as the Commission for Gender Equality and the appointment of feminist activists in key posts, led to the formulation of official policies and formal processes for women's inclusion and a strong official rhetoric around gender equity. She argues that the functioning of these machineries was undermined by political appointees who had little experience or expertise in gender equality, the divisiveness and power struggles within the gender machineries, a lack of resources, and the (male) resistance within state structures. Fester argues that an excessive focus by feminists on creating state machineries and policy reform dissipated their energies. Feminists have failed to embed their agenda in the bureaucratic structures, and this in turn has weakened their voice and transformative potential.

Besides dissipating energy on a failed attempt to infiltrate state structures, an excessive focus on policy may divert feminist attention from exploring alternative channels and spaces for strengthening and channelling feminist voice. In Bangladesh, feminist activists have selectively targeted parts of the state – rather than the political arena and political actors – to channel their demands. This is because close associations with political parties lead to a loss of credibility and legitimacy among their allies in a partisan and polarized civil society (Nazneen and Sultan, this volume). To some extent this skirting of one kind of unproductive tension and pressure has also reduced the momentum within the feminist movement to explore alternative channels and forums for engagement and making demands. Giving state and policy change primacy and focusing less on alternative channels creates difficult conditions for feminists in contexts where the state fails or is reluctant to deliver on gender equity. Failure to explore alternatives for channelling feminist voice may limit activism to promote wider social change in attitudes and perceptions. For example, Nazneen and Sultan's analysis in this volume shows that the Bangladeshi feminist movement for CEDAW ratification, which targeted changes in legal frameworks and policy changes, did not explore alternative channels effectively, and failed to create a wider social debate on CEDAW or a large support base for unreserved ratification of the convention.

In repressive contexts, excessive focus on policy change and over-reliance on the state enmeshes activists in practices that may in the long run hamper credibility of feminist demands and voice. Tadros argues that in Mubarak's Egypt the invisible power structure (state security apparatus) that constrained feminist voice and activity, and the way QUANGOs dominated the gender equity agenda, compelled feminist activists to use their personal networks and connections with the political elite to promote their agenda. Tadros argues that managing these various relationships to attain policy goals has come at the cost of creating consensus around policy change and a support base. It has also led feminists to engage in manipulative practices. Lack of consensus building around particular policies had a devastating impact on gender equity when the Mubarak regime ended. For example, a reservation for women in the national parliament was reversed by the transitional government as quotas were perceived as a policy promoted by the former First Lady and not a collective public demand.

Representation: exclusionary practices and creation of differentiated solidarity

Has this excessive policy focus led feminists to ignore new ways of organizing by women who do not fall under the elite, middle-class feminist activist umbrella? Elitism and middle-class bias within the feminist movement is much debated within all these country contexts and has been highlighted by all contributors. These biases within the movement raise questions about representation. Whose agenda and interests are voiced through feminist activism? And how does power operate to exclude certain demands?

A combination of gender mainstreaming, NGO-ization and

other forces has created processes, mechanisms and structures (such as UN consultation or poverty-reduction strategy processes, or debates in the social media) that require certain skills, technical knowledge and resources of activists seeking to channel their demands. These processes and structures can be exclusionary for groups that lack the technical skills and resources. Moreover, even when the forms and nature of engagement within these processes appear inclusive, the configuration of power relations within the different groups that occupy these spaces may silence voices.

The contributions in this volume present a mixed picture when it comes to practices around solidarity, how power is exercised within the feminist movement, and exclusionary outcomes. In Brazil the national women's conferences (in 2002, 2004 and 2007) led to the formulation of the Feminist Political Platform and the National Women's Public Policy Plans I and II. About 300,000 women participated in these conferences. The focus was on creating '*differentiated solidarity* among women, a solidarity built on awareness of both common and different interests' (Jónasdóttir and Jones 2009: 18). This does not imply that conflicts were absent, but that there was a conscious effort to ensure that participation by various groups was not only for 'illustrative purposes'. There was space for activists to debate collectively the always-contested meanings and goals of feminism and its relationship to other struggles for rights and social justice in Brazil. Fester's chapter on South Africa highlights the collaboration between feminist academics and grassroots women over a campaign for change in customary laws to align women's rights with gender equity clauses in the new constitution. Similarly, in Morocco feminist academics and activists involved in the nationality campaign collected life stories of grassroots women and their families to illustrate how gender-biased nationality laws adversely affected the lives of women married to foreign-born spouses, and their children.

Not all national meetings and conferences engendered this form of participation and differentiated solidarity. In Bangladesh,

Nazneen and Sultan explored coalition building by the three national feminist organizations around three different issues. Despite the intent to be inclusive and participatory, voices of the smaller, local groups based outside the capital were marginalized. As one feminist organization leading such a coalition stated, 'organizations outside of Dhaka were easier to manage as they were more compliant and less vociferous'. This form of control was accepted as a trade-off by the smaller groups to ensure participation in networks that highlighted their presence in the national arena. It was justified by the lead organizations because, firstly, they had the necessary expertise and resources to 'do it properly'. Secondly, they feared that otherwise their agendas might be co-opted and misrepresented. In Egypt, the feminist activists failed to connect with the workers' movement around pay rises and livelihood issues during the Mubarak regime. Clearly, power operates across many divides within the feminist movement and voices that are less powerful may be excluded from the process or silenced. Or, as shown in the case of Brazil, providing space for debate and contention by socially powerful activist groups may create differentiated solidarity.

What also comes across in different chapters is that broad coalition building within the feminist movement and with allies in the civil and political sphere is pursued in order to demonstrate numerical strength and support for the movement's agenda. However, coalition-building processes require complex negotiations, pragmatic decision making and, at times, compromise over feminist ideals. For example, in Morocco, the activists in the women's nationality campaign centred their demands on the impact of gender-biased nationality laws on the family members (foreign-born husbands and children) and not on women as liberal subjects who should have equal rights with men. This allowed them to subdue male resistance and garner support. In Bangladesh the movement supporting justice for acid survivors focused on the suffering inflicted on victims and their families to create empathy among policy makers, legal workers and the police. The feminists did not directly challenge societal notions addressing the comportment of adolescent girls (most of the attacks were by men whose attentions had been rejected). These pragmatic approaches allowed feminist voice to gain space and wider acceptance in society around particular issues. They also highlight the point that *what* is voiced by feminists publicly may not always reveal the underlying feminist agenda: only the compromises are showing.

The effectiveness of pragmatic strategies, illustrated above, was also influenced by changes in overall political opportunity structures. In Morocco the terrorist attacks of 2003 reduced sympathy for Islamists, who were potential opponents of the nationality campaigns, and created space for feminists to raise their demands. The support of the monarch and his interest in reforming the law and countering resistance also proved to be a strong force in pushing through legal reform. In Egypt the policy gains made by feminists during the Mubarak regime were partly fuelled by the regime's need to create legitimacy in the international arena. In South Africa, negotiations around customary rights were possible because of women's significant participation in the anti-apartheid struggle, which created political entitlement in the eyes of the state; the political elite, too, was willing to contest traditional conservatism over gender equity.

Challenges: infiltrating political arenas and building intergenerational movements

Where the feminist activists have been less effective across these selected countries is in engaging with political society and reaching out to younger feminists. Both of these issues have been debated in feminist literature (Goetz and Hassim 2003; Basu 2010; Roy 2012). Democratization processes have created new spaces and opportunities for women's participation. In repressive contexts, such as Pakistan and Palestine, and in post-Mubarak Egypt, our contributors show that these spaces have been captured by Islamist women. The presence of a liberal/secular voice in these formal political spaces has weakened over the years. In countries where strong state feminism exists, such as Brazil, or where women have long campaigned for political empowerment and created reservations for women, such as Bangladesh, feminists have not made effective links with political actors. Even in countries where women have a strong presence within the incumbent party, such as the African National Congress (ANC) in South Africa, women representatives have towed the party line on gender equity (see Fester's discussion of Zuma's trial). As Goetz and Hassim (2003) point out, despite the creation of the women's quota, party lists and other measures, political parties are entrenched patriarchies. Feminists have had difficulty infiltrating this arena, and this has led them to focus on state and civil society arenas as key sites for channelling their voice and activism. However, lack of a feminist constituency, or a constituency that pressures political actors on women's rights in the political arena, allows political parties to compromise on gender equity when they face a crisis.

Finally, creation of an intergenerational movement is of key importance for sustaining feminist voice and activism. The chapters in this book show that new forms of engagement and ways of organizing are being deployed by younger feminists, whose vibrancy and radicalism are often a theme (see Fester, Zia, Sardenberg and Costa). However, these newer forms of engagement and their dialogues with the older (second wave) vanguard are marked by anxieties over issues such as class, race, sexuality and (urban or rural) location. They are also marked by the older vanguard's denial of space to younger voices and insistence on measuring younger women's activism against the normative ideal of autonomous or voluntary ways of organizing. Their verdict is that the younger (urban and professional) feminists fall short on this count (Roy 2012). This does not mean that there is a lack of interest or commitment among the younger generation of feminists, but that in the post-NGO-ization phase the nature of engagement has changed. And the idealization of activism based on unpaid voluntary labour needs to be rethought. Another phenomenon that has confounded feminist activists is that a larger number of young women are engaging with religious discourses as a frame for women's rights. As Zia points out, this is not surprising in the political context post-9/11. How the rise of this new generation of Islamist female activists will modify feminist voice remains to be seen.

Conclusions

In this chapter we have tried to summarise the insights from various country cases on the relationship between feminist voice and activism. These insights challenge assumptions made in development policy discourse about the linear relationship between creating a public voice while building a stable constituency for promoting gender equity, on the one hand, and creating pressure for the attainment of gender equity on the other. This assumed positive relationship between feminist voice, constituency building and the attainment of empowerment is posited about democratic countries where spaces and opportunities exist for feminists to voice gender equity concerns. What the country cases that have undergone a democratic transition show is that this relationship between voice creation, constituency building and the promotion of gender equity is not always linear. Nor does voice always have a positive influence in promoting women's interests. In fact, an examination of relationships between feminist activism, voice, and constituency building in the country case studies (both those that have experienced democratic transition and those under repressive rule) reveals interesting paradoxes. For example, Brazil has a very strong feminist movement and state machineries, but very weak representation of feminists and feminist voice in the formal political arena. In Mubarak's Egypt some feminists had a very influential voice through using personal networks, but it was a conforming voice and they did not have the support of a mobilized popular constituency. In Bangladesh, feminists have an influential voice within certain policy circles but do not enjoy a massive popular support base. These paradoxes indicate that the assumptions and prescriptions arising in development discourse about the positive relation between voice, constituency building and positive change are too simplistic.

All our chapters show the strategic importance for feminist action of a multi-layered constituency of potential allies located within and outside the state agencies and other regional and international actors. The feminist movement and women's organizations do play key roles in channelling women's voice and building constituencies – whether during democratic transitions or in repressive contexts. However, these processes are complex – riddled with difficulties, exclusionary practices within the movement, and pragmatic compromises. Their success also relies on changes in political opportunity structures, both in the international and national context, which create space for negotiating demands. This book attempts to reflect cross-regionally on how feminist voice is organized and legitimized from an insider's perspective. However, the discussion in the previous section indicates that there remains a need for further and systematic research to gain insight into the complex relationship between voice, constituency building, and empowered agency.

Notes

1 This is not a new point and has been discussed by post-modernists in understanding the relationship between giving voice and empowerment (see Lazreg 2004).
2 The definition of a collective voice is based on Hirschman (1970).
3 These aspects of movement building and negotiations have been discussed extensively in social movement theories (see Tarrow 1998; McAdam *et al.* 2001).
4 Fourth World Women's Conference, organized by the UN in Beijing in 1995.
5 Malala Yousufzai's incident is widely known.
6 See Mukhopadhyay and Eyben (2011). Funding for multilaterals and intermediary funding bodies may increase – which would target the state to work on gender, but direct funding for women's organizations is decreasing.

References

Agarwal, B. (2011) *Gender and Green Governance*, Oxford University Press, Oxford.

Al-Ali, N. (2002) 'Women's Movement in the Middle East: Case Studies of Turkey and Egypt', Working Paper, United Nations Research Institute for Social Development, Geneva.

Al-Ali, N. and N. Pratt (2009) *Women and War in the Middle East: Transnational Perspectives*, Zed Books, London and New York, NY.

Alvarez, S. (1998) 'Latin American Feminisms Go Global: Trends of the 1990s and the Challenges for the New Millennium', in S. Alvarez, E. Dagnino and A. Escobar (eds), *Culture of Politics and Politics of Cultures: Revisioning Latin American Social Movements*, Westview Press, Boulder, CO.

—— (2000) 'Translating the Global: Effects of Transnational Organizing on Local Feminist Discourses and Practices in Latin America', *Meridians: Feminism, Race, Transnationalism*, Vol. 1, No. 1, pp. 30–1.

Azim, F., M. Menon and D. M. Siddiqui (2009) 'Negotiating New Terrains: South Asian Feminisms', *Feminist Review*, Vol. 91, pp. 1–8.

Basu, A. (ed.) (1995) *The Challenges of Local Feminism: Women's Movement in a Global Perspective*, Westview Press, Boulder, CO.

—— (2010) 'Introduction', in A. Basu (ed.), *Women's Movement in a Global Era*, Westview Press, Boulder, CO.

Beaman, L., R. Chattopadhyay, E. Duflo, R. Pande and P. Topalova (2008) 'Powerful Women: Does Exposure Reduce Bias?', NBER Working Paper Series No. 14198, Massachusetts Institute of Technology, Cambridge, MA.

Chattopadhay, R. and E. Duflo (2004) 'Women as Policymakers: Evidence from Randomized Policy Experiment in India', *Econometrica*, Vol. 72, No. 5, pp. 1409–43.

Childs, S. and M. L. Krook (2009) 'Analysing Women's Substantive Representation: From Critical Mass to Critical Actors', *Government and Opposition*, Vol. 44, No. 2, pp. 125–45.

Di John, J. and J. Putzel (2009) 'Political Settlements Issues Paper', http://www.gsdrc.org/docs/open/EIRS7.pdf, GSRDC, International Development Department, University of Birmingham.

Goetz, A-M. (ed.) (1997) *Getting Institutions Right for Women in Development*, Zed Books, London.

Goetz, A-M. and S. Hassim (2003) *No Short Cuts to Power: African Women in Politics and Policy Making*, Zed Books, London.

Goetz, A-M. and C. Nyamu-Musembi (2008) 'Voice and Women's Empowerment: Mapping a Research Agenda', Pathways Working

Paper No. 2, Pathways of Women's Empowerment RPC, Brighton.

Hirschman, A. O. (1970) *Exit, Voice, Loyalty*, Cambridge, Cambridge University Press.

Htun, M. and S. C. Weldon (2010) 'When Do Governments Promote Women's Rights? A Comparative Framework for Analysis of Sex Equality Policies', *Perspectives in Politics*, Vol. 8, No. 1, pp. 207–16.

Jayawardana, K. (1986) *Feminism and Nationalism in the Third World*, Zed Books, London.

Jónasdóttir, A. and K. Jones (eds) (2009) *The Political Interests of Gender Revisited: Redoing Theory and Research with a Feminist Face*, United Nations University Press, New York, NY.

Jones, K. B. (1993) *Compassionate Authority: Democracy and the Representation of Women*, Routledge, London.

Kanter, R. M. (1980) *Men, Women and Corporations*, Basic Books, New York, NY.

Keck, M. E. and K. Sikkink (1998) *Activists Beyond Borders: Advocacy Networks in International Politics*, Cornell University Press, Ithaca, NY.

Lazreg, M. (2004) 'Development: Feminist Theory's Cul-de-Sac', in K. Saunders (ed.), *Feminist Post-Development Thought, Rethinking Modernity, Post-Colonialism and Representation*, Zed Books, London.

McAdam, D., J. D. McCarthy and M. N. Zald (eds) (2001) *Comparative Perspectives on Social Movements*, Cambridge University Press, Cambridge.

Molyneux, M. (1985) 'Mobilization without Emancipation: Women's Interests, State and Revolution in Nicaragua', *Critical Social Policy*, Vol. 4, No. 10, pp. 59–71.

—— (2001) *Women's Movement in International Perspective: Latin America and Beyond*, Palgrave, London.

Molyneux, M. and S. Razavi (2005) 'Beijing Plus Ten: An Ambivalent Record on Gender Justice', *Development and Change*, Vol. 36, No. 6, pp. 983–1010.

Mukhopadhyay, M. and R. Eyben (2011) *Mobilising Resources for Women's Rights: The Role of Resources*, Pathways of Women's Empowerment RPC and Royal Tropical Institute (KIT), Brighton.

Nazneen, S. and M. Sultan (2012) 'Contemporary Feminist Politics in Bangladesh: Taking the Bull by the Horns', in S. Roy (ed.), *New South Asian Feminisms: Paradoxes and Possibilities*, Zed Books, London.

Phillips, A. (1991) *Engendering Democracy*, Polity Press, Cambridge.

Rai, S. (1998) 'Women and the State in the Third World: Some Issues for Debate', in S. Rai and G. Livesley (eds), *Women and the State: International Perspectives*, Taylor and Francis, London.

Randall, V. and G. Waylen (eds) (1998) *Gender, Politics and the State*, Routledge, London.

Roy, S. (ed.) (2012) *New South Asian Feminisms: Paradoxes and Possibilities*, Zed Books, London.

Staudt, K. (1990) *Women, International Politics and Development: The Bureaucratic Mire*, Temple University Press, Philadelphia, PA.

Tamale, S. (1999) *When Hens Begin to Crow: Gender and Parliamentary Politics in Uganda*, Westview Press, Boulder, CO.

Tarrow, S. (1998) *The Power in Movements: Social Movement and Contentious Politics*, Cambridge University Press, Cambridge.

Waylen, G. (1997) 'Women's Movement, the State, Democratic Transition: The Establishment of SERNAM', in A-M.Goetz (ed.), *Getting Institutions Right for Women in Development*, Zed Books, London.

1

Well-Chosen Compromises?

Feminists Legitimizing Voice in Bangladesh

Sohela Nazneen and Maheen Sultan

> *To build something is not the same as dreaming of it: building is always a matter of well-chosen compromises.* (Amitav Ghosh, *The Hungry Tide*, 2005: 249)

In this chapter we analyse the strategies and choices of feminist activists in organizing voice and mobilizing support in post-authoritarian Bangladesh. We asked two broad questions about three national-level feminist organizations. How do they 'create meaning' (justify, represent and negotiate) around an issue for constituents, co-workers and coalition partners?[1] And how do they create support for their cause amongst potential supporters and allies (Ryan 1992)? We provide an analytical narrative of how these organizations packaged their demands strategically to appeal to different actors; built coalitions with other civil society actors; used personal networks to access politicians and state actors; and created transnational links to exert pressure on the state. We argue that feminist activists gained legitimacy and influence using these strategies through a clear analysis of the 'opportunity structure' within which feminist organizations function (McAdam *et al.* 2001) – particularly the nature of the state, the role played by partisan politics in civil society, the space created by the Beijing process, and the rights-based discourse. Feminist organizations also identified the most basic criteria for each issue on which members and allies could agree in order to create solidarity, and assessed incentives influencing the behaviour of other actors (such as allies within civil society or the state bureaucracy). These assessments enabled the women's organizations to make strategic and pragmatic decisions that work in the Bangladeshi context. We also argue that these strategic choices sometimes entailed compromises and trade-offs that at times limited their activism, particularly in the mainstream political arena, and led others to question their role in representing women's interests. Overall, however, their activism has enhanced the legitimacy of feminist voice in Bangladesh over the last two decades.

We define voice as 'acts or arguments that influence public decisions' (Goetz and Nyamu-Musembi 2008: 2). Feminist activism refers to principled interventions with the intention of challenging and changing gender power structures. Contrary to existing literature, which argues that feminist voice weakens after democratic transition from an authoritarian regime (see Jaquette 1994; Waylen 1996; Goetz and Nyamu-Musembi 2008), we show that in Bangladesh both feminist activism and voice gained legitimacy and influence in the post-authoritarian period. Our analytical framework considers both structure (the political, social and international context) and agency (the strategies used by activists) in order to bring out the implications for feminist voice. This analysis addresses an important gap in the literature on feminist activism in Bangladesh since the 1990s. Most of the existing literature on feminist and women's organizations[2] in Bangladesh is either descriptive or narrative-based (Begum 1998).[3] Some writers have focused on specific issues or aspects of the movement. For example, Karim commented on the NGO-ization of feminist mobilizations as she explored the production of neo-liberal subjects through the governmentalities exercised by development-focused NGOs (Karim 2011). Others have explored the nature of transnational influences on movement building around specific issues, such as the acid survivors' movement (Chowdhury 2011). But analysis that specifically explores the relationship between feminist activism, voice and constituency building in the Bangladesh context is missing. We focus on the last two so-called 'golden decades' of feminist activism. During this period, along with democratization, changes in the national and international contexts – such as the rise of the rights-based approach, the maturation of the NGO sector in Bangladesh, and preparatory processes for the United Nation's Fourth World Women's Conference in Beijing – created the scope for women's organizations to engage with diverse social actors and the state, and influence their agendas.

The selected case study organizations are among the leaders of feminist activism in Bangladesh: Bangladesh Mahila Parishad (BMP), a mass-level women's movement organization; Nari-pokkho (NP), a feminist activist organization; and Women for Women (WFW), a feminist research and advocacy organization. They are diverse in nature and structure, which allows us to gain general insights about the mobilization strategies used by feminist organizations. In what follows we draw on insights gained as feminist movement 'insiders' in Bangladesh, and comment on the legitimacy of and space for feminist voice, and on representation within the movement.[4]

The context of feminist activism in Bangladesh

Bangladesh has a long history of feminist activism that can be traced back to the anti-colonial nationalist movement, first against the British and then against the Pakistanis. In the post-liberation period (1971 onwards), the movement focused on a broad range of issues such as political empowerment, economic equality, legal reforms of customary and gender-biased laws, violence against women and reproductive rights (Jahan 1995; Kabeer 1989).

Though Bangladesh has a vibrant feminist movement, gender equity and women's rights issues do not have currency in mainstream politics. The state has displayed a contradictory attitude towards gender equity, at times enacting progressive laws and at other times acting to sustain male advantage (Jahan 1995). Women's presence in politics is weak, even though the two major parties, the Awami League (AL) and the Bangladesh Nationalist Party (BNP), are led by women and a third of the seats in the different elected bodies are reserved for them. The repressive and confrontational nature of politics has led many feminist organizations to avoid engaging in formal politics and to engage with the state bureaucracy instead.

Islam was established as the state religion through a constitutional amendment in 1988. In the last two decades the two centrist parties, AL and BNP, have entered into overt and tacit alliances with Jamaat-e-Islami – the Islamist party – to win elections and form governments (Nazneen 2008). This allowed Jamaat to gain ground and made it difficult for women's rights organizations to negotiate with the state on issues that challenge religious prescriptions and laws. As we will show, this had particular implications for how the ratification of the Convention on Elimination of All Forms of Discrimination Against Women (CEDAW) was negotiated by WFW.

The Bangladeshi state is built on a social structure that is hierarchical by gender and class (Goetz 2001). Patron–client relationships still remain the dominant form of social organization for structuring relationships between the classes. The politicization of the civil bureaucracy has increased the control of the ruling parties. This has resulted in civil society actors, including feminist organizations, relying on personal networks for accessing the state bureaucracy.

Feminist organizations have strong links with human rights, cultural activist and development organizations, which developed during the anti-authoritarian movement during the 1980s. Coalition building is a strategy that feminist activists pursue in order to promote gender justice. However, they are wary about whom they choose as allies or coalition partners – anxious to protect their credibility as non-partisan actors and unwilling to share the party affiliation of many civil society organizations. In Bangladesh, the ability of civil society groups to counter the state and promote their collective interest is significantly undermined since the two major political parties, AL and BNP, have managed to penetrate these organizations, whether professional, non-governmental or local. Interactions between political parties and civil society organizations are dominated by concerns on the part of the latter about how the relationship will affect their own legitimacy and autonomy, and feminist organizations share this caution. The state has emerged as the key actor with whom the civil society organizations negotiate directly rather than pursuing their agendas within the formal political sphere.

State dependence on international aid in the 1970s and 1980s significantly helped the proliferation of gender and development projects implemented by the government. In this context links with the donors and the international development agenda were strategically used by feminists to create pressure on the state to implement reforms promoting gender equity. The flip side of this is that, on the whole, women's rights issues have been interpreted by scholars and the public either as a 'Western import' or as a development issue promoted by the donors (Nazneen and Sultan 2009). Feminist organizations have been questioned by non-NGO civil society actors and the wider public regarding their commitment and legitimacy as representatives of women's interests.

Interpreting women's rights issues as development issues was encouraged by the growth of a large NGO sector fed by the availability of donor funding since the mid-1980s. Civil society space came to be dominated by NGOs (Rahman 2006), among whom feminist and women's organizations could recruit allies and form coalitions to exert pressure on the state. In many cases, however, the NGO-ization process and the use of external funding led to a depoliticization of the women's rights agenda (Nazneen and Sultan 2009). For feminist organizations, the key challenges are ensuring that they are not labelled as development NGOs, and that their strategies for strengthening voice help to attain the transformative goals of the movement.

Case study organizations

The case study organizations are different in size, ideological leanings, organizational structures, resources (time, expertise and money), and the societal support they have received. Table 1.1 provides details: year of establishment, membership strength, nature of the organization, and key demands.

Table 1.1 Case study organizations

Name and membership	Successful campaign chosen as research focus of this chapter	Strategies	Results/effects
Bangladesh Mahila Parishad Formed in 1970 150,000 voluntary members	Women's political empowerment	• Injustice framing • Coalition building • Use of media to raise awareness • Use of personal linkages	• Demands reflected in political party documents, but lack real commitment • Reform of the Peoples' Representation Ordinance (PRO) during 2006–9 • Increased media coverage and more informed reporting
Women for Women Formed in 1973 46 voluntary members	Advocacy on CEDAW, seeking removal of reservations (on articles 2 and 16 (1)(c)) and an explanation of the article implementation of the Convention	• Framing as international legal obligation • Coalition building • Use of transnational linkages • Use of personal linkages	• Increased awareness in the state and by women's organizations • Removal of a few reservations in 1997 • State commitment to reviewing remaining reservations with a view to removal • Greater awareness amongst civil society about CEDAW

Naripokkho Formed in 1983 120 voluntary members	Movement against acid violence[5] against women and girls	• Framing emphasized social justice and solidarity • Use of media to raise awareness • Awareness raising amongst survivors • Monitoring state service provision • Legal cases against perpetrators • Coalition building • Use of personal linkages	• Commitment to fighting acid violence mentioned in political party documents • State commitment evidenced in formulation of laws, provision of services and resources • Approach of monitoring state services developed and transferred to other organizations • Increased media coverage and more informed reporting • Public awareness of issue

Strategies used for mobilizing support and organizing voice: gains, trade-offs and compromises

Framing the issues

One of the key strategies used by all three case study organizations for mobilizing support and organizing a collective voice was to 'name and frame' or package (Gamson 1975) the issues in a manner that created a 'common understanding' and feelings of solidarity and trust amongst the participants of the movement (Tarrow 1998). This was done through identifying and negotiating minimum criteria upon which everyone agreed, and sometimes by deciding to leave certain issues out of the debate. At times this led to a focus on the practical needs of women, de-emphasizing women's more contentious strategic interests (Moser 1993).

The framing strategies were also influenced by the types of emotions the organization wanted to evoke in people. Issues were framed differently for different participants by taking into account variations from the organization's core constituency.

BANGLADESH MAHILA PARISHAD (BMP)

BMP framed the issue of women's political empowerment for its core constituents of elected female representatives, BMP members, and women's or civil society organizations as a matter of entitlement. They emphasized that women's equal participation at all decision-making levels was a precondition for women to be able to gain equal rights in economic and social spheres. Barriers to women's political empowerment were framed as a collective injustice to women. This 'injustice framing' was crucial to building a collective identity amongst the core constituents.

> [M]aking our members and women realize that unless women have the decision-making power they cannot change their economic and social position…. The women representatives were discriminated against by their male colleagues and at the institutional level. They were angry. We wanted to support them and create a general awareness among women about this injustice. (Interview, BMP 1, 14 July 2008)

BMP approached political party leaders and state officials strategically, focused on their election promises about reserved seats and direct elections, and highlighted gender biases within the political system that hinder women's full participation. Increasing women's political participation through reservation and capacity building for women representatives were the minimal criteria upon which all the constituents had agreed.

This strategic framing also marked a shift in how BMP perceived its role and the context within which political parties and state officials operated. BMP positioned itself as a lobbying organization, a shift from its earlier more confrontational approach, to interact with the state apparatus and political parties in the post-authoritarian period. It realized that the state's executive branch was a key instrument for change that needed to be lobbied. Though the major political parties did not share the same commitment towards women's political empowerment, they might respond to lobbying if BMP were able to highlight the benefits of supporting this agenda. Also, the changes in the 'political opportunity structure' ushered in by the caretaker government in recent years[6] (with reforms of state agencies and, particularly, the election commission) were seen as opening up spaces for policy advocacy through lobbying (Interview, BMP 1, 14 July 2008).

The impact of this package of strategies on legitimacy and space for feminist demand has been mixed. BMP has created a strong sense of solidarity and trust amongst its core constituents and the legitimacy of these demands is widely recognized. However, the strategic framing approach to negotiating with state officials and political parties has had limited impact. Making political parties accountable for their electoral promises is difficult since they do not perceive that failing to meet feminist demands can lead to any significant loss of votes or support. Also, BMP's framing strategy was unable to address the perceived high political costs for the parties associated with increasing the number of reserved seats for women or direct elections to these seats. Such costs could include an opposition within parties to designating, rotating or reserving constituencies for women, as that could mean lost opportunities for male politicians; and a fear of losing seats to other parties who might field capable female candidates in these reserved seats.

NARIPOKKHO (NP)

Like BMP, NP varied its framing strategy for the acid survivors' movement according to whether it was addressing core or non-core constituents. The minimum criterion was to create a sense of solidarity for the cause of acid survivors by presenting the matter as an issue of social justice. The emphasis on social justice stemmed from the fact that the need for medical treatment, rehabilitation and justice for the survivors may overshadow the goals of social awareness against this crime. Thus it was necessary to refer to acid survivors as 'survivors' and not 'victims' of acid violence. This meant stressing how the 'personhood' of a survivor is violated by the crime and the consequent suffering that the survivor and her family experience. It also required engagement with the survivors to change society's perceptions, and extensive negotiations with the media and state machineries. This process created a space for making demands on how the healthcare and legal needs of the survivors are met, as well as raising awareness to prevent this crime.

For the survivors, framing the issue in this way legitimized their demands for medical treatment, justice and rehabilitation. For the other constituents, framing the issue along the lines of 'social justice' emphasized the need for reflecting on the nature of a society that gave rise to, enabled and tolerated such a heinous crime (Interview, NP 3, 13 September 2008). Using this framing, NP deliberately tried to evoke empathy for, and protectiveness towards, the survivors amongst the judges, police personnel and doctors. This was to motivate the service providers into increasing their service quality and creating an enabling environment for the survivors. One NP activist explained:

> [O]ur target was to use emotions, we encouraged the girls to speak out, to describe their traumas, pains, their family [this was also a part of a healing therapy]. It is difficult to ignore if you see it, hear it, if they are a person to you. (Interview, NP 2, 10 September 2008)

The other reason for using this strategy was to circumvent judgements from these service providers about the moral character of the survivors (usually teenage girls or young women), and speculations about premarital 'romantic' involvement. This was particularly useful in court, where such issues were malignantly introduced by the defendants' lawyers. One NP member, a lawyer, detailed her strategy:

> If I had tried to challenge society's views about what the comportment

of a good girl is, I would have hit a wall! Instead I argued that whether one was romantically involved did not mean that she deserved to have acid thrown at her. Her misdemeanour does not match the treatment she received. That the defendant's lawyer who is like her father/ brother… should not be making such dirty insinuations.... (Interview, NP 3, 14 September 2008)

However, the stress on evoking empathy for the survivors by highlighting their suffering involved a strategic compromise: leaving certain issues out of the debate. The movement against acid violence did not challenge the social definition of the acceptable behaviour of a 'good girl' head on. Issues around adolescent romance and sexuality were explored with the survivors in 'safe' environments and not in the public domain, to avoid being labelled as promoting what are perceived as 'Western' norms around sexual behaviour (Interview, NP 4, 2 December 2008).

WOMEN FOR WOMEN (WFW)

WFW, in framing demands for full ratification and implementation of CEDAW, also distinguished its approaches to core and other constituents. State obligation to ratify the convention was identified as the minimum criterion for action, agreed after extensive discussions with the core constituents, National Coalition for Beijing Process members (see the following section). CEDAW was presented as a 'bill of rights for women' to the core group (interview, WFW 1, 30 July 2008). Articles from CEDAW were linked to the different articles of the Platform for Action, in order to contextualize and illustrate the nature and types of discrimination women faced. This helped to concretize the issue at the grassroots level. A WFW member explained:

> In the field, we started by saying CEDAW was a dalil [legal document], and the women thought it was a deed for land! So we decided to link CEDAW's articles to women's experiences of discrimination and to the PFA which concretized the issue. (Interview, WFW 3, 30 July 2008)

However, in public forums and during negotiations with the

bureaucracy, WFW deliberately chose to frame the removal of reservations on Article 2 of CEDAW and the state obligation to ensure gender equality as mandatory clauses, because the state is a signatory to the convention. The demand to ratify the remaining articles of the convention was based on the following arguments: (1) CEDAW does not violate the constitution, and is in fact in accordance with it; (2) other Islamic countries have reformed Islamic laws; (3) Bangladesh does not have an Islamic constitution but a secular one; and (4) many of the current personal laws in Bangladesh are discriminatory. These arguments also allowed WFW to avoid being labelled as imposing 'Western' values and norms or pushing a donor-driven agenda. A WFW member observed:

> We tried to convince a person logically through examples showing how the religious personal laws can be discriminatory; why the government is accountable under CEDAW to address gender inequality.... We used the constitution ... we approached the state diplomatically, because of the conservative elements.... (Interview, WFW 1, 30 July 2008)

This 'legalistic' approach reflects a clear understanding of the 'political context' – the role played by Islam and the Islamic parties in politics, and the conservatism that exists within the bureaucracy. WFC emphasized state obligation, examples of reform in other countries, and the Bangladesh constitution to circumvent accusations of being anti–Islamic and to create space for negotiations with the state. The reference to international obligations and the Platform for Action was useful in the context of the pre- and post-Beijing process. WFW was able to maintain an even pressure on the conservative bureaucrats up until the early 2000s without inviting any backlash from fundamentalist quarters. Many members and their acquaintances were in key positions in the bureaucracy, which sustained their ability to exert pressure. But this 'legalistic' framing involved trade-offs. The stress on the state being under international legal obligation and on secularism limited the issue to specific women's groups, state officials and sections of civil society.

It was not accepted by any of the political parties as a mainstream issue, specifically because this involved changing religious personal law – a move that could be deemed anti–Islamic and be unpopular politically. There was no debate or inclusion of this issue in the wider civil society arena, either. In fact, this lack of debate within the civil and political society proved costly, particularly with the rise of *madrassah*-based Islamic platforms like Hefazat-E-Islam, which have specifically targeted CEDAW and campaigned against feminist demands for changing religious personal laws.

The following key insights emerge from our analysis of the framing strategies of the three organizations. 'Packaging' strategies created a sense of solidarity amongst the core constituents of the case study organizations. These were also effective in ensuring the support needed from other civil society groups, particularly on women's political empowerment and the acid survivors' issue, but less so on CEDAW. An important reason for this success was that the issues were packaged in an uncontroversial manner (leaving out contentious issues), so that the cost of supporting these causes publicly would be low.

The strategic approach taken by BMP and WFW, and the 'experiential' approach of NP helped them to avoid controversy and access state officials. This encouraged state officials to view these issues as worthy of addressing and to realize that doing so would not jeopardize their positions within the state structure. It also indicates that the case study organizations possessed a clear understanding of how to appeal to the state, and of the space that had been created by changes in the political or international context. However, the strategic framing process involved negotiations and the exclusion of contentious issues, which meant there were trade-offs on each issue. The 'package' of strategies had limited impact on strengthening the feminist agenda and voice within political parties. The political costs of addressing these issues remain high as they entail dealing with issues that might be unpopular with the electorate and with male politicians. The case study organizations therefore failed to address the issues directly with the political parties.

Coalition building

Coalition building with civil society actors, particularly women's and human rights organizations, emerged as a key strategy used by all three case study organizations. The impetus for coalition building came from the need to build support for their cause, demonstrate the strength of their movement, and thereby increase pressure on the state. Coalitions and networks amongst civil society actors increased as the democratization process unfolded in the 1990s. In a context where civil society is polarized and partisan, coalition building can be problematic and risky, because the legitimacy and credibility of any organization can be affected by the alliances and coalitions it creates or joins. The feminist organizations have been careful in selecting their individual allies and coalition members, looking for those who subscribed to similar ideologies, were 'perceived' to have a non-partisan position, and were therefore considered trustworthy. The feminist organizations also needed to control and set the agenda to avoid co-option by partisan members of the coalition or political parties. On the flip side, coalition building by the feminist organizations meant the avoidance of a close engagement with political parties for fear of losing credibility, and having an excessive focus on lobbying the state. The compulsion to control the agenda also arose from the need to separate rights-based coalitions from development networks, as feminist organizations feared losing credibility by being labelled as development NGOs.

Our analysis shows that all three organizations had to establish their legitimacy to work on a particular issue and take on the leadership role in an alliance. This was done by demonstrating their expertise and experience, their ability to lead, and their command of the necessary resources such as connections with the state bureaucracy, media, international agencies and human resources. This raised the question of hierarchy amongst the coalition members, as certain organizations were seen as having greater credibility and resources, which created power asymmetries. The initiator of the coalition usually held the power to set and control the agenda. Such power asymmetries were most evident in the case of coalitions with smaller women's organizations based outside the capital that had little chance of making their voices heard. This was in contradiction with the unspoken but implicit expectation of reciprocity in entering into and forming alliances (an expectation that the coalition would be mutually beneficial to the initiator and to those joining, and that lending organizational support entitled them to receive support in return). However, reciprocity did not always follow and this created tensions amongst the leaders of the coalitions and its members. We use the case of coalition building by BMP to illustrate these points.

BMP set up the Shamajik Protirodh Committee (SPC or Social Resistance Committee) in 2001 in response to electoral violence against minorities, and later adopted the issue of women's political empowerment too. BMP felt that by using this 'umbrella' organization the visibility of the issue would increase and their own vulnerability in case of a backlash would be lessened.

This coalition has grown to 46 members and operates as a 'loose' (informal) platform that concentrates on three issues proposed by BMP: post-election violence against women and minorities; the revision of the Women's Advancement Policy; and seeking reserved seats for women in Parliament. BMP initiates the programme procedures and takes decisions in consultation with members, who share the expenses. Since BMP serves as the secretariat of the coalition, it has a greater say than any other member. One BMP interviewee pointed out that '[w]hoever writes the minutes controls the agenda' (Interview, BMP 2, 18 July 2008). BMP's leadership in this coalition is based on their track record and capacity to coordinate and lead. The committee, which includes human rights organizations, cultural organizations, women's organizations and development NGOs, recognizes that not everyone can contribute or be equally active.

Although BMP's leadership is recognized within the coalition, acceptance by other established feminist organizations and development NGOs within the coalition of its leadership role and the norms of reciprocity varies. Development NGOs do not contest BMP's interpretation of the issues and programmatic decisions, and are largely content to participate in the greater movement, which legitimizes their claim to work on women's political empowerment. This is also largely true of small local-level women's organizations. However, other established feminist organizations, such as NP or WFW, are more critical of the process as well as the formulation of the agenda. They acknowledged BMP's leadership in the SPC but were critical that it was not playing by the same rules as other members of the alliance. They felt that BMP was not reciprocal and did not recognize their leadership in other areas.

Although BMP wishes to set the agenda, it also engages in consensus building. This is done through identifying issues to which the members easily respond and on which they readily agree to take a common position. BMP is conscious of differences of opinion within the coalition and has made conscious efforts to manage and address these differences. There is an increased acceptance of differences of approach and members are more willing to negotiate and come to a common understanding. One BMP interviewee pointed out:

> Organizations have a more similar understanding of issues than before, and perhaps the context has brought together organizations and helped them to work together.... There is greater unity and maturity now and demands are stronger. Government not keeping its promises has raised people's awareness.... The coalition between organizations has become much stronger. (Interview, BMP 1, 14 July 2008).

Their strategy of reaching out to various civil society organizations and individuals and forming coalitions has given the feminist organizations additional visibility, presence and credibility, and increased their outreach beyond their organizational membership to smaller and often local-level women's organizations (Goetz and Hassim 2003). The coalitions have not been restricted to women's rights organizations but have enlisted a broader membership, including men. This has served the mutual interests of the case study organizations as well as their coalition members, the latter gaining information and access to national networks.

However, a major consequence of the lead organization controlling the agenda is that the voices of smaller women's organizations and their local issues are marginalized during the negotiation processes. For example, issues and organizations that represent a marginal position, such as ethnic and religious minority women within the existing political systems, or discrimination faced by a particular section of women workers, such as sex workers or informal agricultural workers, do not receive adequate attention. This is generally accepted as an internal trade-off by both parties, especially since the small local organizations do not have the convening capacity and resources required to voice issues within these coalitions and at the national level.

Use of personal networks

Given the patron–clientelist nature of Bangladesh politics and society, using personal networks emerged as an effective strategy for these three organizations to access state officials, political party officials and civil society groups. Familial or other types of personal connections create a sense of obligation to reciprocate and evoke trust, which are key factors in influencing people to act (Tarrow 1998). These networks opened up policy and organizational spaces for the feminists to voice their demands.

The primacy of personal networks for advancing feminist voice is also influenced by the following factors. The state has a contradictory position on gender equity issues, because of the 'moral conservatism' (Nazneen 2008) that exists within civil bureaucracy and the state's unwillingness to 'rock the boat' on issues around religion. The use of insiders within the bureaucracy has created space and opportunities for furthering the feminist agenda and overcoming resistance. Secondly, the polarization of civil society actors into two camps makes it difficult to induce trust and mobilize support unless a sense of obligation is invoked.

Although this is a common strategy, we discuss WFW here since this example illustrates these points best. The reservations placed by Bangladesh on CEDAW related to personal laws, which in Bangladesh are based on religion. The resistance to reforming these discriminatory laws within the bureaucracy and from political parties is high, due to the fear of backlash from religious groups. Since 1996, both centrist parties have formed tacit and overt alliances with Jamaat for winning elections and forming governments (Nazneen 2008), making advocacy for the ratification of CEDAW a difficult proposition.

Despite these constraints, WFW successfully used personal networks to lobby the state to ratify CEDAW. Many of their members are academics teaching at the university. They have family members or former students working within the civil bureaucracy. This created an opportunity for the organization to lobby key people and access state machinery. A WFW member explained:

> All of us have links with the bureaucracy.… [A] lot of the government secretaries are our students. Our family members are state officials.… If we made a request … they could not overlook it. They felt obliged. (Interview, WFW 1, 30 July 2008)

Moreover, in the 1990s when WFW started working on the full ratification and implementation of CEDAW, many of their members were in key positions in the civil bureaucracy. Having insiders within the state structure allowed them to raise gender equity issues in various state forums, build rapport with key officials, and avoid bureaucratic resistance. A WFW member observed:

> We had the right people in the right places. One member was a government adviser … we were in the Planning Commission, and in donor agencies. We could bring in gender issues at different levels of policy-making process. So we did not face bureaucratic resistance. We could negotiate.… (Interview, WFW 2, 16 August 2008)

Like WFW, the other two organizations also used personal networks to access state officials. NP used familial ties and friendships developed through advocacy networks to access the health and law ministers. This not only provided high coverage of the issue but also allowed the organization to overcome any resistance they faced when trying to access and monitor state services provided to acid survivors. BMP interviewees also pointed out that it was an effective strategy to garner support from political parties. The organization approached specific people who they felt would be more receptive, despite the overall reluctance within political parties to address women's political empowerment. One BMP interviewee explained:

> We try and work with people who are progressive within the party, who we know…. They do not subscribe to our philosophy but we have a personal claim on them. (Interview, BMP 2, 18 July 2008).

Though the use of personal networks expedited the process of accessing the state, and in certain cases ensured collaborative relations, using personal networks was not effective for dealing with the political party leadership. This is partly due to the fact that for some of the organizations, such as WFW, the party leaders were not from the same social background. The experience of BMP in dealing with political parties shows that their issues were marginalized in mainstream politics. All of these organizations (BMP to a lesser extent, perhaps) have kept their distance from political parties for fear of losing credibility and legitimacy as members of civil society. While this is pragmatic, it limits the possibility of mainstreaming the feminist agenda within the larger political debate.

As shown above, personal connections induce a sense of obligation, reciprocity and trust, and help to mobilize support from a range of actors. The organizations stressed that the 'personal claim' and 'sense of obligation' such networks evoke among state officials allowed them to further their causes. Relying on personal links also implies that these links needed to be identified, cultivated and maintained. Depending on particular individuals means that if they are absent or lose their positions of authority, the effectiveness of the organizations is threatened. In spite of this risk, using personal networks in the Bangladeshi context is an effective strategy, since insiders within the state structure help to overcome bureaucratic resistance in addressing feminist concerns.

Use of transnational linkages

Using transnational networks also emerged as an effective strategy for following up on commitments made by the state. These linkages allowed the case study organizations to establish themselves as legitimate interlocutors on certain issues. It created space for the women's rights agenda in different national forums and put pressure on the state. The example of WFW and its efforts to remove state reservations placed on articles of the CEDAW convention illustrates these points.

CEDAW was the creation of an international feminist movement. It was intended that this internationally binding convention would support the demands of national-level women's movements, while also making each state accountable to an international body for meeting these demands. As we have seen, the international context and pre- and post-Beijing processes created the space and opportunities for WFW and other feminist organizations to interact amongst themselves at the national level, as well as with international feminist organizations, the state, and UN bodies. In Bangladesh the Beijing process also coincided with democratization, which increased interest in and awareness of the country's CEDAW reporting process, thereby strengthening its capacity. From the mid-1990s the feminist movement began to interact with the state on CEDAW reporting and preparing alternative reports to the CEDAW committee. The convergence of these political and international opportunities created a context in which feminists could pressurize the state to fulfil its international obligations and remove discrimination against women.

It was in this context that WFW was formed and became a member of the various regional and international forums working on issues related to CEDAW as well as on gender equality. It helped that a number of the WFW members had worked as 'experts' internationally on these issues (Gaventa and McGee 2010). Their expertise placed them as legitimate interlocutors in relation to CEDAW, for the government as well as for the feminist movement.

WFW had been the convener of the National Preparatory Committee for the Beijing NGO Forum and it represented the Bangladeshi organizations in international forums. It had many opportunities to participate in international processes related to the Beijing Conference and its follow-up. These included coordinating the national alternative report for Beijing Plus Fifteen and the CEDAW reporting and monitoring process, where WFW had facilitated government reporting and had also been at the forefront of NGO reporting to the CEDAW committee. Effective use of these transnational linkages allowed WFW to strengthen its legitimacy as an actor and further its agenda in creating pressure on the state.

Conclusions: implications of these strategies for feminist voice

What can be said about feminist activism and voice in Bangladesh, on the basis of the analysis presented above? We focused on 'political opportunities' (changes in the national political environment) and the international context, as well as on mobilizing structures (such as personal networks or formal movements) and framing strategies (McAdam *et al.* 2001). We explored how feminist activism and voice (agency) unfold within various structural constraints and opportunities. We showed how feminist organizations in Bangladesh used different strategies based on a clear assessment of existing opportunities within the national context. We assessed the political costs and trade-offs involved in employing each strategy and choosing to target amenable parts of the state. The influence of the context is clear in how the case study organizations – despite their differences in membership, organizational structure, outreach and size – use similar strategies in negotiating with the state bureaucracy, political parties and civil society actors. These include targeting responsive parts of the state selectively, establishing wider platforms and coalitions with like-minded civil society actors, ensuring autonomy from the political parties, and using personal relationships to overcome difficulties in accessing different constituents. These strategies were effective for channelling feminist voice and building a constituency for a feminist agenda. In tandem with these strategies all three organizations created new structures for mobilization (such as new coalitions) and amplified their voice by making their constituency visible and building consensus amongst the actors, whether within the state or as part of civil society. Effective use of these strategies also helped the organizations to establish a leadership role in advocating a particular agenda. Internal politics within the alliances, however, often entailed a suppression of minority feminisms (Menon 2007) and marginal voices.

The discussion below focuses on the compromises and gains made by the feminist organizations while advocating their agenda, and the implications of these outcomes for feminist voice in Bangladesh. The effectiveness of their strategies is illustrated by policy gains and increased awareness around the issues they tackled. Table 1.1 listed the results – changes in government policy on women's representation such as the public representation order; the removal of some of the reservations on CEDAW articles; the creation of health care and legal services for acid survivors; and the increased public debate on these issues.

At the beginning of the chapter we pointed out that mobilizing support is a matter of strategic decisions based on well-chosen compromises. Our discussion of the strategies that the case study organizations used – whether in framing, using networks, or building alliances – showed that all three organizations made various compromises. In most cases these were well chosen since they were based on a clear assessment of the national context and political opportunities; a correct analysis of the incentives that may induce action; and an ability to weigh the trade-offs involved, with a willingness to bear certain costs in order to secure corresponding advantages.

Thus the organizations decided to 'create meaning' or frame an issue by identifying minimum criteria for all supporters; packaging issues differently for different groups (particularly for state officials, so that their involvement did not jeopardize their position); and leaving out certain issues that were contentious given the social and political context (not debating the role played by religion; not challenging assumptions about the comportment of a 'good girl'). This, at times, led to emphasizing 'practical' matters such as increasing reserved seats for women in Parliament or the international obligations of the state to ratify CEDAW. Although this raised the issue in public, it did not press certain debates in the political arena. Without the engagement of political parties and acceptance from the general public, progressive legislation or policies have a limited impact on women's rights.

The political context – particularly the polarization of civil society actors into two party camps, the risk of losing credibility as an actor by being associated with any particular political party, and the rise of Islam in politics – influenced how the organizations selected their allies within civil society, and explains why they chose not to engage closely with political parties. Asserting their autonomy when dealing with political parties and their affiliates, and ensuring control over their own agenda in this context, was crucial for establishing organizational legitimacy as representatives of women's interests. This specific context and bureaucratic resistance also led them to use personal networks to induce a sense of obligation and trust amongst the state officials, and to work through insiders within the state bureaucracy to overcome resistance and moral conservatism.

Another question which the case studies raise is about which women within the coalition represent and voice the feminist agenda in the various policy spaces. Admittedly, the organizations we chose are composed of urban, intellectual elite, educated, middle-class women (or are led by them in the case of BMP), which is not unusual since such women lead feminist activism in many countries (Basu 2010). When engaging in policy and civil society spaces, these groups of women are perceived as 'experts' because of their knowledge, skills and experience, which confers a legitimacy to their voice. Questions inevitably remain about whether and how women from other classes or located in rural areas access policy and decision-making spaces, and how their agenda and priorities are represented. Are certain issues – for example, rural livelihoods or informal sector work – adequately and effectively addressed by elite, urban, educated, middle-class feminists in Bangladesh who claim they represent different constituencies through their alliances? Our analysis shows that, in fact, within coalitions the voices of smaller local organizations are marginalized.

Although political parties talk of women's political participation and the need to address acid violence, it is no more than rhetoric, and the risk of political association with parties has led to non-engagement or limited engagement in the formal political arena. While this may have allowed feminist organizations to maintain their autonomy and legitimacy as actors, the trade-off has been that the feminist agendas (aside from the Women in Development agenda) have not entered the mainstream political arena. Admittedly, though, engaging with political parties does not guarantee these issues will enter the public debate. Moreover, the presence of Women in Development and Gender and Development agendas in the political arena is perhaps linked to the overwhelming influence of the gender and development discourse, actors, and projects.

The feminist organizations have also elected to engage more thoroughly with the state bureaucracy. This appears to be less costly in terms of credibility and allows them to establish their legitimacy as actors. This was facilitated by the convergence of the democratization process and the international context (pre- and post-Beijing), which created the scope and space for effective engagement with the state. This does not imply that influencing the state has been easy, or that it has taken place on the terms set by feminist organizations. In fact, it is the state that mainly sets the terms of negotiations. However, over-reliance on the state and perhaps an excessive focus on policy has limited the organizations from exploring alternative forums, such as the media, where feminist voice could have been effective and legitimate.

On the whole, despite the different trade-offs, the strategies used by feminist organizations have furthered their agenda, created legitimacy and expanded the space for feminist voice over the last two decades. However, the very success of these strategies, as the discussion has shown, has limited the exploration of alternative forums and has been achieved at the cost of marginalizing smaller voices and excluding certain agendas. In 2013, with the rise of Hefazat-E-Islam (a loose platform of Islamist groups), this lack of alternative fora for channelling feminist voice – together with a limited presence in the formal political arena, and over-reliance on the state bureaucracy – have created a precarious position for feminist activism in Bangladesh. This has raised the question of whether these strategies will remain as 'well-chosen' in the coming years.

Acknowledgements

We are grateful to Adrian Leftwich, Rounaq Jahan and the participants at the Bellagio conference for their incisive comments. Pathways of Women's Empowerment RPC funded the research for this chapter.

Notes

1 Members of an organization may not necessarily be a constituent group. Constituents of an organization, if it is an 'another-serving' organization (Batliwala 2008), are those groups whose interest the organization tries to meet. So the organization's members may work for and with the constituents.
2 By 'feminist organization' we mean those who explicitly state that they are feminist and focus on changing gender power structures. Women's organizations may work to address women's practical gender interests (Molyneux 1985), but may not necessarily aim to change gender power structures.
3 Some of these studies include retrospective analyses of factors that led to change, or the differences between various feminist groups and their engagement with the state (Kabeer 1989; Jahan 1995).

4 Our position as insiders made it easier to access the organizations and build trust. However, it also led to difficulties such as sensitivities about interpretations. One of us is a member of NP and the other is closely linked with WFW and BMP. Our research primarily relied on in-depth interviews and document analysis. However, to minimize our personal biases we conducted repeated interviews, used field memos, held validation workshops with the organizations, and presented our findings and analysis to key resource people – both academics and activists – who work in feminist movements in Bangladesh. The research was conducted during 2008–9 under the Pathways of Women's Empowerment Research Programme Consortium.

5 Acid throwing is a form of violent assault. Perpetrators of these attacks throw acid at their victims (usually at their faces), burning them, and damaging skin tissue, often exposing and sometimes dissolving the bones. In Bangladesh women were often targeted if they turned down romantic proposals.

6 For example in 2006, when an interim government was formed, an initiative was taken to reform the Public Representation Ordinance – whereby a number of measures were proposed and accepted to increase the party nominations of women to committees and for elections.

References

Basu, A. (2010) 'Introduction' in A. Basu (ed.), 'Revisiting Women's Movement in Global Perspective' (draft MS).

Batliwala, S. (2008) *Building Feminist Movements and Organizations: Clarifying Our Concepts*, AWID, Toronto.

Begum, M. (1998) *Banglar Nari Andolon* (Women's Movement in Bangladesh), Shomoy, Dhaka.

Chowdhury, E. H. (2011) *Transnationalism Reversed: Women Organising Against Gendered Violence in Bangladesh*, SUNY Press, NY.

Gamson, W. (1975) *The Strategy of Social Protest*. Homewood, IL.

Gaventa, J. and R. McGee (2010) 'Introduction', in J. Gaventa and R. McGee (eds), *Making Change Happen: Citizen Action and National Policy Reform*, Zed Books, London.

Ghosh, A. (2005) *The Hungry Tide*, HarperCollins, New York, NY.

Goetz, A. M. (2001) *Women Development Workers*, UPL, Dhaka.

Goetz, A. M. and S. Hassim (2003) *No Short Cuts to Power: African Women in Politics and Policy Making*, Zed Books, London and New York, NY.

Goetz, A. M. and C. Nyamu-Musembi (2008) 'Voice and Women's Empowerment: Mapping a Research Agenda', Pathways Working Paper No. 2, Pathways of Women's Empowerment RPC, Brighton.

Jahan, R. (1995) 'Men in Seclusion and Women in Public: Rokeya's Dreams and Women's Struggles in Bangladesh', in A. Basu (ed.), *The Challenges of Local Feminisms: Women's Movements in Global Perspective*, Westview Press, Boulder, CO.

Jaquette, J. S. (1994) *The Women's Movement in Latin America: Participation and Democracy*, Westview Press, Boulder, CO.

Kabeer, N. (1989) 'Subordination and Struggle', *New Left Review*, No. 168, pp. 95–121.

Karim, L. (2011) *Microfinance and Its Discontents: Women in Debt in Bangladesh*, University of Minnesota Press, Minneapolis, MN.

McAdam, D., J. D. McCarthy and M. Zald (2001) *Comparative Perspectives on Social Movement*, Cambridge University Press, Cambridge.

Menon, N. (ed.) (2007) *Sexualities*, Women Unlimited, New Delhi.

Molyneux, M. (1985) 'Mobilization without Emancipation: Women's Interests, State and Revolution in Nicaragua', *Critical Social Policy*, No. 4, p. 10.

Moser, C. O. N. (1993) *Gender Planning and Development: Theory, Practice and Training,* Routledge: London.

Nazneen, S. (2008) 'Gender Sensitive Accountability of Service Delivery NGOs: BRAC and Proshika in Bangladesh', PhD thesis, Institute of Development Studies, University of Sussex.

Nazneen, S. and M. Sultan (2009) 'Struggling for Survival and Autonomy: Impact of NGO-ization on Women's Organizations in Bangladesh', *Development*, Vol. 52, No. 2, pp. 193–9.

Rahman, S. (2006) 'Development, Democracy and the NGO Sector: Theory and Evidence from Bangladesh', *Journal of Developing Societies*, Vol. 22, No. 4, pp. 451–73.

Ryan, B. (1992) *Feminisms and Women's Movement*, Routledge, London.

Tarrow, S. (1998) *The Power in Movement: Social Movement and Contentious Politics*, Cambridge University Press, Cambridge.

Waylen, G. (1996) *Gender in Third World Politics*, Open University Press, Milton Keynes.

2

Feminisms in Brazil
Voicing and Channelling Women's Diverse Demands

Cecilia M. B. Sardenberg and Ana Alice Alcantara Costa

Over the last four decades, feminist and women's movements in Brazil have made significant advances towards achieving gender justice, securing rights and reforming public policy. Yet the combined effects of sexism, racism, lesbophobia, ageism and other currents of inequality and domination that course through a very skewed class society have kept the gaps among women quite wide, even though gaps between men and women have narrowed. This is why, along with the fight for gender equality, women must wage struggles for social and economic justice in other arenas to address inequalities based on class, race and sexuality. As a result, different identity 'feminisms' – and a corresponding gamut of feminist voices – have arisen in Brazil, creating the need to deal not only with tensions due to existing inequalities, but also with the task of devising strategies to channel very diverse women's demands.

In this chapter we discuss how feminisms in Brazil have responded to this challenge. We look at the national conferences for women held over the last decade – the Conference of Brazilian Women (2002) and the National Women's Public Policy Conferences I and II (2004 and 2007) – and examine their products: the Feminist Political Platform and the National Women's Public Policy Plans I and II. We contend that the highly participatory character of these events, which mobilized close to 300,000 women all over Brazil, allowed for the formulation of policies for women that recognize the diversity of experiences, identities, and existing inequalities among women, as well as catering to the needs and demands of the less privileged. We further contend that in redefining feminist struggles to incorporate these specific demands, feminisms in Brazil have been revitalized. This demonstrates that putting to work what Anna Jónasdóttir calls a '*differentiated solidarity* among women, a solidarity built on awareness of both common and different interests' (Jónasdóttir 2009: 58) is fundamental to strengthening feminist voice in contemporary capitalist societies.

This is a crucial point to take into account as we assess feminist and women's movements in Latin America. Just a decade ago, Nikki Craske lamented that re-democratization processes in the region, following the long periods of dictatorship that some countries such as Brazil experienced, operated as a 'dispersion factor' for social movements. 'By the 1990s,' she stated, 'it is increasingly difficult to speak of a "women's movement". Rather it is diverse, plural and complex as its different constituent elements seek ways of furthering their goals on the new institution terrain' (Craske 2000: 5). She was concerned with the weakening of 'the mobilizing capacity of the women's movement', observing that a change was taking place in the relationship between women's movements and the state: 'There has been a shift from making demands on the state to negotiations with it' (*ibid.*: 6). According to her, this shift came accompanied (and in turn fostered) by a proliferation of non-governmental organizations (NGOs), who became 'major actors in the women's movement, almost to the point that these are becoming proxies for other actors whose voices are being drowned' (*ibid.*: 6). Others have expressed similar concerns (Lebon 1997; Razavi 2000).

We agree that, along with other Brazilian social movements, feminist and women's movements ebbed during the early 1990s. However, this was only for a short period. By 1995, feminists were very active again, particularly within the women's movement, creating networks and coalitions in preparation for the Fourth World Conference for Women in Beijing (Sardenberg and Costa

2010). Women's organizing in Brazil has been very active in the last 15 years. As detailed later in this chapter, during this period feminism in Brazil also expanded its scope of action by diversifying its grassroots membership – a move which, instead of weakening the movement, actually strengthened it.

Writing about the relationship between feminist and women's movements in the mid-1990s, Soares *et al.* (1995: 309–10) spoke of how they reflected 'the many dimensions of women's subordination as well as the social, cultural, ethnic, and generational diversity of its participants'. In addition to being heterogeneous, they noted that women's movements in Brazil were also 'spontaneous', which led to 'a varied presence in the national arena and sometimes to ambiguous and contradictory demands' (*ibid.*: 310). Arguing that, despite diversity, the common ground women's movements shared was 'the discovery of a common identity as women and the emphasis on daily life', Soares *et al.* suggested that 'each part of the women's movement could be analysed as a social movement in itself, with its own dynamics and modes of expression. These parts intersect, interrelate, and, at times, conflict' (*ibid.*: 310).

Their observations remain valid: the feminist movement is still 'but one expression of a broader women's movement' (*ibid.*: 310). Nonetheless, as we hope to demonstrate in this chapter, it has become increasingly difficult to define borders and limits between them, in terms of the people involved, as feminists are active in all 'expressions' of the broader movement. Likewise, the feminist movement too has expanded considerably, including within its widening wings an increasing number of women from other segments of the broader women's movements (Sardenberg and Costa 2010).

In what follows, we briefly outline the major strides and challenges of contemporary feminisms in Brazil, highlighting the processes that gave rise to the National Conference of Brazilian Women and the First and Second National Women's Public Policy Conferences. We then focus on the products of these conferences – the Feminist Political Platform and the First and Second National Women's Public Policy Plans. We analyse these as expressions of feminist voice, showing how both solidarity and conflicts have characterized women's struggles in their diversity. In so doing, we hope to contribute to a better understanding of what improves the effectiveness of feminist voice in a context of deep inequalities among women. For us, carrying out this task has special meaning and implications: for over three decades, we have been feminist activists in different arenas and social movements, have participated in the aforementioned conferences, and have been involved in implementing and monitoring the public policies for women included in the national plans analysed here. We, too, constitute a 'feminist voice'.

Feminisms and feminist voice in Brazil: the recent past

The expression 'feminist voice' is widely employed, but it is rarely clear what is meant by it. In some instances, it is merely applied in reference to somebody who openly stands for women's rights and interests in a particular setting or context – for example, 'She is the feminist voice in the Bureau'. Yet it can also be expanded to include different forms of expressions in the struggle for greater gender justice, including the use of silence as resistance (Hartley 2011). Although we agree with Hartley that 'any expression that seeks to end sexism and promote gender equality' should be considered as 'feminist voice', and believe that all these expressions are relevant and deserving of greater analysis, in this chapter we focus only on expressions of 'collective' voice – that is, 'acts and arguments' of feminist and women's movements to influence public decisions towards the achievement of gender justice (Goetz and Nyamu-Musembi 2008).

Women's activism in Brazil has manifested itself in a wide range of social movements. However, by *women's movements* we refer only to those that centre on gender-based interests or, as Maxine Molyneux puts it (1998: 231–2), only to 'those arising from the social relations and positioning of the sexes and therefore pertaining, but in specific ways, to both men and women'. According to Molyneux, women's interests may be further distinguished as 'practical' and 'strategic'; the former defined as those 'based on the satisfaction of needs arising from women's placement within the sexual division of labour', whereas the latter involves 'claims to transform social relations in order to enhance women's position and to secure a more lasting re-positioning of women within the gender order and within society at large' (*ibid.*: 232). Following this distinction, we define *feminist movements* as those that are centred on women's strategic gender interests, recognizing, however, that these interests are always contextually defined, and vary in time and space, socially as well as geographically.

Contemporary feminisms emerged in Brazil in the context of democratic struggles and resistance against the military regime that came to power after the coup in 1964. The feminist movement was a part of the wide and heterogeneous movement that included women's struggles along with the fight for the country's re-democratization. Women's strategic discourses were diluted in the discourses of other anti-state social movements, which saw the military dictatorial regime as a common enemy that had to be brought down. Nevertheless, feminist organizations emerging in this period strove to amplify feminist voice by bringing new issues – domestic violence, discrimination against women in the labour force and their exclusion from decision-making spheres – into public debate. This involved redefining the concept of politics in order to include the 'personal' in the realm of the exercise of citizenship, so that everyday life practices would also be included – a perspective not easily accepted even by progressive forces at that time (Alvarez 1990).

By the late 1970s and early 1980s other important social movements had made their appearance on the political scene, and claimed 'autonomy' from political parties. Among them were the feminist, black, gay, ecological, and landless people movements, as well as those supporting the separation of indigenous territories – all seeking to expand 'the political terrain and the concepts of citizenship, democracy, equality, and participation' (Pitanguy 2002: 2–3).

The 1980s saw the re-democratization of the country and emerging social movements played an important role in forging demands that were made on the state. Amnesty was granted to political prisoners and those in exile were brought back to Brazil. They included activists from the political left, many of whom were women who had been active in feminist groups in Europe and the USA. At the same time, reforms in the Brazilian political party system paved the way for negotiations and alliances with members of newly created and more progressive parties, as well as for the acceptance and implementation of women's demands (Pinto 2003). In this new context, feminists were successful in including a feminist agenda in public policy and normative frames (Pitanguy 2002). Among them was a major women's health programme that opened dialogue between officials in the Ministry of Health and feminist activists (Villela 2001). Also, as a result of negotiations with opposition candidates, the first Council for the Status of Women was created in São Paulo in 1983. This was followed by the first police station for assaulted women, in 1986. By 1992, there were 141 such police stations across the country, which have now grown to over 400 (Pinto 2003; Gomes *et al.* 2009). The creation of local and state councils for women's rights did not follow at the same pace, but it is important to highlight the creation of the National Council for Women's Rights (CNDM) in 1986. These were certainly important results of the expression of feminist voice.

Participation in the newly formed institutions and supporting state policies for women brought new challenges for feminists, particularly the need to rethink the movement's position in relation to the state, which was no longer identified as the 'common enemy' (Costa 2005). Feminists had to recognize that the modern state was capable of influencing society not just through coercive means, but also through progressive policies. It was evident that it was important to recognize the relevance of progressive legislation, social and economic policies, and the different cultural regulation mechanisms in education and public communication processes; and to look at the state as a potential ally for women's empowerment (Molyneux 2003: 68).

When feminists recognized this it became possible for them to become involved in a movement to define a new constitution for Brazil. Feminists were successful in obtaining approval for 80 per cent of women's demands in the new constitution through direct action (promptly identified by the media as the 'lipstick lobby'), which included social mobilization and political pressure. Support from the CNDM, and the role of the *bancada feminina* (Women's Caucus) in the National Congress were fundamental factors. Although only 26 women were elected to the 1986–90 legislature from the various political parties, and only one of these was a self-declared feminist, the *bancada feminina* was able to 'rise to the occasion', assume a supra-partisan identity, and present 30 amendments defending women's rights in the new constitution (Pinto 2003: 74–5). They were supported by women's groups from all over the country. Once again, 'feminist voices' created echoes all over the country and advocated for gender justice.

The 1980s saw an emergence of new branches within the wider women's movement. At the 1987 National Feminist Meeting (*encuentro*), for example, nearly 79 per cent of the participants affirmed that they were active in 'labour unions, in the Black movement, in neighbourhood associations, in mothers' clubs, in the church, and in political parties' (Soares *et al.* 1995: 309). At this *encuentro*, Black women publicly claimed a specific space for their struggles both against sexism and racism (Ribeiro 1995).

When the arena for public politics expanded for women, the demand for professionals increased too. Over the years this led to the emergence of feminist NGOs, who took the lead in lobbying the state, thus bringing new challenges and dilemmas for feminist movements (Alvarez 1998b).

The last two decades

The beginning of the 1990s was a time of growth for a diversity of feminist organizations and identities (Lebon 1997). Women articulated their demands through various channels: working-class women used neighbourhood associations; factory workers used the women's departments of their unions; and national union coalitions and rural workers campaigned through their respective organizations. These different segments of the women's movement began to identify themselves with feminism. Black women's feminist organizations continued to grow and strengthen the feminist political agenda as well as the parameters of feminist struggle. Feminism was widening its reach and becoming more 'popular'. The growth of 'popular feminism' had significant consequences for the wider women's movements: it diluted the ideological barriers and resistances to feminism and 'amplified' feminist voice.

The preparations for the Fourth World Women's Conference in Beijing in 1995 helped to articulate Brazilian women's and feminist movements. Although since the 1980s formal and informal networking had brought together feminists across Latin America and the Caribbean (through the feminist *encuentros*), Beijing gave Latin American feminisms the opportunity to participate in a world conference as an integrated and well-organized regional network for the first time (Sternbach *et al.* 1992; Alvarez *et al.* 2003).

The experiences of Brazilian feminisms in these and other transnational spaces introduced new strategies and discourses into national activism (Alvarez 1998a, 2000). The advancements in information and communications technology fostered networking as a major organizational strategy and, during the 1990s, a number of networks emerged in Brazil, most of which are still active.

One of the positive consequences of Brazilian feminists' presence in these and other international/transnational spaces − perhaps invoking what Alvarez (2000: 3) identifies as 'transnational activists logics' − was that their legitimacy in the fight for public policy for women was boosted locally and nationally. This is what Margaret Keck and Kathryn Sikkink (1998) call the 'boomerang pattern' of influence, explained by Alvarez as the kind of influence 'whereby transnational coalitions of non-governmental, governmental and inter-governmental actors put pressure on more powerful states and international government organizations (IGOs) to bring pressure to bear in turn on a particular government which violates rights or resists the desired policy change' (2000: 3).

Indeed, the national and transnational articulation of feminists in the Beijing Conference process eventually paid off, with the creation of the National Secretary of Women's Rights (SEDIM) in 2002 – the last year of President Fernando Henrique Cardoso's term (Sardenberg 2004). One of its first tasks – one that was being undertaken more than ten years behind schedule – was Brazil's first report to the CEDAW Committee. This was a response to the feminist NGOs' mobilization to monitor the ratification process of the Optional Protocol[1] to CEDAW as part of the world campaign – 'Women's Rights Are Not Optional' – on the Brazilian government's behalf. Although CEDAW's Article 18 affirmed that all member countries that had signed CEDAW (passed in 1982) should report every four years, it was only in 2002 that the Brazilian government first responded to that obligation and commissioned a number of feminist NGOs to fulfil it. Following the practice established by the CEDAW committee, a network of feminist organizations drew together more than 400 entities to produce Brazil's 'Shadow Report', which was presented alongside the official report to the CEDAW committee in New York. This process brought together activists in the feminist and women's movements across the country to prepare for the expression of a 'feminist voice' at the National Women's Public Policy Conferences that followed.

Voicing diversity

The pre-Beijing Conference process, which began in 2001, also helped to bring together different feminist organizations and networks to draw up the Feminist Political Platform (Plataforma Política Feminista-PPF). The idea for such a platform emerged during the Second World Social Forum in Porto Alegre, when a group of feminists participating in the 'Female Planet' session met to discuss women's participation in the upcoming presidential elections. Inspired by the 'Lipstick Lobby' process and a letter to women written in 1986 with the support of feminist groups from all over the country, they decided to produce a similar document.

A national organizing committee was created to launch the process of drawing up a Charter of Principles and key themes. More than 5,000 women active in local women's forums throughout Brazil's major cities participated in state-level conferences during the formation of this platform. This culminated in the National Conference of Brazilian Women held in Brasília, 6–7 June 2002, where resolutions and proposals from 26 state conferences were presented and discussed by 2,000 women from around the country. The final version of the PPF was presented at the conference, and later formally delivered to all candidates contesting elections for national and state office.

The PPF was published in 2002 (CNMB 2002), distributed widely around the country, and discussed in local women's forums. It started with the 'Charter of Principles', and was followed by the themes listed below:

1 Political democracy
2 Democratic state and social justice
3 Brazil's participation in the international arena
4 Democratization of social life
5 Sexual and reproductive freedom

The largest section, on 'social justice', dwelt on issues ranging from the effects of 'structural adjustments' on deepening social inequalities to paragraphs that focused on social justice and women's work (ss.152–172), including a special section on women's domestic work (ss.173–183). Of particular note are the paragraphs dedicated to racial and ethnic justice (ss.136–151), in which Brazilian feminists denounce the profound existing inequalities:

s.141 Due to the discriminatory character of Brazilian society, black and indigenous women have benefited very little from the achievements of Brazilian women in the last 70 years. Black women still occupy the bottom of the social pyramid: they are engaged in the least prestigious occupations; present the highest rates of unemployment; and receive the lowest wages among the economically active population, even when reaching the same educational levels as white women and men. Black women present illiteracy rates three times higher than white women. Indigenous women remain marginal to the process of social inclusion; in addition to presenting high rates of illiteracy, few of them have access to professional occupations outside of those available in their villages. (CNMB 2002)

Overall, the PPF expressed the need to combat existing inequalities among women in Brazil; it also defined a feminist stance against racism, lesbophobia and homophobia, as well as against the class hierarchy and inequalities that characterized Brazilian society.

When Luiz Inácio Lula da Silva was elected President, the possibility of transforming the PPF into public policies for women became more real. Feminists involved in the presidential campaign and in the new government were instrumental in prompting Lula to declare 2004 the 'Women's Year'. One of the key events of this *Ano da Mulher* was the First National Conference on Policies for Women in Brasília, organized by the Special Secretariat for Public Policies for Women (Secretaria Especial de Políticas para Mulheres, or SPM), a government portfolio that was elevated to cabinet status in 2003.

Modelled on the National Conference of Brazilian Women and the formation of the PPF, the First National Conference on Policies for Women was attended by nearly 300,000 women from throughout the country, mobilized through municipal and state conferences. Nearly 2,000 delegates to the state conferences were nominated to attend the national conference in Brasília in July 2004. The purpose of this nation-wide process was to establish a dialogue between civil society and government – from the municipal to the federal levels – for formulating the First

National Plan of Public Policies for Women (I Plano Nacional de Políticas para Mulheres – I PNPM) for eradicating gender inequalities in Brazil.

All over the country, feminist activists with different affiliations participated in this process, conscious that it could revitalize the feminist movement as an actor on the national political scene and would be an important platform for 'feminist voice'. However, feminists were also aware of the risk of being used 'for a merely illustrative participation, with few concrete results as to definitions of the future plans' (AMB 2004a: 01). In order to avoid falling into this situation, the Articulação de Mulheres Brasileiras (AMB) devised participation and intervention strategies for feminist delegates in the municipal and state preparatory conferences. This was in order to guarantee that the largest possible number of delegates identified themselves as feminists and thus ensured that the demands of the PPF were incorporated into the First National Plan of Public Policies for Women. This was a successful strategy because, at all the state conferences with only one exception, the legalization of abortion on demand was approved by a wide margin (Sardenberg 2005). The First National Conference on Policies for Women approved it too, and recommended its inclusion in the plan. It said that the

> feminist position affirms the state's responsibility for financing, formulating and implementing public policies for women; establishing links between social and economic policies (both with a distributive character); maintaining budgetary links to health and education; keeping affirmative action relevant; upholding the principles of equality, equity and the secular nature of the state; recognizing the need for inter-sectoral linkages in order to implement such policies; and thereby emphasizing the need for all areas of the government to participate. (AMB 2004a: 01, our translation)

In the evaluation of the conference outcomes, the AMB recognized that feminist intervention was crucial:

> Mission accomplished. We consider that many of the challenges in the Feminist Political Platform have been translated into principles

> for public policies for women. Delegates from women's and feminist movements present at the First National Conference on Public Policies for Women affirm the historical struggles of feminism, such as women's autonomy and abortion rights…. In making a valuable contribution to the democratization and transformation of the Brazilian state, activists from all segments of the women's and feminist movements were able to act together in an articulated manner, demonstrating our great capacity to do politics even when facing innumerable objections and obstacles created by an array of forces … at the different levels of the federation, especially in those governance contexts in which the hegemonic power holders are uncompromisingly opposed to justice and democracy. (AMB 2004a: 01)

According to the SPM, 239 proposals were approved at the conference, which later translated into 199 actions taken by the committee that drafted the First National Plan of Public Policies for Women. This committee was made up of representatives from various ministries, the CNDM, and women's bureaus from across the country, who worked together for three months to consolidate the plan. It was launched on 8 December 2004 and was to be effective until 2007, when a second conference was to be held.

In August 2007, the Second National Conference for Public Policy for Women (II CNPM) was held, involving preparatory processes similar to the previous one. This time, 2,559 members were elected in the 600 municipal, regional and state conferences that were a part of this process. Once again, over 300,000 women from across the country were involved directly and/or indirectly in the process. In the final document, some important achievements, such as the launching of the Pact against Violence and the passage of comprehensive legislation to combat domestic violence (known as the Maria da Penha Law) were recognized and reaffirmed. The demand for the legalization of abortion was also reasserted by a wide margin (Sardenberg 2007). Within the new recommendations for the Second National Plan of Public Policies for Women (II PNPM), the following points were welcomed by feminists especially:

- To encourage and implement affirmative action policies as necessary instruments that can enable distinct groups of women to fully exercise their fundamental rights and freedom.
- To address the power imbalances between men and women in terms of economic resources, legal rights, political participation and inter-personal relations.
- To combat the distinct forms of appropriation and exploitation of women's bodies and lives, such as sexual exploitation, sexual trafficking and the consumption of stereotyped images of women.
- To recognize gender, racial and ethnic violence as structural and historical types of violence and as expressions of women's oppression that need to be treated as matters of public security, justice and health. (Brasil SPM 2008: 30, our translation)

In the introduction to the presentation of this plan, the SPM openly states that although the Second National Plan of Public Policies for Women 'expresses the political will of the federal government to unravel the patterns of inequality between women and men' in the country, it is neither merely a plan of the Special Secretariat nor a plan only for women. It is a 'plan of the federal government to benefit the whole society' (Brasil SPM 2008: 7).

Conflict and solidarity

We have seen that approximately 300,000 women from city to federal levels were involved directly or indirectly in the entire preparatory process for the First National Conference for Public Policy for Women. In the 27 state conferences held during May and June 2004, 14,050 women participated as delegates, of whom 2,000 were nominated for participation in the national conference. Of these, 47 per cent were members of organizations involved in the black women's movement, and about 3 per cent were from native indigenous groups, ensuring that race and ethnicity issues were included.

Table 2.1 compares the profile of participants from the National Conference of Brazilian Women – a theoretically 'feminist' space – with the profile of participants who attended the First National Conference for Public Policy for Women, a space that characterized the broader 'women's movement'. Very few differences appear either in terms of their 'location of political activity' or their 'area/segment of activity' (that is, the major cause they defended). It is worth noting that, in both the conference spaces, NGO members were not the majority. A large number of members from government organizations attended the I CNPM, as it was a conference organized by government to build the support needed for implementing changes. But they were not the majority. Participants declared themselves active in a variety of political locations, and those active in social movements had the largest representation. This is consistent with Sonia Alvarez's observations regarding new trends of feminisms in Latin America:

> Feminism – like many of the so-called new social movements that took shape in the region during the 1970s and 1980s – can today more aptly be characterized as an expansive, polycentric, heterogeneous *discursive field of action* which spans into a vast array of cultural, social and political arenas. The 1990s saw a dramatic proliferation or multiplication of the spaces and places in which women who call themselves feminists act, and wherein, consequently, feminist discourses circulate. After over two decades of struggling to have their claims heard by male-dominant sectors of civil and political society and the state, women who proclaim themselves feminists can today be found in a wide range of public arenas – from lesbian feminist collectives to research-focused NGOs, from trade unions to black and indigenous movements, from university women's studies programmes to mainstream political parties, the state apparatus, and the international aid and development establishments. (Alvarez 1998b: 2)

Reflecting on the *encuentros* in another work, Alvarez (2000: 6) stresses the 'increasingly expansive, polycentric, heterogeneous Latin American feminist field' and observes that the *encuentros* 'have brought together thousands of women active in a broad

Table 2.1 Profile of participants in major women's conferences – Brazil

Location of political activity of participants	National Conference – PPF (2002)[a] %	I CNPM – I PNPM (2004)[b] (more than one choice) %
Social movements	34.7	34.0
NGOs	32.19	27.0
Political parties	20.21	25.0
Government organizations	7.53	29.0
Universities	5.37	5.0
Autonomous	–	7.0
Other	–	5.0
Total	100.0	0
Area/segment of activity	*National Conference – PPF*	*I CNPM –I PNPM (more than one choice)*
Feminist movement	34.22	35.0
Popular movement	16.59	25.0
Other	–	17.0
Labour unions	11.89	12.0
Black women	12.78	10.0
Senior	2.3	10.0
Youth	4.22	9.0
Rural women	7.2	7.0
People with disabilities	1.2	5.0
Domestic workers	2.14	4.0
Lesbians	1.46	3.0
Indigenous women	3.03	3.0
Homosexuals	–	2.0
Midwives	2.97	1.0
Total	100.0	

Source: Table compiled by authors from the following sources: a CNMB (2002); b Brasil SPM (2004).

range of public spaces – from lesbian-feminist collectives, to rural and urban trade unions, black and indigenous movements, landless movements, research NGOs and university women's studies programmes, guerrilla organizations and mainstream political parties'. Besides, as she notes, irrespective of their self-identifications, 'the *encuentros* provided a unique space for activists to debate collectively the always-contested meanings and goals of feminism and its relationship to other struggles for rights and social justice in the region'. She concludes that the *encuentros* have played 'a critical role in fashioning common discourses, fostering a shared (though polysemic) Latin American feminist political grammar, and providing activists in individual countries with key theoretical and strategic insights and symbolic resources which they subsequently "translated" and redeployed locally'.

This is also true of the national feminist meetings; and indeed a 'feminist discursive field' also unfolded at the national level in Brazil. This is important, as despite the crossover of activists from women's movements into feminist activism and vice versa, the distinctive struggles, issues and discourse of feminism are clearly demarcated. Table 2.2 (opposite), sourced from a bulletin by the AMB, draws out differences between the National Conference of Brazilian Women (CNMB) and the CNPM. In the same bulletin, the AMB clarifies that its objectives in participating in one conference differed from of its reasons for attending the other. In the CNMB they wanted to affirm that the feminist and women's movements were political actors in the presidential electoral context, who presented their own propositions, whereas in the I CNPM they wanted to reaffirm the incorporation of the feminist perspective in national public policies for women, to 'make them promoters of effective equality and justice'.

Brazilian feminisms are said to be anti-sexist, anti-racist and anti-homophobic, and to stand for anti-capitalist, radical transformations in the social relations of production. These principles have been incorporated thoroughly in the PPF and are also very strongly affirmed in the guidelines defined for the First and Second Plans of Public Policies for Women. These guidelines

Table 2.2 Differences between the CNMB and CNPM

	2002 – CNMB	*2004 – I CNPM*
Nature of conference	Civil society	Governmental
Organizers	10 national networks of the women's movement	SPM
Objective	Build a feminist political platform	Propose guidelines for the National Plan of Public Policies for Women
Content	Analysis of the Brazilian social context and affirmation of the propositions of the different movements to transform Brazilian society and women's condition	Debate on Brazilian reality and evaluation of governmental actions for development at municipal, state, and national levels
Participants	Close to 2,000 delegates from state conferences plus representatives from the national networks	Total of 1,993 delegates from governmental organs and civil society, elected at the state conferences, plus members of CNDM and the federal government
Principal norm	Charter of principles	Internal regiment and by-laws
Main characteristic	Public space for the dialogue, disputes and alliances between women's movements	Space for public dialogue, disputes and alliances between the government and civil society

Source: AMB 2004b, our translation from the Portuguese

respond to a number of demands from distinct segments of the women's movements, such as: 'black women, indigenous women, white women, *quilombolas* (women in communities established by those escaping the grip of their slave masters), Roma women, *quebradeiras de coco* (members of the movement struggling for usufruct rights for the *babaçu* nut), community leaders, lesbians, disabled people, new and historical activists, etc.' (Brasil SPM 2008: 08, our translation). However, this does not mean that arriving at them has been a process free from tensions and conflicts, if not public rifts. On the contrary, 'social movements fields are constituted by continuous contestations – discursive and strategic' (Alvarez 1998a: 19).

Indeed, feminist voice in Brazil has not necessarily been harmonious. A major source of conflict since the 1970s has been the 'party politicking' within the women's movements. In the early 1980s, traditional leftist parties in Brazil, such as the Brazilian Communist Party (PCB) and the Communist Party of Brazil (PCdoB), still regarded feminism as a 'bourgeois' expression and considered women's struggles to be subordinate to the 'general' struggles of society. Although they have since become supportive of feminist struggles, the practices of political party women within the feminist and women's movement clearly indicate that they put party interests above those of the respective movements. Until the late 1980s, the Brazilian feminist movement, in contrast to other sections of the broader women's movement, was composed primarily of white, middle-class women. However, as Cecilia McCallum (2007: 67) observes, whereas a number of works highlight the supposed 'historical split between black feminists and mainstream white feminists and underline the latter's failure to address the issue of race during the 1980s, the PPF 'gives extensive and unprecedented space to discussing racial discrimination and proposing measures to combat it'. Furthermore, in following up the events and processes that unfolded in Salvador, Bahia, in preparation for the 2002 CNMB, McCallum (2007: 80) was witness to the fact that:

Black, white, middle-class and working-class feminists meet, work together, exchange ideas, and provide support, easing – if not overcoming – tensions. [S]eparate identities and the recognition of difference is also a basis for solidarity.

Turning to class, some authors, referring to what has happened in other countries, suggest that relations established between middle-class feminists and women in the popular movements during the 1970s and 1980s were severed with the 'professionalization' of feminisms, particularly as feminist NGOs emerged (Razavi 2000). However, in Brazil other dynamics seem to be at play, as suggested in the research carried out by Nathalie Lebon (1997) on feminism and women's groups in São Paulo. Likewise, Millie Thayer (2001) studied the relations between the Rural Women Workers' Movement in the north-eastern state of Pernambuco and SOS Corpo – a major feminist NGO operating out of the large urban centre of Recife, Pernambuco. She witnessed the bubbling of tensions and conflicts between the two groups, but adds that they were resolved because the relationship was a mutual one, both organizations gaining from it (Thayer 2001: 261). She nevertheless calls attention to the fact that funding to women's organizations in Brazil 'while small in relation to overall foreign aid', was an 'indispensable condition of survival for many of them, given the lack of local philanthropy and scarcity of state funds'. She further notes that

> along with funding came ways of conceptualizing feminism that grew out of US and European movements and that became part of the discursive terrain on which Brazilian women defined their politics. The unequal distribution of these material and conceptual resources among women's movements aggravated previously existing hierarchies among them, granting visibility and power to some, while marginalizing others. (*Ibid.*: 253)

Awareness of this course of events has led some of these organizations to try to bridge the gap. During the 2005 National Feminist Encounter held in São Paulo, SOS Corpo held a workshop to discuss feminism and popular organizations, centred on the question: 'What are some of the challenges that the situation of poverty and extreme inequality (of gender, race, class) place to feminism?' For the SOS educators, this was a major survival challenge not only in terms of the survival of feminists in popular groups, but also of their own organizations. Thus, middle-class feminists, working in consolidated organizations, had to ask of them/ourselves how both types of groups were contributing to the building of feminism (Andrade 2006). This is certainly a question that we, as academic feminists, should also always have in mind when thinking of feminisms in Brazil.

Conclusion

In their reflections for the Pathways programme on researching 'feminist voice', Anne-Marie Goetz and Celestine Nyamu-Musembi (2008: 4–5) point out that, despite various attempts, the relationship between 'women's voice in public debates and positive social and economic outcomes for women as a gender is not yet established'. Contrary to general belief, for instance, they stress that there is no direct correlation between the number of women in formal politics, and the level and quality of public policies for women. They bring together findings from studies indicating that in many instances these policies come in response to efficient national machineries for women, and very often to the actions of women's movements.

This is clearly the case with regard to Brazil. Despite a very low representation of women in the National Congress, the Brazilian national constitution abides by the principle of gender justice, and crucial policies and legislative initiatives such as the Maria da Penha Law, which is geared towards combating domestic violence against women, are being implemented (Sardenberg *et al.* 2010). Clearly, these achievements stem from effective 'voice' for gender justice and against other inequalities highlighted by feminist and women's movements in the country, as we have shown in this chapter.

We believe that feminist voice has also had an important influence on public opinion. This is suggested by the results of a survey conducted in 2001 with a representative sample of 2,502 women in Brazil (Venturini *et al.* 2004) that focused on a number of issues affecting women in public and private spaces in Brazil. The survey included questions about the interviewees' views on feminism and *machismo*. Respondents were asked: (1) Did they consider themselves feminists? and (2) What was their understanding of feminism? The women were also asked where they believed there was *machismo* in Brazil, and what they understood by it (Soares 2004). Only 28 per cent of the respondents saw themselves as feminists. More young women 15–24 yrs old (35 per cent), with at least a high school education (35 per cent), and living in families with higher purchasing power saw themselves as feminists. This seemed to confirm the assumption that most self-identified feminists were in fact young, professional, middle-class women.

With regard to perceptions on the presence of *machismo* in Brazilian society, however, age, education and income distinctions diminish considerably. Nearly 90 per cent of all the respondents felt the existence of *machismo* in their daily milieu. Among them, 78 per cent correctly defined it as the power of men over women. Respondents also had realistic perceptions regarding the condition of women in Brazilian society and 65 per cent felt that women's lives had improved in the last 20–30 years. They defined 'being a woman' today as entering the labour market, gaining economic independence, freedom and social independence to act according to their desires, making crucial decisions regarding their lives, and achieving equal rights in formal terms. This showed that they were able to identify the major changes that had occurred in women's lives during the period (Soares 2004: 168), and that pointed to a process of women's empowerment. The results showed that the majority of those interviewed 'lived well with the female condition, were conscious of the gains obtained (the right to work and social autonomy), but complained of the burden of a double day; and demanded that all discrimination should end, be it in the labour market or in the home, such as violence, child care and domestic responsibilities' (Soares 2004: 170, our translation).

Although the percentage of women who see themselves as feminists is small, the values and achievements of feminism in Brazil are recognized and appreciated by the majority of women in the study. This, we believe, is a relevant assessment of the growth of feminist voice in Brazil over the last thirty years or so – even though a number of challenges have to be met to secure the transformation of gender relations in favour of women.

Note

1 The Optional Protocol adopted by the United Nations in 1999, and open to adoption by countries that had already signed CEDAW, became valid in December 2000. Brazil joined CEDAW in 1984, signed the Protocol in March 2001, and ratified it in June 2002.

References

Alvarez, S. E. (1990) *Engendering Democracy in Brazil: Women's Movements in Transition Politics*, Princeton University Press, Princeton, NJ.

—— (1998a) 'Latin American Feminisms "Go Global": Trends of the 1990s and Challenges for the New Millennium', in S. E. Alvarez, E. Dagnino and A. Escobar (eds), *Cultures of Politics/Politics of Cultures: Revisioning Latin American Social Movements*, Westview Press, Boulder, CO.

—— (1998b) 'Advocating Feminism: The Latin American Feminist NGO Boom', paper at the Latin American Studies Programme Conference, Mount Holyoke College, MA, 2 May, http://www.mtholyoke.edu/acad/latam/schomburgmoreno/alvarez.html (accessed 10 August 2008).

—— (2000) 'Translating the Global: Effects of Transnational Organizing on Local Feminist Discourses and Practices in Latin America', *Meridians: Feminism, Race, Transnationalism*,Vol. 1, No. 1, pp. 30–1.

Alvarez, S.E., E. J. Friedman, E. Beckman, M. Blackwell, N. S. Chinchilla, N. Lebon, M. Navarro and M. R. Tobar (2003) 'Encountering Latin American and Caribbean Feminisms', *Signs: Journal of Women in Culture and Society* 28: 537–79.

AMB (Articulação de Mulheres Brasileiras – Brazilian Women's Articulation) (2004a) 'Articulando a Luta Feminista nas Políticas Públicas' (Articulating the Feminist Struggle in Public Policy), text for discussion, AMB, Recife.

AMB (2004b) 'Principais Resultados da I CNPM' (Major Results of the I CNPM). *Articulando Eletronicamente*, Vol. 3, No. 90 (20 July 2004).

Andrade, P. (2006) 'Seminário debate feminismo popular e anti-racista' (Seminar debates popular and anti-racist feminisms), *Ciranda da Informação*, 22 April, http://www.ciranda.net/auteur165.html (accessed 10 January 2008).

Brasil SPM (Secretaria Especial de Políticas para Mulheres – Special Secretariat for Public Policies for Women) (2004) 'Conferência Nacional De Políticas Para As Mulheres, 1', http://www.presidencia. gov.br/estrutura_presidencia/sepm/.arquivos/integra_anais (accessed 10 November 2008).

Brasil SPM (Secretaria Especial de Políticas para Mulheres – SpecialSecretariat for Public Policies for Women) (2008) 'II Plano Nacional de Políticas para Mulheres', Brasília, http://200.130.7.5/spmu/docs/Livreto_ Mulher.pdf (accessed 3 October 2009).

CNMB (Conferência Nacional de Mulheres Brasileiras, Brazilian Women National Conference) Feminist Center for Studies and Advisement) (2002) *Plataforma Política Feminista*. Brasília, http://www. articulacaodemulheres.org.br/amb/adm/uploads/anexos/Plataforma_ Política_Feminista.pdf

Costa, A. A. A. (2005) 'O Movimento Feminista no Brasil: Dinâmicas de Uma Intervenção Política' (The Feminist Movement in Brazil: A Dynamic Policy Intervention), *Gênero* (Gender), Vol. 5, No. 2, pp. 9–36.

Craske, N. (2000) 'Continuing the Challenge: The Contemporary Latin American Women's Movements', Research Paper 23, Institute of Latin American Studies, University of Liverpool.

Goetz, A. M. and C. Nyamu-Musembi (2008) *Voice and Women's Empowerment: Mapping a Research Agenda*, Pathways Working Paper 2, Pathways of Women's Empowerment, Brighton.

Gomes, M., Z. Silva, C. Ribeiro and C.M. B. Sardenberg (2009) 'Relatório Parcial de Pesquisa' (Interim Research Report), OBSERVE (Observatório de Monitoramento da Aplicação da Lei Maria da Penha – Observatory for the Monitoring of the Application of the Maria da Penha Law), www.observe.ufba.br.

Hartley, M. H. (2011) 'What Is a Feminist Voice?', http://feminist voice uwindsor.blogspot.com.br/2011/01/what-is-feminist-voice.html (accessed 10 December 2011).

Jónasdóttir, A. (2009) 'Feminist Questions, Marx's Method and the Theorisation of "Love Power"', in A. Jónasdóttir and K. Jones (eds), *The Political Interests of Gender Revisited: Redoing Theory and Research with a Feminist Face*, United Nations University Press, New York, NY.

Keck, M. E. and K. Sikkink (1998) *Activists Beyond Borders: Advocacy Networks in International Politics*, Cornell University Press, Ithaca, NY.

Lebon, N. (1997) 'Volunteer and Professionalized Activism in São Paulo Women's Movement', paper prepared for presentation at the Latin American Studies Association meeting, Guadalajara, Mexico, 17–19 April.

McCallum, C. (2007) 'Women out of Place? A Micro-Historical Perspective on the Black Feminist Movement in Salvador da Bahia, Brazil', *Journal of Latin American Studies*,Vol. 39, pp. 55–80.

Molyneux, M. (1998) 'Analysing Women's Movements', *Development and Change*, Vol. 29, No. 2, pp. 219–45.

—— (2003) *Movimientos de Mujeresen América Latina, Um Estúdio Teórico Comparado* (Women's Movements in Latin America, a Comparative Theoretical Study), Catedra, Universidad de Valencia, Madrid.

Pinto, C. R. J. (2003) *Uma História do Feminismo no Brasil* (A History of Feminism in Brazil), Editora Fundação Perseu Abramo, São Paulo.

Pitanguy, J. (2002) 'Bridging the Local and the Global: Feminism in Brazil and the International Human Rights Agenda', *Social Research*, http://findarticles.com/p/articles/mi_m2267/is_3_69/ai_94227142 (accessed 10 December 2008).

Razavi, S. (2000) 'Women in Contemporary Democratization', Occasional Paper No. 4, United Nations Research Institute for Socaial Development (UNRISD), Geneva.

Ribeiro, M. (1995) 'Mulheres Negras Brasileiras: de Bertioga à Beijing' (Brazilian Black Women from Bertioga to Beijing), *Revista Estudos Feministas* (Feminist Studies Review), Vol. 3, No. 2, pp. 446–57.

Sardenberg, C. M. B. (2004) 'With a Little Help from Our Friends: "Global" Incentives and "Local" Challenges to Feminist Politics in Brazil', *IDS Bulletin*, Vol. 35, No. 4, pp. 125–9.

—— (2005) 'Pedagogias Feministas: UmaIntrodução' ('Feminist Pedagogies: An Introduction'), in L. M. Bandeira (ed.), *Violência Contraas Mulheres: A Experiência de Capacitação das DEAMs da Região Centro-Oeste* (Violence Against Women: Experiences in Capacitation for Battered Women's Police Stations in the Mid-West Region), AGENDE, Brasília.

—— (2007) 'The Right to Abortion: Briefing from Brazil', *Open Democracy*, 26 October, www.opendemocracy.net/article/5050/how_feminists_make_progress (accessed 16 March 2008).

Sardenberg, C. M. B., M. Q. Gomes, M. Tavares and W. Pasinato (2010) *Domestic Violence and Women's Access to Justice*, OBSERVE, NEIM, Universidade Federal da Bahia, Bahia.

Sardenberg, C. M. B. and A. A. A. Costa (2010) 'Contemporary Feminisms in Brazil: Achievements, Shortcomings, and Challenges', in A. Basu (ed.), *Women's Movements in the Global Era: The Power of Local Feminisms*, Westview Press, Boulder, CO.

Soares, V. (2004) 'O Feminismo e o Machismo na Percepção das Mulheres Brasileiras', in G. Venturini, M. Recaman and S. Oliveira (eds), *A Mulher Brasileira nos Espaços Público e Privado* (A Brazilian Woman in Public and Private Spaces), Editora e Fundação Perseu Abramo, São Paulo.

Soares, V., A. A. A. Costa, C. Buarque, D. Dora and W. Sant'Anna (1995) 'Brazilian Feminisms and Women's Movements: A Two-Way Street', in A. Basu (ed.), *The Challenge of Local Feminisms: Women's Movements in Global Perspective*, Westview Press, Boulder, CO.

Sternbach, N. S., M. Navarro-Aranguren, P. Chuchryk and S. E. Alvarez (1992) 'Feminisms in Latin America: from Bogota to San Bernardo', *Signs*, Vol. 17, No. 2, pp. 393–434.

Thayer, M. (2001) 'Transnational Feminism: Reading Joan Scott in the Brazilian Sertão', *Ethnography*, Vol. 2, No. 2, pp. 243–71.

Venturini, G., M. Recaman and S. Oliveira (eds) (2004) *A Mulher Brasileira nos Espaços Público e Privado* (A Brazilian Woman in Public and Private Spaces), Editora e Fundação Perseu Abramo, São Paulo.

Villela, W. V. (2001) 'Expanding Women's Access to Abortion: The Brazilian Experience', in B. Klugman and D. Budlender (eds), *Advocating for Abortion Access: Eleven Country Studies*, Johannesburg: University of Witwatersrand: 87–108.

3

The South African Revolution
Protracted or Postponed?

Gertrude Fester

When South Africa held its first democratic elections in 1994 many well-wishers throughout the world celebrated. Nelson Mandela became the first President, South Africa had a human rights and gender-sensitive constitution, and the number of women in Parliament rose by 300 per cent. Yet, 19 years later, the feminist voice in South Africa is fragmented and faint. This is especially paradoxical given the strong women's movement within the national democratic struggle and women's participation in formulating the new constitution. On the evidence of the statute book and a far-reaching national gender machinery, many have hailed this as a 'women friendly' country. That gender mainstreaming and democracy do not necessarily lead to a strong and vibrant feminist movement is confirmed by writers (Goetz and Hassim 2003). This chapter will examine how the fragmentation of feminist voices occurred, and discuss the implications of sectoral and divided feminist activism for feminist voice in South Africa.

First I define voice in South Africa – how and when we achieved it, under what circumstances it was sustained, and whether it has been – or can be – amplified. I raise other concerns. How is it used, and by whom? Who sets the agenda(s) of the movement(s)? Who represents whom? In what specific context is one assessing these things, and how much does that matter? I also highlight my own positionality as a feminist activist, and use my own experience in politics and as a former Member of Parliament and Commissioner for Gender Equality. I have been involved in politics for most of my life – first in the anti-apartheid movement, when we highlighted the importance of women's liberation within the national liberation struggles. This was not always easy, as there were often accusations that we were 'dividing the struggle'. In post-apartheid South Africa (the first democratic election was in 1994) I had various political deployments (1997 to 2006): Member of Parliament, gender and transformation consultant to the Minister of Minerals and Energy, adviser to the African National Congress Mayor of Cape Town, and Commissioner for Gender Equality.

I respond to the above questions by highlighting three phases in contemporary South Africa[1] that correspond to three presidencies: Nelson Mandela (1994–9), Thabo Mbeki (1999–2008) and Jacob Zuma (2008 to the present). It is ironic that this chapter about feminist voice is structured by periods that refer to male leaders, but this reflects the prevailing patriarchy. These periods, however, are not distinct and events may overlap; tendencies may have commenced in one period and intensified in the next. I preface this three-phase journey with an account of the grassroots women's struggles of the 1980s, which gave voice to women's struggles in the 1990s. Provincial and local government politics will not be covered in this chapter, but the contradictions I detect in national politics can be found at those levels too.

Apartheid era (1982–90)

Grassroots women's voices emerged nationally in structures post-1976, after the students' uprisings.[2] In what is now Western Cape Province, black African[3] women like Mildred Lesia and Dorothy Zihlangu from the African National Congress Women's League (ANC WL, formed in 1943) – many of whom were without formal education and were employed as domestic workers – mobilized women into the United Women's Organization

(UWO), established in 1981. UWO was a unitary structure and had branches in all areas of the Western Cape. A minimum of ten members could form a branch if they were committed to the aims of the organization and were ready to work for the empowerment of women and a South Africa free from apartheid. Despite the rigid apartheid, UWO was non-racial in its membership. About 90 per cent of the women were grassroots and black African, while a few branches had middle-class white and coloured members. In 1986 UWO became the United Women's Congress (UWCO) when it joined up with the Women's Front (grassroots black Africans only). The programme of action was decided by the majority. At the 1984 conference it was argued by the Gardens (white) branch that the programme was not feminist enough. This was countered by grassroots women and a debate emerged on what feminist, women's and people's issues *are*. Although some of us used the word feminist then, it was always controversial; it is less so now. The conference accepted Whitey Pokwana's words as a resolution:

> These problems of women – children, contraception and so on – are all part of a bigger system. The passes hit us first. (UWO, conference minutes, 1984)

It was clear that the voice setting the agenda was that of black African working-class women. At an emergency meeting at Hewat Training College[4] Mildred Lesia, always an outspoken political leader, stated: 'We will not be dominated by intellectuals!' This was perhaps a euphemism for white. And perhaps, as we were trying to build 'non-racialism', she never used the word white.

In the 1990s, a new surge of energy and excitement hit South Africa. Nelson Mandela was freed, and the ban on the ANC, the Pan Africanist Congress (PAC) and the South African Communist Party (SACP) was removed. On a personal level, the charges of treason and terrorism against 13 others and me were dropped and we were released from prison after a trial that had lasted nearly three years. UWCO was dissolved to form the African National Congress Women's League (ANC WL). The ANC WL initiated the National Women's Coalition (NWC) to unite women's voices during the negotiations period and to ensure our input into the constitution. This was the specificity of the context. One could ask who set the agenda(s) of the movement(s), and who was representing whom? One cannot underestimate the history of racial exploitation and abuse of more than three centuries. The NWC, despite its successful 1994 'Women's Charter for Effective Equality' campaign, which consisted of key demands of women for the new South Africa, was riddled with race, class and personal conflicts and challenges. There was a cautious atmosphere in meetings. We were in the same room – black women, women of colour and a few white women from the liberation movements such as ANC and PAC – planning strategies together with white women from the Nationalist Party (which had legislated apartheid) and the Democratic Party (white liberals who were in the apartheid Parliament). In terms of race and class politics, the whites who joined had resources and often were not engaged in wage labour. This meant that they were free to volunteer work such as typing the minutes of the meetings. These created particular kinds of exclusionary dynamics, described below. For example, at a NWC meeting, a Democratic Party member, Kate Birch, announced that as she had typed the minutes, she drew up the agenda and would also chair. It was all done very fast and other members, including myself, were too tired from everyday work and activism even to protest. On another occasion we needed three delegates and a white woman nominated three other whites. I raised concerns and repeatedly had to explain why we had to have a more representative delegation, but they saw nothing wrong with three whites. Eventually the delegation was changed. At meetings in Cape Town, continuing the culture of the 1980s where we always had translations, we proposed translations. This became difficult. The new breed of professional women (both white and coloured) who had recently joined the women's movement did not see the need for translation as it 'was a waste of time and we had lots to do'. Xhosa-speaking women stopped attending these English-only meetings. I actually had to beg grassroots women leaders like Dorothy Mfacu (Chair of the UWC) to attend.

At a national level this also took place. During the negotiations the Congress of Traditional Leaders of South Africa (CONTRALESA) wanted customary law to supersede the central equality clause of the constitution. Nationally within the NWC, women mobilized to counter this. Ann Letsebe, executive member of the NWC, recalled:

> Some … white women [said], 'No … it's going to waste time, because of … negotiations … there's so much to do'.… We said … if black women's issues are not taken on board at the same time with everything else, you can forget it. (Quoted in Abrams 2000: 49)

However, despite this, the NWC managed to promote the concerns of the poorest and most marginalized women through its charter campaign. The Women's Charter stated in its preface that women's demands were diverse and mediated by race, class, sexualities, (dis)abilities and other axes of oppression. Nevertheless it was often a battle to ensure that grassroots and black women's voices were heard. Some women and I still contend that despite the successes of the NWC, it 'empowered' some already empowered women even more.

The Mandela period (1994–9)

The negotiations for a new South Africa succeeded despite various hiccups and resulted in a gender-sensitive constitution and a substantial increase in women's representation in the Parliament. This was lauded by local and international feminists (Seidman 1999; Geisler 2000, 2004; Hassim 2004; Gouws 2004a, 2004b), who agreed that the national discourse was decidedly 'gendered equality'.

Despite the claimed commitment to gender equality, it was not a feminist resolution. The private/public divide, and culture and religion specifically, mediated women's inequality, thereby limiting women's citizenship. The rhetoric was about gender equality, but the reality was different. I thought then that this was a part of the process. This was the period where various women's groups, committed to making the theoretical contents of the constitution a reality, worked together constructively.

An example of this was the Rural Women's Movement appealing to feminist academics at the Centre for Applied Legal Studies (CALS) to work on submissions to Parliament on customary marriages which relegate women to permanent minors. Within customary marriage women do not have access to land and are not entitled to their children in the case of separation or divorce. A partnership between the Joint Monitoring Committee on the Improvement for the Quality of Life and Status of Women (JMC) in Parliament, grassroots rural women, and feminist lawyers at CALS culminated in the Recognition of Customary Marriages Act 120 of 1998. This act addresses the equality of women within customary unions and ensures access to constitutional rights. In retrospect, though, it has inherent weaknesses and has not radically changed rural women's lives.

This was also the time during which the various mechanisms of the National Gender Machinery (NGM) were set up. These included the Commission on Gender Equality (CGE) (Act 120 of 1996), the Office on the Status of Women (in the presidency), Gender Focal Points/Gender Desks in departments, a Gender Responsive Budget as well as policy and legislation on affirmative action. Despite an advanced NGM (Geisler 2004; Seidman 2003), there is still a lack of capacity and skills (Republic of South Africa 2005: 7; Serote 2004: 5). I agree that the picture is a very uneven one, as Gouws asserts (Gouws 2005: 11). We in the feminist movements abdicated our roles – the agenda was being set by 'femocrats' within a patriarchal ANC. All our attention was focused on making the government legislate and implement.

The Gender Responsive Budget in South Africa was called the Women's Budget Initiative (WBI). This was because there is no word for 'gender' in the vernacular languages. It had very few achievements and many shortcomings. The government accepted recommendations selectively, not necessarily assenting to those that would contribute to a real transformation. It is lamentable that this project lasted only as long as there was donor funding, and this makes one question the state's commitment to gender equality. Another setback for poor and marginalized people was when the Reconstruction and Development Programme (RDP) – a radical transformation programme for the poor to make decisions about their communities – was replaced by the neo-liberal Growth, Employment and Redistribution Strategy (GEAR). Hassim (2006: 232) points out that women cabinet ministers did not object to this programme and this had disastrous consequences for women and the poor. (I must add that I did not object, either.) Maybe the women cabinet ministers and women in positions of power had trusted this 'government of the people' to uphold gender equity concerns? The women's structures I was part of never debated GEAR, which was drawn up in 'somewhat secretive conditions and presented as non-negotiable' (Hassim 2006: 231). Or was it that at that early stage there was already awareness that the agendas were drawn up by the male executive and that the women's caucus might not have any power *per se*?

On reflection, I realized that at that time I was preoccupied with other struggles and especially the restructuring of the education system, specifically at the tertiary level and teacher training institutions. I personally challenged the education policy maker, David Shepherd, about the lies and deception we were being fed on the future of training colleges. The other major struggle many others and I were battling with simultaneously was around the interim constitution, which had to be finalized in the same year – 1996. There was the danger of losing the equality clause that was to enjoy primacy over all other clauses in the constitution.

This pull in different directions created an overwhelming feeling of fatigue among feminist activists. The feminist energy of the 1990–4 period had dissipated. Many feminists were Members of Parliament (MPs) for the first time, and they faced new challenges constantly. I recall periods of frustration due to far too many, too long and often unnecessary meetings chaired by incompetent 'senior' men. Business that could be concluded within thirty minutes took three hours because of this poor chairing. I do concede, though, that it was a difficult time for everyone. It was the first time that we as 'soldiers', former political prisoners and activists were in Parliament – making democratic laws and repealing unjust ones from the apartheid statute book.

It was a concern that the NGM and many feminist NGOs were seriously under-resourced. Thus Seidman's words 'that feminist rhetoric mask[s] patriarchal intent' are perhaps prophetic (2003: 542). But the situation in South Africa was much more complex. Was it just a case of 'masking patriarchal intent'? Were women's and gender structures functioning strategically and effectively and, if not, were the structures themselves to blame? The institutions set up to promote gender equality could have had a far-reaching impact. If they had functioned optimally they could have contributed to some transformation. But the tensions amongst women leaders in the NGM consumed us/them. We need to stress, however, that facilitating citizenship for women needed more than just the NGM. Transformation has to be holistic and the private/public divide and gender hierarchy have to be overcome. The culture of Parliament and most institutions remained patriarchal. The NWC disbanded in 1996 and feminist activism was steered into sectoral projects like the Women's Legal Centre and the Women's Health Project.

The patriarchal nature of Parliament also constrained the ability of women MPs to promote gender equity concerns. Parliament had a Joint Monitoring Committee on the Quality of Life and Status of Women (JMC) for promoting gender equity concerns, and the chairperson of the JMC, Pregs Govender, was very committed. Through her dedication the committee became an important vehicle for feminist voice. However, it was exasperating that it often lacked a quorum, as members chose to prioritize other meetings taking place at the same time. I recall a few meetings with only two members present. How do we interpret this? Did this mean that other members did not consider the JMC meeting important enough? And what pressures did the chairpersons of the other meetings place on members to ensure their attendance?

Despite this obstacle, the JMC nevertheless was a unique experience. We regularly received submissions and enjoyed participation from civil society women's structures, and discussed strategies for empowerment with them. The JMC also had oversight power to monitor budgets and priorities of ministers. This committee, together with the Office on the Status of Women in the Presidency, drew up the National Policy Framework for the Empowerment of Women and Gender Equality. And this framework informed all policies in South Africa.

However, despite these formal powers, our ability to voice and influence decisions was constrained not only by the patriarchal culture but also by informal rules of business through which parliamentary affairs were conducted. Sexual harassment and violence against women continued, even at the level of decision makers in Parliament. I use the following examples to illustrate these points.

At a meeting during which the Ministers of Finance and Trade and Industry presented their programmes, I questioned the strategy that tourism was being seen as the panacea for problems in South Africa. Members of civil society were sitting behind the ministers, and included in this group was Sally Timmel representing Fair Share, an organization that interrogates budget priorities. I was later informed by Timmel that the ministers were not happy with my line of questioning and that one minister said to the other, 'She is asking the wrong questions.' I became aware then – but did not know how to deal with it – that although we had open discussions and proposals as a ruling party, the ultimate decisions were made elsewhere or by the executive.

I also served as a member of the Finance Portfolio Committee working on the National Development Agency Act that aimed to eradicate poverty, and to fund NGOs and civil society projects to consolidate democracy. The processes through which these bills were discussed, however, were not empowering either to me or, I believe, to others. In retrospect it is strange that we never even discussed it as women MPs. Initially draft bills as drawn up by the Finance Department were discussed. They were then interrogated by MPs in order to assess whether the bills satisfied the criteria set by the constitution and the policies of the country – that is, to 'improve the quality of life of citizens and free the potential of each person' (preamble to the constitution) and that 'the state may not unfairly discriminate directly or indirectly against anyone on one or more grounds, including race, gender, sex, pregnancy, marital status, ethnic or social origin, colour, sexual orientation, age, disability, religion, conscience, belief, culture language and birth' (Chapter 2, clause 9(3), Constitution Act 108 of 1996). We then proposed changes to improve the bills. My experience of the portfolio committee was that as soon as a bill was read the hands of four 'pale male' members, all from different parties including the ruling ANC, would shoot up. They would deliver long dramatic monologues critiquing the bill. By the time they were done, all the most obvious comments would have been made, and often there was almost nothing to add except the most obscure and complex points that only an accomplished economist could bring to bear. By then I and the others (the novices) could not participate. Outside of the committee I, as a timid new member, approached the chair of the committee to suggest that a limit on speaking times might give more people a chance to participate. However, throughout my time as member, this was routine. Based on my experience of Parliament, therefore, I found that aspects of the very vehicle charged with facilitating democracy in South Africa did not always function democratically, and occasionally may have muted the feminist voice inside Parliament.

The Mbeki period (1999–2008)

During this period, many women took on prominent positions. There was a larger contingent of women in the cabinet, and later a woman Deputy-President (Mlambo-Ngcuka)[5] was appointed. But this period was also characterized by less debate within the ruling party and the ominous AIDS-denialist period of Mbeki and the woman who was Minister of Health, Tshabalala-Msimang. It was ironic that the media vilified Tshabalala-Msimeng, who was executing Mbeki's policies, but not the President to the same extent. The conflict gave rise to the emergence of powerful social movements of AIDS activists like the Treatment Action Campaign (TAC). The campaign was initially dominated by men. We in the women's movement have often challenged the women in TAC because of their secondary status in the structure. Recently, though, women members of the TAC have become much more prominent in leadership.

Goetz distinguishes between women's 'infiltration' and the 'assimilation' of women in political parties (Goetz 2003: 138–9). When women infiltrate they intervene and change the patriarchal agenda, whereas with assimilation they are subsumed into the political 'party' agenda, which often marginalized women. Women in political parties tried hard to intervene, but were not always successful. I see a dilution of women's influence despite increased numbers in decision making in the post-2000 period. But Pregs Govender, ANC MP and chair of the JMC, courageously challenged the ruling party on their commitments to women and HIV/AIDS in the light of a notorious arms deal on which billions of rand were spent. She resigned in 2002.

Goetz (2003), Tsikata (2004) and others argue for a change in the 'culture of the institutions'. Even though there have been three consecutive women Speakers of Parliament, my personal observation is that the culture has not changed significantly. Without such change, women cannot be effective enough, and they remain 'descriptive representatives' as opposed to 'substantive or strategic representatives' (Goetz and Hassim 2003: 5) who can make major interventions. In Parliament, senior and middle managers were often men[6] and it is at this level that transformation had to be operationalized.

Hence, there was no sustained feminist voice. Through the NGM there was an emphasis on government structures and policies that applied in the 'public' world only, as opposed to the private world of women. There is also no evidence to date that the NGM has made any appreciable difference to *all* women's lives in South Africa. During our travels, especially in the rural areas, we met many women who had not heard of the CGE. Fortunately, the national Afrikaans radio station, *Radio Sonder Grense* (Radio without borders) gave me a weekly slot. Through this I was able to reach many in the rural areas where this language was mostly spoken. In retrospect, we misplaced a great deal of energy in building the NGM and not promoting the voices of civil society and the independent women's movement. Gender equality has, to a certain extent, benefited those employed in this new 'gender industry' (femocrats, middle-class women, NGO personnel and the new elite) but again only in their 'public' worlds.[7]

Women's lives, despite their positions and powers, are influenced profoundly and negatively by religion and culture. The outcome of women's agency is that they have contributed to the new democracy and gender-sensitive constitution, but despite this many women are still polarized – as 'gender divas'[8] and poor women. New contradictions have emerged in the new South Africa. In addition to the residual black/white dichotomy, new class divides developed amongst blacks in general, and black women in particular. New government positions, including the 'gender industry' and corporate positions, created a *nouveau riche*, while the majority remained poor.

But the state is not homogeneous. Elements within the state may be dedicated to making gender equality a reality (albeit limited), but there may also be sections that do not accept it. South Africa's bifurcated legal system with its radical Bill of Rights alongside the conservative traditional chiefs and customs, which are acknowledged constitutionally, concretely symbolizes the difficulty of reconciling multiculturalism with democracy and full citizenship. Apart from these diverse interests there are also competing demands on the state: extreme poverty and underdevelopment, economic apartheid, debt and other problems inherited from the apartheid state affected the reconstruction of the new South Africa. For example, even though a large bulk of the budget is allocated for education, it may not be used as effectively as possible, as crises and challenges within education are prevalent. Welfare grants are not empowering and are only a short-term solution to eradicating poverty. Currently there are 15 million people, including children and child-headed households – one third of the South African population – who receive these grants. This is of concern, as grants are unsustainable in the long term – while more jobs and skills training for the unemployed are not being promoted effectively, either.

Looking at the period 1994–2006, an important lesson feminists learnt was that building sustainable and strong independent women's organizations was important. This had not been done. Many women activists joined Parliament, leading to an over-reliance on 'state feminism'. Independent women's and civil society voices were weakened as a result. The presence of 'femocrats' had indeed de-radicalized the feminist agenda and voice.

In addition to weakening feminist voice because of an over-reliance on state feminism, polarization and other divisions within the ANC also weakened feminist activism. This division became clear when the current President Jacob Zuma (previously Deputy President and then relieved of his post by President Mbeki because of corruption charges) was accused of rape. 'Kwezi', who was known to him and who regarded him as Father (she addressed him as 'Ulama') was allegedly raped by him in his house. South African society at large and the political movements were totally polarized on this issue.

Outside the court there was as much drama as there was inside. Busloads of supporters came from rural areas of KwaZulu-Natal, Zuma's home province, which has a majority Zulu population. These were mostly young Zulu men (wearing '100% Zulu boy' t-shirts) and women. Many young men carried Bibles and crosses, and these 'Bible-clad' boys 'shouted unprintable slogans with references to women's body parts' (Motsei 2007: 143). There were women at the forefront, burning effigies of 'Kwezi' while shouting 'Burn the bitch!' They accused 'Kwezi' of being disrespectful as she had accused her 'Chief' (Zuma). Some women like MaMkhize achieved celebrity status through her support for Zuma. According to her, instead of accusing Zuma of rape, 'Kwezi' should have been 'grateful' 'and if she (MaMkhize) had been raped she would not have bathed her bosom (where he'd lain) for days' (*ibid.*: 31). However, there were also other women outside the court supporting 'Kwezi', and protesting in favour of a fair trial.

The situation was aggravated, particularly as 'Kwezi' was a lesbian and feminist, which traditionalists found difficult to accept. She was questioned severely by the prosecution and her entire sexual history was interrogated. Ministers of religion of the theological institute where she had studied accused her of 'being mad' and needing 'treatment', which was used as evidence against her.

Zuma was found not guilty of rape. After the trial National Intelligence representatives warned 'Kwezi' to leave South Africa and Africa, as they could not guarantee her safety. This has multiple implications for the priorities and values of the average South African. 'Kwezi', who had expected a fair trial in a 'gender-sensitive country' – South Africa – now lives in Europe. Research from People Opposing Women Abuse (POWA 2010) suggests that fewer women are willing now to report rape because of the trauma of 'secondary rape' as seen in 'Kwezi's' trial, especially if the alleged rapist is a public figure.

Most women in the ANC political movements were silent during that period. Even today some believe fervently it was a political ploy by Mbeki's supporters to prevent Zuma from becoming President. This tension continues.

The Zuma period (2008 to present)

Currently the discourse in South Africa is largely anti-women and misogynistic. Political leaders, especially those of the ANC Youth League (YL), speak with impunity against women. It was the Equality Court (March 2010), and not the feminist movement or women's voices, that termed the ANC YL President Malema's[9] comments about women who are raped 'hate speech'. The expert witnesses said his words were 'gender-insensitive and trivialized rape. It perpetuated male sexual entitlement and was obviously sexist and would have upset many South Africans – including the survivors of rape.' Magistrate Collis found that 'given the totality of the evidence' the court was satisfied that the words 'could reasonably be construed as hurtful, harmful and demeaning to women' and hence constituted hate speech (Equality Court judgment, March 2010).

An NGO – Sonke Gender Justice – brought a case of hate speech and harassment against Malema. The court papers confirm that Malema referred to the case of 'Kwezi', implying how survivors of rape should or should not behave after such a crime. He said that 'Kwezi' was not a victim of rape and claimed that the fact that she stayed in Zuma's house and asked for breakfast and taxi money the morning after, proved it.

This illustrates the contradictions of contemporary South Africa. There is no united feminist voice that can challenge misogyny, but there are a few NGOs doing sterling work. For example, another NGO – the New Women's Movement – held a march challenging government policies regarding poor women and children, on National Women's Day, 9 August 2010.

Constitutional structures such as the Equality Court do make positive interventions, as the above example illustrates. Similarly, the Constitutional Court ensures that practices and laws uphold the constitution. In a judgment on 10 September 2002, the Constitutional Court ruled that the Black Administrations and Child Care Acts that prevented same-sex couples from jointly adopting a child were unconstitutional. The judgment states that '[28] [The two acts] ... perpetuate the fiction or myth of family homogeneity based on the one mother/one father model. It ignores the developments that have taken place in the country....' Many other constitutional court judgements overturned laws relating to primogeniture and inheritance law (see Fester 2007).

Given the contradictory, divisive and fragmented nature of

feminist activism and voice in South Africa, are there new areas of activism and voice emerging? How are the younger generation of feminists mobilizing? And around what issues? What are the implications of these activities for feminist activism in South Africa? I use the following campaign examples to explore these questions. These examples include feminist campaigns that started as a reaction to localized incidents that highlighted the state failure in addressing women's rights, and also those that were inspired by international protocols.

The 'One in Nine' campaign

The negativity of Zuma's trial helped in the emergence of some positive feminist voices. The One-in-Nine Campaign was established in February 2006 at the start of Zuma's rape trial in solidarity with 'Kwezi' as well as other women who speak out against rape and sexual violence. The study on sexual violence conducted by the Medical Research Council (MRC) in 2005 (Abrahams *et al.* 2012) indicated that only one out of every nine rape survivors reports the attack to police. This statistic gave the campaign its name. Statistics also indicate that the rapists are convicted in less than 5 per cent of the cases that do get to the courts. Hence, lobbying the Department of Justice and advocating for women's rights were needed urgently. The One-in-Nine Campaign works for social justice in order to ensure that the sexual rights of women are respected, upheld and advanced. Campaign activists work in a holistic way – incorporating HIV/AIDS, violence against women, women's rights, human rights, and lesbian, gay, bisexual, trans- and intersexed (LGBTI) activism to ensure that the sexual rights issues of all are addressed (Women's Net, no date).

The Triple-7 campaign

Marginalized people like women from rural areas, or those with disabilities and non-heteronormative sexual orientation, remain sidelined. Lesbians are especially vilified. This happens both at legislative and community levels. Watson, a senior researcher in

Parliament, shared her disappointment at the increasing levels of homophobia amongst ANC parliamentarians since 2001 (interviewed 29 June 2010). Because of an increase in hate crimes, especially against Black lesbians, the Triple-7 Campaign was initiated by the Joint Working Group (a national network of organizations focusing on lesbian, gay, bisexual, transgender and intersex issues). This campaign aims to highlight the violence perpetrated against lesbian women. It derives its name from the dates of the murders of 'out' lesbians, Sizakele Sigasa and Salome Masosa, who were brutally killed in Soweto on 7 July 2007. The 07–07–07 campaign is national, and different organizations take responsibility for it in various parts of the country. They provide legal counsel and support for survivors of rape and violence, and to their families/partners. They also lobby and monitor the justice system, as there seems to be a reluctance to punish perpetrators of hate crimes. The trials of various cases have been postponed repeatedly at the courts and eventually thrown out for 'lack of evidence.' This shows that despite gender-sensitive legal reforms, the justice system requires a serious overhaul.

The South African Feminist Forum

While some campaigns and feminist voices were initiated through local incidents such as those discussed above, others were inspired by international protocols like the SADC Protocol Alliance or the Association for Women's Rights in Development International (AWID) conference (Cape Town, 2008). At the AWID conference, South African feminists had a workshop which resulted in a public statement condemning current misogyny and patriarchy. The South African Feminist Forum was formed in response to AWID's call to further the concerns raised at the conference. This is coordinated by the Feminist Forum (Western Cape). Other partners, such as Women's Net, Gender Advocacy Programme, World Women's March, New Women's Movement and Women's Hope Education and Training Trust (WHEAT) have not been active for different reasons. This highlights one of the concerns for effective feminist activism: inactive and inefficient partnerships. The project is entitled, 'Amplifying Feminist Voices and Movements in South Africa: Actioning the AWID 2008 Statement of South African Women'.[10] Unfortunately, uniting feminists and amplifying their voices is a protracted and demanding task, and organizations are too busy to go through this process. They were encouraged to used their core functions in such a way as to present a feminist voice, but this has still not occurred.

The Feminist Forum aims, amongst other things, to promote a feminist agenda, unite the disparate women's and feminists structures for effective lobbying and advocacy, and promote a feminist movement. Unfortunately, workload pressures have prevented the forum from expanding nationally. A lesson to be learnt from this is that organizations need to prioritize and be specialized. Too many women's organizations aim to do everything – including training, women's empowerment programmes, the prevention of violence against women, etc. – thus duplicating tasks and making coordination difficult. The feminist voice at the national level is waning; indeed it is barely heard. The Feminist Forum has now partnered with the South African NGO Coalition (SANGOCO) and a provincial meeting in December 2010 of more than fifty organizations was a positive development. The outcome of this dialogue is contained in a statement on 1 December 2010. It was based and built on that of the South African Feminist Forum statement of 2008.[11]

In terms of raising voices around LGBTI issues, a few NGOs such as Triangle, Gender Dynamix, and Inclusive and Affirmative Ministries have made constructive and meaningful interventions. The first two are led by feminists.

However, attempts to strengthen inter-generational dialogue and to include younger women's organizations have not always been successful. After several attempts, I managed to speak to Josephine, the Coordinator of the Girl Child Movement, and she shared her frustration about the absence of administrative support and infrastructure, which was a result of their funding crisis. According to her and from the interviews she conducted with members, the most pressing concerns for young girls were lack of education and poverty. Young girls were being forced to leave school, or attended school irregularly, because of household and family chores. They could not afford sanitary towels as a result of poverty (interviewed 14 October 2010).

Bonga from the Young Women's Chapter of the New Women's Movement said:

> We, young sistaz and youth in general, have lost a sense of who we are. Our lives have been defined by 'stuff', we have given our choices to the media to let the media decide how we must look, what to wear, how to act and how to be. And this has greatly been influenced by a lack of strong female structures in our homes and in the society. (Interviewed 14 October 2010)

The Girl Child Movement and the New Women's Movement are going through funding and other crises and hence have not always been able to respond to calls for partnership. The irony is that such partnerships could support them.

On 21 and 22 October 2011, about twenty feminists from different parts of the country met with the goal of bringing together a South African Feminist Forum (SAFF) for reflection, alliance building and planning a nation-wide programme. It is too early to assess the effect of this initiative but it is positive that it occurred.

Feminist voice in South Africa: fragmented and challenged within the state and the political arena?

Feminist voices within bureaucracy and state

The above analysis of state feminism and the NGM shows that, despite its commitment to attaining gender equality, it did not achieve this; nor did it amplify a clearer feminist voice in South Africa. Admittedly, there is no 'quick fix' after centuries of patriarchal colonialism, culture, religion and education. The complexity and the interrelatedness of gender inequalities in the very marrow of our religions and culture in South Africa, as elsewhere, will not be easy to unravel and transform. On the contrary, in this 'new South Africa', only muted women's voices emerge from women within government and the state-run women's movement such as the Progressive Women's Movement of South Africa (PWMSA), and often only at election time. The ANC Women's League (WL) seems voiceless, in contrast to its fraternal organization the ANC YL, and this is a clear indicator of the powerlessness of women as a constituency.

At present, the voices that sometimes do emerge are not always constructive. The new machineries such as the CGE have been 'underground' except for occasional media briefs on 'mismanagement', or 'disclaimers' by the auditor-general. Their 'voices' were heard in June 2010 via accusations and counter-accusations between CGE commissioners and the former chair of CGE (CGE Commissioners 2010; Gasa 2010). Despite gross violations of women's and gender rights in South Africa over the past two years, the CGE is under a self-imposed and self-censored silence. In fact, the Public Protector (a constitutional position, and a neutral term for the ombudsman), the advocate Thuli Madonsela, stated bluntly that the CGE has 'deteriorated to the extent that its operations have come to a standstill' and asked for the urgent intervention of Parliament and the Treasury in the affairs of the commission (Masando 2010).

Currently the voices that emerge are increasingly those of the state feminists. In May 2006, women in Parliament launched the '365 days of no violence against women' movement under the auspices of the Deputy Minister of Social Development, Nomatyala Hangana. In November 2008, Women's Spaces was launched by the then Deputy Speaker of Parliament, Nozizwe Madlala-Routledge. However, to date nothing has materialized from these two structures.

Without any analysis or evaluation of the previous NGM structures, South Africa added a Ministry of Women, Children and Persons with Disabilities. This Ministry was introduced in

May 2009, and a year later had proved as ineffective as some aspects of the NGM had been. Many women activists feel that it is overwhelmed by its mandate (Mataboge 2009a). In the past, the three 'marginalized issues' of gender/women, children and disabilities had separate structures within the presidency, with negligible or limited success. Now the new Minister has to address all three with a token budget. The Minister appointed had no experience of gender or feminist activism and her constituency was COSATU (the ANC Alliance partner), which was well known for its neglect of analysis or activism in relation to gender.

It is also difficult to see how the Minister can resolve some of the intractable earlier problems which continue within the NGM. Overlapping mandates, uncertainty as to where oversight functions reside, a lack of autonomy to take the government to task over non-compliance with the gender agenda, and a lack of implementation of gender policies and legislation are only some of the problems. However, the new Minister of 'the three marginals' (as someone coined it), Lulu Xingwana, who was appointed as Minister of Women, Children and Persons with Disabilities in November 2010, in a short time added some constructive and innovative activities, while speaking out strongly on discrimination against women and the perpetuation of patriarchy. The new chair of the JMC, Barbara Thompson, also encouraged public participation by women, following the pattern we had seen in the past (Watson, interview, 29 June 2010). These developments seemed to indicate some progress by the femocrats in raising and addressing issues of gender justice.

Feminist voice/women's voice within political parties

Compared with how the feminist voice and agenda have fared within the state machinery, the situation within political parties is even more constraining. The gender equity agenda has been used in an opportunistic manner by the main opposition parties. Gouws (2009) highlights the contradictions of the political arguments between the ANC and the opposition. Gender equality emerged as the first serious issue for conflict between the

ANC and the Democratic Alliance (DA – the opposition party which won the Western Cape Province in April 2009). This happened even though gender equality was totally absent from issues campaigned for during the elections. Two main opposition parties have women leaders: the Independent Democrats (Patricia de Lille) and the Democratic Alliance (Helen Zille),[12] but neither of them has raised any gender issues. This is a key lesson – not to essentialize women as caring, or especially likely to raise women's issues. This should also be noted by the 50/50 campaign – transformation is beyond numbers.[13]

The DA was never in favour of having quotas for electing MPs, as they saw themselves as being defined on the basis of merit. There was an outrage when Zille appointed ten men as ministers in her provincial government in 2009. Gouws (2009) does not discuss how race and gender intersect when she critiques Zille's cabinet of seven white and three black men. What subliminal message does this female political party leader send out when she says she has to choose a cabinet based on merit: that women and black people are not meritorious? With the exception of the ANC, no political party has a quota system.

In South Africa there have been a few women's political parties since 1994, but none of them managed to gain any seats. The most recent one – Women Forward – contested the national and some provincial elections in the 2009 elections and lost its deposit. A detailed analysis of the political scenario is needed to see what strategy would best suit a feminist agenda.

The ANC, with all its contradictions, still has the majority of seats and the majority of women MPs, except in the Western Cape Province. As the oldest liberation movement in Africa (launched in 1912) it still elicits historical and emotional loyalty. It is also the only political party which reserves 50 per cent of its seats for women representatives as a policy.[14] MPs from this party also include historically marginalized persons, like people with disabilities.

The voice that often shouts the loudest in contemporary South Africa is that of the Conservatives. It is a myth that South

Africa is unique. Like many parts of the world, South Africa too has seen the emergence of new conservative movements. The African Christian Democratic Party (ACDP) has not embraced quotas but it has women in key positions – thus illustrating the argument that Goetz and Nyamu-Musembi (2008) make about conservative movements using women to give the impression of promoting equality, while actually strengthening the confines of patriarchy. But many women have also internalized patriarchy, and hence do not mind being part of this conservative movement. In South Africa women not only participate in conservative structures but are also in the forefront of starting conservative movements, emulating the conservative agendas of men. Angus Buchan started the 'Mighty Men's Movement', in which 200,000 men participated in order to assess their roles and become 'real men' again. Then Gretha Wiid launched its cohort: a 'Mighty Women's' conference. Her aim was to fill the vacuum left by Angus Buchan who spoke only to men. She complemented his message by saying: 'Mighty men should have worthy women' (News24 2009) All this was done within a very narrow interpretation of Christianity: that a woman should support her man, the head of the house. Radical women of faith are not really very vocal in South Africa.

The Zionist Church is the biggest of all churches in South Africa, and women promote it through their weekly prayer meetings. Conservative movements in other faiths like Islam and Judaism, are also increasing, albeit in smaller numbers.

The strength of the ANC in the past was that it was a broad organization incorporating Catholics, Communists, conservatives and radicals, which united diverse forces during the anti-apartheid struggles. However, as a ruling party its straddling act must attempt to satisfy capitalists and labour, and other forces with conflicting interests. So it has alliances with the traditional leaders as well as with progressive women's groups.

The ANC initially had a strong relationship with the South African Council of Churches (SACC), which also played a key anti-apartheid role. The SACC consists of the mainline churches like Anglicans, Protestants and Catholics. The SACC lost its place within the ANC alliance as it refused to be the ANC's mouthpiece (Mataboge 2009b). It has critiqued the ANC for its failure to eradicate poverty. The Catholic Bishops' Conference criticized Zuma and questioned his use of culture as justification 'to defend bad moral behaviour' – Zuma is a polygamist and recently had a child out of wedlock (News24 2010). Zuma, meanwhile, had called for new links between church structures and the National Interfaith Leadership Council (NILC) was launched in 2009. It was initiated by Pastor Ray McCauley, a staunch Zuma supporter (Charisma Magazine 2010). The NILC's agenda is one that can impede women's and gay struggles as its first priorities are to reverse legislation on abortion and same-sex unions. Nthabiseng Khunou, an ANC MP and member of the NILC secretariat, told the *Mail & Guardian* that the council would 'play a role' in revisiting legislation that legalizes abortions and gay marriages. Khunou, a pastor, said the laws were very unpopular in South Africa's churches: 'I know most churches want them abolished, so the reason for the NILC is to give a voice to people who don't have it' (Mataboge 2009b).

How far the ANC will be able to counter the conservative agenda and create and sustain initiatives for gender equity depends on how it weathers the series of political crises it has faced in recent years. The ANC has been fractured by the formation of a breakaway Congress of the People (COPE), which was formed by supporters of former President Mbeki. The most recent rupture the ANC faces is the Economic Freedom Forum (EFF), formed in June 2013 by expelled ANC YL president Julius Malema and his supporters.[15] The EFF claims to be a platform for debate and discussion, and that it has no intention of contesting the elections in 2014. The ANC is also trying to counter new political forces such as the Agang (Sotho for 'togetherness') political party, formed on 13 February 2013 by Dr Mamphela Ramphele, which has the support of middle-class whites and academics. It is speculated that she may attract more supporters from the main national opposition, the white-led Democratic Alliance (DA).

The formation of these new political forces has been influenced by dissatisfaction with the ANC over corruption, service delivery failure, economic policies (denationalization of the mines), and police brutality to quell resistance.[16] The feminist and women's voice in this new political arena will be affected by how women participate and the agendas they mobilize around.

Service delivery failure in the Western Cape has angered people at the grassroots (including women) and the DA has capitalized on that. Selective targeting of state projects for ANC-governed provinces has created massive protests. The controversial Black Economic Empowerment (BEE), it is argued, only enriched the government elite and those close to them. The gap between rich and poor continues.

The question is how have feminists responded to these crises and debates on pro-poor politics and the economy? In terms of civil society and feminist voices, South Africans have raised their voices mostly around service delivery concerns but also around wage labour and salaries. But the most vocal, large-scale dissatisfaction is heard from the South African poor. Many state that feminist voices have been muted, yet there have been many protests against the continuing violent rapes and killing of women, often within their homes and committed by family members.[17]

The analysis above shows that the ANC has shifted its position on gender equity. It would have been inconceivable during the 1994–2004 period that some of the events and developments described above would ever have taken place in Parliament. Feminists, including myself, were naïve to believe that with the impressive constitution and the NGM we could effect some change. What we have seen in the above analysis is that, though the structures of the NGM were comparatively advanced, their functioning was hopelessly inadequate because too many political appointees had little experience or expertise in gender equality (Serote 2004; Gouws 2004a, 2004b, 2005). The politics of power and patriarchy are still thriving in this gender-sensitive country, and so are the inherent contradictions. This will be a long and protracted struggle.

Our ideas about activism have also changed. Initially we believed that we should consolidate the NGM. But, as we have seen, over-reliance on state feminism, with many ANC women leaders promoting party interest over gender equity concerns, divisiveness within the gender machinery, and the rise of conservative forces, all created an unpropitious political landscape: the gender equity agenda began to fall between cracks that turned into fissures, and the feminist voice was weakened. For example, research commissioned by the joint portfolio committee, the JMC, confirmed that most of the work on countering violence against women was financed by NGOs and not the government.

Though the government has created the CGE to channel women's/gender equity demands, it has never functioned effectively given the ambiguity in terms of staff and commissioners' roles, and power struggles between commissioners and other staff. The contradictions in the constitution that created both the CGE and a Commission on the Promotion and Protection of Culture, Religion and Linguistic Communities, whose mandates were potentially contradictory, created insurmountable difficulties. There were major problems with monitoring government departments in order to assess the progress of gender equality. Ministers did not submit information to the CGE on time. The information provided in reports was limited to internal structures and not their service delivery in communities. It was largely a numbers game and the inherent patriarchal cultures were never interrogated. Budgets for gender desks were minimal or non-existent, the gender focal person (GFP) also held another portfolio and she was the GFP because of her personal passion. If a formal GFP existed within the structures it was always at the lowest levels of the bureaucracy, and the impact was minimal.

Feminists who engaged with these state machineries in South Africa initially believed (or wanted to believe) that the strategy of mainstreaming empowered women in a democratic state, albeit a liberal democracy, would result in radical progress. But the bureaucracy we engaged with is essentially masculine, hierarchical and unresponsive to attempts to promote gender equality. This limited the impact of femocrats and activists engaging with the state to promote gender equity in a post-apartheid state (Ferguson 1984).

Conclusions

Unity amongst women has always been problematic, but generally at certain phases during a political struggle alliances have formed that gave voice to feminist concerns. Leaders in the NWC were mostly middle-class, but grassroots women's structures like UWO and UWCO had leaders from the African working class. Although the NWC was relatively successful, it was clear that certain groups were marginalized. For example, debates on customary law nearly split the fragile alliance when some white women's groups felt the issue was too complex and could 'protract' the progress of the NWC. Feminist voices were strengthened within the context of negotiations for a new constitution for South Africa, but there was always a danger of women being marginalized. Nineteen years after 'freedom', the scenario is still quite frightening. Homophobia increases as the religious right grows. Violence against women and children has become almost epidemic in scale, as Mama observed many years ago. 'South Africa's high representation of women ... sits alongside the worst figures for gender-based violence and some of the most shocking manifestations of sexual abuse (often fatal against women of all ages)' (Mama 2004: 3).

Pockets of feminist activity can be found. Currently the women's movements in South Africa are very fragmented and are organized by sectors. In the Western Cape more dynamic and visible structures have emerged through NGOs. The Women on Farms project has given rise to a farm workers' trade union – Sikhula Sonke. Although it is a trade union for men and women, it is women-led and the agenda is radical. Nationally, the Network on Violence against Women is most dominant, but its effectiveness varies from region to region.

Many perceive a hierarchy amongst feminists, which is true.

Most women's interest groups are organized but often there is no communication amongst them. As mentioned earlier, black lesbians are the most marginalized at all levels. It would seem that violence against women is privileged but that violence against black lesbians is not. At a meeting of the Concerned Women's Network[18] in May 2009, at former Western Cape Premier Lynne Brown's official residence, Leeuwenhof, a black African lesbian questioned the ANC WL ('our mothers in the ANC') for the message it was sending out to the country by remaining quiet when 'we are raped and murdered just because we are lesbians'. At another meeting in June 2009, held by the Network on Violence against Women, a participant made the distinction between 'big feminists like you, and us minor ones'. This is food for thought. Do we, as feminists with a longer history of participation in feminist struggle, give the impression of being more 'relevant' than or superior to younger feminists, thus contributing to the hierarchy amongst feminists? It also needs to be emphasized that the word 'feminist' is still controversial and in some cases it is still associated with urban, middle-class, white or Western women. Some prefer the word 'womanist'[19] to describe their analysis.

But whatever women choose to call themselves, the sad reality of a once women-friendly country is that women's radical voices are almost absent. We promoted the NGM while neglecting to build grassroots and civil society movements. Now we battle to build women's movements – this has become a struggle in itself. There used to be times when I felt that my participation/our participation made a difference: but this feminist voice has not been sustained.

When I interviewed the feminist academic, Amanda Gouws, she said:

> Now it's more about sectoral women's structures, e.g., violence against women, poverty, etc. Now there seems to be no urgency, as we had in past – the impetus that we had when we formed the NWC. We lost our feminist discourse and activism and we also lost the single issue of the Women's Charter that united us. There are different discourses now: a masculinist discourse. The populist

discourse is quite vulgar re women's issues. Nothing seems to be getting to us to show solidarity around some of these issues, even the crude misogynism of Malema (ANC YL leader). I myself am puzzled. We must not forget the impact that neo-liberal capitalism has on situations and why there is no unity. Neo-liberal capitalism leads to the managerialist way of managing issues – it de-radicalizes activism (one such tool is gender mainstreaming). We have lost radical feminism (I think). Now we are into identity politics. (Interviews March and June 2010)

Pregs Govender (former chair of the JMC) is the current vice-chair of the Human Rights Commission of South Africa. She asserts that the 'honeymoon' is over in South Africa. According to her it is evident in a number of ways, including the fact that recent and current legislation is anti-women. She also refers to President Zuma's meeting with the House of Traditional Leaders and the regressive discourse emerging from there. 'We're in serious trouble if this continues,' she said, and also shared her dismay about the ineffective performance of the then Minister of Women, Children and People with Disability at the Commission on the Status of Women meeting in New York (interview 13 March 2010).

Feminists are also tired after all these difficult struggles. Perhaps we underestimated the energy required to rebuild a new society. I am reminded of the lines from Giles Pontecorvo's famous film on the Algerian national war of liberation – *The Battle of Algiers*: 'It's difficult to start a revolution; more difficult to sustain it. But it's later, when we've won, that the real difficulties will begin' (quoted in McClintock 1995: 388). The current situation is not without a sober poignancy, especially for women. Also, there are many personality differences amongst feminists – and many of my interviewees agree that such differences are obstacles to consolidating feminist activism and subsequent feminist voices. One interviewee said, 'When certain women call meetings or it is known that they will attend, others boycott the action.' However, such happenings are not necessarily to be ascribed to women only.

From my interactions with women's organizations I can see that most of them are experiencing crises involving funding or some other life-threatening challenge. Many women's NGOs have closed over the past few years and some are on the verge of closing down. The DA-ruled Western Cape Province, led by a woman Premier, has stopped funding to many women and feminist NGOs. Many NGOs and women's structures feel insecure, and others are too busy even to respond to invitations. It is ironic that we – who aimed to give solidarity a new meaning when we set out – have not come together to help and support one another.

Stark differences amongst women have prevented a united feminist voice from emerging. Grassroots women said: 'While you feminists are concerned with getting out of the kitchen, our fight is to get a kitchen' (Mtintso 2003: 572). But are these differences real or assumed? Are we being blinded by our prejudices? Will these differences ever be reconciled? Audre Lorde leaves us with some hope:

> It is not our differences that separate women but our reluctance to recognize these differences and to deal effectively with the distortions that have resulted from ignoring and misnaming these differences.… As Paulo Freire shows so well in *The Pedagogy of the Oppressed*, the true focus of revolutionary change is never merely the oppressive situations that we seek to escape but that piece of the oppressor that is planted deep within each of us and that knows only the oppressor's tactics, the oppressor's relations. Change means growth, and growth can be painful. But we sharpen self-definition by exposing the self in work and struggle together with those whom we define as different from ourselves, although sharing the same goals. For black and white, old and young, lesbian and heterosexual women alike, this can mean new paths to our survival … develop[ing] new definitions of power and new patterns of relating across difference. (Lorde 1997: 379–80)

We have overcome major battles in the past by uniting. Many still speak about the South African 'miracle'. I strongly believe in it and am committed to working towards uniting the feminist voice in the future. Together with diverse groups and especially younger women and girls, we will amplify our feminist voices. No revolution is possible without strategic unity and if we as feminists do not raise our united voice in a critical solidarity, we will be contributing to postponing the revolution. We should also learn from other struggles and build transnational feminism. There are miracles on the horizon, waiting to happen.

Notes

1   South Africa experienced more than 350 years of colonial and capitalist apartheid. Although apartheid was legislated in 1948, it was a part of the colonial system and was introduced by the Dutch Reformed Church in 1857 through its separate race churches. The British introduced the pass system, which curtailed the movements of black people. The African National Congress (ANC) was formed in 1912 to challenge the power of white settlers who usurped mineral-rich land. After the 1913 Land Act, 87 per cent of the land belonged to the whites and 13 per cent of poor arid land to the black indigenous majority. The twentieth century in South Africa was marked by liberation struggles. Women, like other parts of the society, were also highly organized and this culminated in the 1956 Women's March (in which women of all races – including a few whites – took part), which challenged the extension of passes to black African women. Passes curtailed people's freedom of movement. Millions were imprisoned because of pass offences. The Federation of South Africa Women, which organized the march, focused on the issues concerning the poorest and the majority of women. As mass protests increased, all liberation movements like the ANC, the Pan Africanist Congress (PAC) and the South African Community Party (SACP) were banned by the apartheid government in 1960.
2   In 1976 students boycotted classes when the apartheid government imposed Afrikaans as a medium of instruction in schools. Afrikaans was seen as the language of the oppressors. The boycotts spread nationally.
3   'Black African' refers to the indigenous population who speak Bantu languages like Xhosa and Zulu, classified as African by the apartheid state. They were the most oppressed in terms of the hierarchy of race oppression. I use these apartheid labels to illustrate the class and race positions in order to highlight whose

voices are prominent. In this pecking order of apartheid laws, the statutes governing Indians and coloureds (of mixed race, including descendants of slaves and indigenous First Nations) were less restrictive. During the political struggles we used the generic word 'black' to refer to all oppressed groups. This was a legacy of the Black Consciousness Movement of the 1970s, in which all oppressed persons were identified as black in order to unite against apartheid. In fact the Freedom Charter of 1956, drawn up as a result of national consultations amongst the oppressed, states in its preamble, 'South Africa belongs to all who live in it, black and white'. However, during the 1992 period new tensions and ethnic awareness arose. At a woman and gender meeting, Pregs Govender (Indian) and I (slave/First Nation descendant) were on a panel with one white and two Xhosa-speaking women. A member of the audience shouted that there were not enough 'blacks' on the panel. Govender and I were shocked, as it was the first time in our more than 20 years of political struggle that we were not seen as 'black'. These race tension and identity issues continue in contemporary South Africa, especially in relation to who qualifies for affirmative action positions.

4   The power and roles were quite clear. We were building a movement led by the African working class. Some of the tasks white and middle-class women were responsible for were getting venues. This was where I lectured.

5   Phumzile Mlambo-Ngcuku is now the UN Women's Director.

6   Although the Speakers were women from 1994 to 2009.

7   African women within this new South Africa have achieved leadership positions. Nosimo Balindlela, Premier of the Eastern Cape (2004–8), is a concrete example of the schizophrenic existence of women in public office – Premier in the public world and dutiful mother and wife in private. Even though she was the first citizen of the Eastern Cape Province she is a woman and as a woman she knows her place. The elders bequeathed her the title of 'an honorary man': 'It was the elders' way of showing that I am a pillar of strength in the family, the mother of the family' (Cohen 2005: 19). In an interview, Nomaindia Mfeketo (in 2004, the deputy speaker of the national Parliament) pointed out that Balindlela had to 'seek permission first before she could use the family name in her public duty'.

8   Patricia McFadden coined this phrase, referring to women who flit around the world on a gender ticket but have no accountability to poor women. Chandra Mohanty (2003) refers to 'feminist careerists'.

9   It has been widely interpreted that the ousting of former President Mbeki, which coincided with the return to leadership politics of Jacob Zuma, was orchestrated with the massive and very vocal support of the President of the ANC YL, Julius Malema and his team. Tension between the ANC and the ANC YL sharpened, culminating in the expulsion of YL President Malema. Subsequently, Malema promised to ensure that ANC leaders who oppose his efforts to put the country's mines in state hands are removed. He launched the Economic Freedom Forum, a political platform, in early June 2013, and committed himself to fighting poverty. Meanwhile his properties, worth millions, are being sold as the South African revenue authorities are demanding unpaid taxes.

10 The statement, pictures and information can be found at http://womensnet.org.za/south-african-feminists.

11 This can be found on http://www.sangocowc.org.

12 They have since amalgamated (August 2010) and the Independent Democrats will be phased out by 2014.

13 The 50/50 campaign, initiated in 2004, is global and coordinated by WEDO, New York. In South Africa it has been coordinated by the Gender Advocacy Programme. The aim is to have 50 per cent representation of women in all decision-making bodies, especially in government. We have added a rider – not just numbers, but quality and a commitment to raise feminist issues.

14 Initially it was 33 per cent, and was changed by former President Mbeki to 50 per cent. There are many women MPs who are doing sterling work.

15 It was with the ardent support of populist orator Malema and the ANC YL that Zuma came to power after the ousting of Mbeki. Malema was expelled for bringing the ANC into disrepute. He called for regime change in Botswana and supported the land grab of Mugabe (Zimbabwe's president). This is contrary to ANC policy.

16 One these confrontations was on 16 August 2012, when police shot and killed 35 protesters at the Marikana mines in the north of the country.

17 In 2013 the Olympic 'Blade Runner', Oscar Pistorius, was arrested for fatally shooting his girlfriend.

18 A loose temporary alliance of progressive women, many of them ANC supporters, formed in Cape Town prior to the April 2009 national elections, in response to the confusion and disillusionment of women about whom to vote for when a misogynistic discourse

was in evidence amongst many political leaders. They no longer meet. It was assumed that they would re-convene in 2011 for local government elections, but this did not happen. South Africa is even more fragmented in 2013. It will be interesting to see whether radical feminist voices will emerge in the 2014 elections.

19 See 'Womanism' by Emmagunde:
'Womanist is to feminist as purple is to lavender' – Alice Walker
'Womanism is a feminist term coined by Alice Walker. It is a reaction to the realization that "feminism" does not encompass the perspectives of Black women. It is a feminism that is "stronger in color", nearly identical to "black feminism". However, womanism does not need to be prefaced by the word "black", the word automatically concerns black women. A womanist is a woman who loves women and appreciates women's culture and power as something that is incorporated into the world as a whole. Womanism addresses the racist and classist aspects of white feminism and actively opposes separatist ideologies.' http:// afeministtheorydictionary.wordpress.com/2007/07/17/womanism/ (accessed 29 July 2013).

References

Abrahams N., S. Mathews, R. Jewkes, L. Martin and C. Lombard (2012) 'Every eight hours: Intimate femicide in South Africa 10 years later', research brief, South African Medical Research Council, August 2012.

Abrams, S. K. (2000) 'Fighting for Women's Liberation during the Liberation of South Africa', unpublished M Phil dissertation, Wadham College, Oxford.

CGE Commissioners (2010) 'Gasa's Flights of Fancy', *Mail & Guardian*, 18–24 June, p. 25.

Charisma Magazine (2010) 'South African Pastor Ray McCauley to Divorce', http://www.charismamag.com/index.php/news/26182-south-african-pastor-ray-mccauley-to-divorce (accessed 28 June 2010).

Cohen, L. (2005) 'Barefoot Premier Gets down to Earth', *Weekend Argus*, 2 January, p. 19.

Emmagunde (2007) 'Womanism' 'http://afeministtheorydictionary. wordpress.com/2007/07/17/womanism/ accessed 29 July 2013.

Ferguson, K. E. (1984) *The Feminist Case against Bureaucracy*, Temple University Press, Philadelphia, PA.

Fester, G. (2007) 'Reconciling Multiculturalism for Democracy: Challenges for the new South Africa', in B. Arneil, M. Deveaux, R. Dhamoon and A. Eisenberg (eds), *Sexual Justice/Cultural Justice*, Routledge, London.

Gasa, N. (2010) 'Mr President, I Stand Accused…', *Mail & Guardian*, 11–17 June, p. 33.

Geisler, G. (2000) 'Parliament is another terrain of struggle: women, men and politics in South Africa', *Journal of Modern African Studies* 38, pp. 606–30.

—— (2004) *Women and the Remaking of Politics in Southern Africa – Negotiating Autonomy, Incorporation and Representation*, Nordiska Afrika Institutet, Oslo.

Goetz, A.-M. (2003) 'Women's Political Effectiveness: A Conceptual Framework', in A.-M. Goetz and Shireen Hassim (eds) (2003), *No Shortcuts to Power: African Women in Politics and Policy Making,* Zed Books and David Philip, London, New York, NY and Cape Town.

Goetz, A-M. and S. Hassim (eds) (2003) *No Shortcuts to Power: African Women in Politics and Policy Making*, Zed Books and David Philip, London, New York, NY and Cape Town.

Goetz, A-M. and C. Nyamu-Musembi (2008) 'Voice and Women's Empowerment: Mapping a Research Agenda', Pathways Working Paper No. 2, Pathways of Women's Empowerment, Brighton.

Gouws, A. (2004a) 'The Politics of State Structures: Citizenship and the National Machinery for Women in South Africa', *Feminist Africa*, No. 3, pp. 1–18.

—— (2004b) 'Shaping Women's Citizenship: Contesting the Boundaries of State and Discourse', in A. Gouws (ed.), *(Un)thinking Citizenship*, Ashgate, Burlington, VA.

—— (2005) 'The State of the National Gender Machinery: Structural Problems and Personalized Politics', in J. Daniel and R. Southall (eds), *The State of the Nation 2005–2006*, HSRC Press, Cape Town.

—— (2009) 'Wanneer vroue beter mans as mans word' (When women become better men than men), *Die Burger,* 14 May 2009, p. 16.

Hassim, S. (2004), 'Nationalism Displaced: Citizenship Discourses in the Transition', in A. Gouws (ed.), *(Un)Thinking Citizenship*, Ashgate, Burlington, VA.

—— (2006) *Women's Organisations and Democracy in South Africa: Contesting Authority*, University of KwaZulu-Natal Press, Scottsville.

Lorde, A. (1997) 'Age, Race, Class and Sex: Women Redefining Difference', in Anne McClintock, Aamir Mufti and Ella Shohat (eds), *Dangerous Liaisons: Gender, Nation and Postcolonial Perspectives,* University of Minnesota, Minneapolis.

Mama, A. (2004) 'Editorial', *Feminist Africa,* No. 3, pp. 1–5.

Masando, S. (2010) 'Gender Commission Grinds to a Standstill', www. timeslive.co.za/local/article699597.ece/Gender-commission-grinds-to-a-standstill (accessed 10 October 2010).

Mataboge, M. (2009a) 'Women's Ministry Drowning', *Mail & Guardian*, 13 November.

—— (2009b) 'Why the ANC Dumped the Council of Churches', *Mail & Guardian*, 18–23 September, p. 5.

McClintock, A. (1995) *Imperial Leather*, Routledge, New York, NY.

Mohanty, C. (2003) *Feminism without Borders: Decolonizing Theory, Practicing Solidarity,* Duke University Press, Durham, NC and London.

Motsei, M. (2007) *The Kanga and the Kangaroo Court,* Jacana Media, Auckland Park.

Mtintso, T. (2003) 'Representivity: False Sisterhood or Universal Women's Interests? The South African Experience', *Feminist Studies*, Vol. 29, No. 3, pp. 569–80.

News24 (2009) 'Women Get Own Mighty Men', http://news24.com/SouthAfrica/News/Women-get-own-Mighty-Men, 19 July (accessed 28 June 2010).

—— (2010) 'Churches Slate Zuma's Morals', http://www.news24.com/SouthAfrica/Politics/Churches-slate-Zumas-morals-2100212 (accessed 28 June 2010).

POWA (2010) 'Criminal Injustice: Violence against Women in South Africa: Shadow Report on Beijing + 15', prepared by People Opposing Women Abuse (POWA) with the AIDS Legal Network (ALN) on behalf of the One in Nine Campaign and the Coalition for African Lesbians (CAL), http://www2.ohchr.org/english/bodies/cedaw/docs/ngos/POWA_Others_SouthAfrica48.pdf (accessed 29 July 2013).

Republic of South Africa (2005) *South African Beijing +10 Report*, The Presidency, Pretoria.

Seidman, G. W. (1999) 'Gendered Citizenship: South Africa's Democratic Transition and the Construction of a Gendered State', *Gender and Society*, Vol. 13, No. 3, pp. 287–307.

—— (2003) 'Feminist Interventions: The South African Gender Commission and "Strategic" Challenges to Gender Equality', *Feminist Studies*, Vol. 29, No. 3, pp. 541–63.

Serote, P. (2004) South Africa Country Report for the Southern African Development Community (SADC) Needs Assessment for the Capacity Building for National Gender Machineries in SADC Member States, SADC, Gaborone.

Tsikata, D. (2004) 'The Rights-Based Approach to Development: Potential for Change or More of the Same?', *IDS Bulletin*, Vol. 35, No. 4, pp. 134–6. Women's Net (no date) 'One in Nine Campaign: Solidarity with Women', www.womensnet.org.za (accessed 19 October 2009).

4

Voicing Autonomy through Citizenship
The Regional Nationality Campaign and Morocco

Alexandra Pittman and Rabéa Naciri

This chapter focuses on one of the most comprehensive regional coalition-building efforts for nationality reform and citizenship across the Middle East and North Africa (MENA), the Campaign to Reform Arab Women's Nationality ('the nationality campaign'). It explores the politics and dynamics of channelling voice through feminist non-governmental organizations (NGOs).[1] Particular attention is placed on the development of transnational and local discourses and strategies to advocate for women's nationality rights and the creation and strengthening of regional and transnational networks for reform.

We focus on the work of the Moroccan international human rights organization, Association Démocratique des Femmes du Maroc (ADFM) to provide an example of how campaign members adapted regional strategies to their own specific contexts, communicating the need for reform. We also explore the difficulties faced by the Lebanese NGO, Collective for Research and Training on Development – Action (CRTD.A) in campaigning on nationality reform issues against a background of religious and ethnic factionalism, political instability and conflict. We conclude by examining some of the central lessons for campaign development and the role of voice in advocacy efforts.

A diverse set of primary and secondary data were used in our research, including interviews, desk research and personal interactions and experiences with feminist activists involved in the campaign. NGO activists are an interesting locus of analysis as they provide a bridge between global spheres of interaction, political society and local communities (Merry 2003). The ability of NGO advocacy work to maintain the delicate balance of translation and authentic representation, often through agendas of elite and middle-class leaders, has engaged considerable debate and critique (see Mariz Tadros's work in this volume). However, there are many innovative advocacy models that build campaign demands based on women directly affected by inequalities, and that foster grassroots capacities within an advocacy campaign framework. The nationality campaign describes such a model for social change, one that combines advocacy with a strong grassroots base and carefully crafted and adaptive political strategies.

Historical aspects of nationality

The process of making feminist voice audible to the state and susceptible to legislative, administrative and judicial provision occurs within a broader discursive and political field. Within this field, social meanings around citizenship and nationality are constructed, negotiated and contradicted (King 2007; Spillman 1995). Notions of who can and cannot claim rights are shaped historically by the way in which specific colonial, patriarchal, religious, political and economic ideologies have interacted and constructed women's status in relation to the state (Joseph 2000; Moghadam 2003). Being able to channel feminist voice effectively – allowing it to be legitimated and recognized by the state and in political society – does not necessarily lead to immediate change, as will be shown through the analysis. Rather, a variety of factors including political opportunities, stability of the socio-political context, existing power structures and constraints, and grassroots alignments shape the possibilities for reform.

While legal frameworks in the Western world base citizenship on the liberal notion of the individualized citizen and his/her rights, in the MENA the arbiter of citizenship rights is the family (Joseph 2000). The family has been a central defining feature of legal structures. In particular the male, as the head of the household and arbiter of the family, has been inscribed in the legal frameworks of many states through a personal status code. Personal status codes are strongly inspired by Muslim rights based on social rules (*fiqh*) that have been derived from the Qur'an and interpreted by Islamic jurisprudence scholars. The codes govern men's and women's behaviour and rights, such as divorce, marriage and inheritance. While there is great religious diversity in personal status codes across the region, some basic similarities emerge, particularly in the way that nationhood is integrally tied to patriarchy (Kandiyoti 1991). The patriarchal norms embedded within personal status codes demonstrate the centrality of male privilege as established and justified through Islam (Ahmed 1992: 242).

In contrast to personal status codes, which draw inspiration from religious law, many constitutions and civil laws across the MENA region, including labour and penal codes, are written in a secular framework. Yet even within this secular legal framework, states have often been clear that their main concern is preserving the family and not the individual as the basic building blocks for their societies. Therefore, women's roles and rights are not seen as independent, but rather are defined in relation to their family roles as wives and mothers: 'This is the major factor in enhancing and promoting both religious and familial control over them [women] and rendering them more dependent on these institutions for representation and security' (CRTD.A 2004: 8). The implication is that only through relational aspects of identity can one gain rights as a citizen (Joseph 2000) as the male head of household bestows nationality and citizenship rights on his family members. This 'second class citizenship' (CRTD.A 2004) revokes women's autonomy and status as independent legal subjects in the eyes of the state.

Typically across the region, constitutions secure women's political, social and economic rights as citizens; however, separate nationality codes based on the family violate these equal rights. In some countries, such as Jordan, Syria, Lebanon and Iraq, women acquire the nationality of their husband after marriage through a legal process, not keeping their own nationality – and so the family would not be able to apply for residency cards in the wife's birth country, since she would have lost her citizenship rights through marriage (Sonbol 2003). In other countries, such as Morocco, legal provisions have allowed naturalized foreign spouses to keep their nationality – meaning husbands and wives could hold different nationalities after marriage. In order to challenge these discriminations at a fundamental level, feminists must deconstruct male privilege as embodied in the law (Abou-Habib 2010a; Naciri 2007a) and address the tension between the liberal individual and relational notions of rights (Joseph 2000).

The regional campaign for women's right to pass their nationality on to their family

The regional nationality campaign was initiated in 2001, drawing together activists in Morocco, Lebanon, Jordan, Egypt, Bahrain and Algeria. Coordinating NGOs in each country include ADFM Morocco, CRTD.A Lebanon, Sisterhood is Global Institute/Jordan (SIGI/J), Forum for Women in Development (FWID), Bahrain Women's Society (BWS) and Centre d'Informatique et de Documentation sur les Droits de l'Enfant et de la Femme (CIDDEF). The campaign aims to coordinate activist efforts to educate and advocate for legislative changes in all MENA countries to support women's full and equal citizenship. Campaign members meet annually to share successful strategies, collaborate to broaden the reach of the campaign, and thus increase their collective political voice and power. These deep relationships, built on mutual trust and respect, are integral solidarity mechanisms, broadening the influence and reach of campaigns. Many of the members of the coalition had been working together for several years in different regional networks and reform projects.

Lina Abou-Habib (2008), the regional coordinator of the

nationality campaign and executive director of CRTD.A Lebanon, describes the iterative process of deciding to focus on citizenship. As campaign activists analysed common concerns and barriers to gender equality, nationality arose as a priority issue for all involved, given the patriarchal and kinship framing of rights. As a starting point, campaign members developed a collective frame[2] of reference for outlining and communicating the need for nationality reform to different stakeholders. Key stakeholders included jurists, elected representatives, and the broader public. Given these stakeholder groups, a major focus of the campaign was on engaging women's political participation and ensuring that publicly elected representatives had women's rights at the top of their agendas (Abou-Habib 2010a).

A key component of the campaign was to develop an over-arching regional voice, strategies, and key entry points that each NGO would adapt, on the basis of opportunities for reform within its own political context (Abou-Habib 2010a). In this way, the campaign operated at two levels, both as a regional solidarity and support mechanism and as a local implementation and advocacy body. Coalition members underscored the importance of diversity as each country context had different state dynamics, political and legal structures, and civic and social spaces available to advocate for reform. For example, in Morocco, activists decided that reform should only ensure that a mother could pass nationality on to her children. In other countries, such as Algeria and Lebanon, it was critical that the woman be able to pass nationality to her children and spouse. By allowing each member to adapt strategy and demands to a unique context, the coalition circumvented unnecessary tensions and power struggles inherent in a universal approach to implementation. This adaptive model also ensured space for multiple voices in the strategy development processes. A diversity of perspectives is not only a mechanism for strengthening transnational organizing efforts, but has also been cited as an emerging component of strong movement building within a country in a specific campaign (Khorasani 2009).

From the outset, members of the nationality campaign

decided not to reference religious or doctrinal arguments, given that nationality laws across various Arab countries are not based on a religious foundation, but for the most part are inspired by colonial laws. After conducting extensive background research into the domestic and international legal codes within their countries, members met to discuss how to frame a persuasive message for reform. The slogan 'My nationality, a right for me and my family' was arrived at in order to highlight the necessity of equality of all citizens and to underscore the current masculine bias in nationality rights. In Arabic, since nationality is a masculine word, the campaign slogan used the feminine translation of 'my nationality' instead.

Locating citizenship in a rights framework has a variety of implications. First, it opens up the possibility of leveraging other fundamental rights secured by the state, such as constitutional rights to equality. Second, the slogan positions citizenship as a family matter, addressing several important issues: the right of a woman to pass her nationality on to her children and husband, the child's right to the nationality of the mother, and, finally, the right of all family members to enjoy equal rights to citizenship (in education, health or employment, for example). Men had always enjoyed the unilateral right to pass on their nationality; now women were demanding that right as well. Third, the framing also aimed to broaden the potential range of supporters for reform – since communicating the necessity of ensuring equal access to rights and resources within a family broadened the potential stakeholders of interest, instead of highlighting this only as a women's rights issue. In effect, activists are subverting the notion of the need for a patriarchal and familial arbiter of citizenship, and replacing it with a call for the need for a liberal individual conceptualization of rights, all the while recognizing the familial ramifications of the relational structure. While some might see this strategy as reinforcing stereotypical notions of woman as mother, in fact, this strategy cleverly subverts that paradigm by securing women's right to autonomy within the family context through matrilineal lineage rights.[3]

An important communication tactic that activists used to argue for nationality reform across the coalition was to highlight the legislative, political and social inconsistencies in the legal structures of each country (Abou-Habib 2008; Idrissi 2008; Nafaa 2008). The focus on jurists as a stakeholder group largely shaped this advocacy strategy. The disconnect between legal frameworks was particularly apparent since, in all of the state constitutions in coalition countries, women and men were granted equality as citizens – and yet nationality codes exempted those equal rights. Intellectually, activists argued nationality laws should be changed as 'we should be able to live within the principles and provisions that our constitutions provide' (Abou-Habib 2010a). Further highlighting the legal inconsistencies, coalition activists leveraged national consensus on gender equality that had been codified in international human rights frameworks, such as the Universal Declaration of Human Rights (UDHR), Convention on the Elimination of All Forms of Discrimination Against Women (CEDAW) and the Convention on the Rights of the Child (CRC).

In order to implement these framing and communication messages, activists brainstormed a range of potential strategies that could be implemented by different NGO partners in their local contexts. Different mobilization tactics included petition drives, public rallies, public debates, political and juridical lobbying, and media campaigns. The regional campaign made significant use of blogs and social networking sites, such as Facebook, building on emerging technological trends as a powerful space for awareness raising, organizing and recruitment (Abou-Habib 2008; Hayek 2008; Goyal 2009; Afkhami 2009). In order to gain a deeper understanding of how regional strategies were adapted to the local campaign context, we explore the campaign process and progress in Morocco.

The nationality campaign in Morocco

As in other states across the MENA, in Morocco there is a complex legal structure consisting of secular laws for constitutional, civil and penal matters and the religiously inspired personal status code governing women's status and relations in the family.[4] Historically, women's rights have been both leveraged and subverted in the name of the state.

During the fight for independence from France, male nationalist leaders in the Istiqlal Party, like Allal al-Fassi, argued for women's rights and emancipation within Moroccan society, linking modernization processes with women's education (Bessis and Belhassen 1992). Women's rights activists played a prominent part in the nationalist movement and it was assumed that women's status and condition would improve in an independent Morocco.

However, women's rights activists' demands for equality and for a progressive and emancipatory legal structure were disregarded when independence was achieved (Rachid 1985). After independence, the nationalist demands were partially met through the abolition of the customary law for the Berber population and the development of the Moudawana (personal status code) by *oulema*, Islamic jurisprudence scholars, in 1957–8 (Buskens 2008). Mounira Charrad (2001) argues that states that relied more heavily on tribes (kin-based networks) for social control and political support after independence, such as Morocco, instated more conservative family laws (based on tribal norms) than states such as Tunisia, where the personal status codes were among the most liberating for women.

The Moudawana

The Moudawana (1957/8–2004) was, and in its reformed form still is, the most important law outlining women's status and rights in Morocco. The Moudawana has been amended twice since its inception in 1993 and more substantively in 2004. The old Moudawana (pre-2004 reform) constituted the primary mechanism for discrimination against women in the private sphere, establishing inequality before marriage (age, legal capacity to marry), during marriage (rights and duties of spouses), upon dissolution of marriage (spousal inequality in access to divorce and its effects) and, finally, inheritance.[5] Moroccan feminist activists have adamantly campaigned for equality in the Moudawana since its instatement (Lemrini 2005).

The eventual reform of the Moudawana in 2004 was precipitated by a number of political events, including King Mohamed VI's aim to align it with the values of justice in Islam as well as Morocco's international commitments concerning human rights. In addition, there was strong political tension and public debate around the necessity of reform, particularly between liberal feminists and progressives and the far right and Islamists, who claimed that the charge to reform was culturally inauthentic. The notion of cultural authenticity has been discussed in depth by Deniz Kandiyoti (1991), who highlights the way in which Western colonial projects in Muslim societies created tensions around family and cultural values, specifically those relating to women. The opposition was incredibly persuasive and barred reform from taking place for many years.[6] In March 2001, following an audience granted by King Mohamed VI, nine women's associations working for the promotion of women's rights decided to create a coalition, 'Printemps de l'Egalité pour la Réforme de la Moudawana' (Spring of Equality for the Reform of Moudawana) (Pittman and Naciri 2007, 2010). In April, the King established an advisory commission, consisting of three women and eleven men, to work on revising the Moudawana. The work took almost two and a half years and was marked by moments of strong tension due to internal conflict between its members and external pressure exerted by the 'Spring of Equality' coalition, which closely monitored the commission's progress.

The Casablanca terrorist attacks in 2003 paradoxically improved the context for reform because they served to weaken the Islamist groups politically. The liberal activists further pushed for the necessity of reform and the King used the opportunity to demand that recommendations for the Moudawana reform be made quickly (Sadiqi 2008). The interaction of these and many other constraints and opportunities culminated in a draft law being passed through Parliament and final legislative changes being made in February 2004. Many of the lessons and experiences activists gained through the Moudawana reform efforts contributed to strategy development in the local and regional nationality campaign.

The Nationality Code

The former Nationality Code did not automatically grant women, as was the case for men, the right to pass nationality on to their children – unless the father was unknown, or they were stateless (Article 6.2 or 7.1 respectively). However, Article 9.1 states that a child can acquire Moroccan nationality if, within the two years preceding his/her majority age, he/she declares the desire to do so. This applies to every child born in Morocco of a Moroccan mother and foreign father, as long as at the time of the declaration he/she has a permanent and regular residence in Morocco. The foreign wife of a Moroccan man could acquire nationality through a declaration to the Minister of Justice after two years of regular legal residence in Morocco, but a foreign husband was subject to the naturalization process (long and complex, with the outcome not guaranteed, Article 10). Members of ADFM and Moroccan human and women's rights activists involved in the local campaign wanted to reform the Nationality Code so that women could transmit their nationality of origin to their children without any limitations or conditions related to age, residence, or nationality of the father. Moreover, they demanded a retroactive application of the law.

These practices of Moroccan citizenship as codified were not in alignment with the country's constitutional laws or international agreements. Article 5 of the Moroccan constitution states: 'All Moroccan citizens shall be equal before the law.'[7] And Morocco has ratified a number of international declarations that have the potential to influence women's status, such as the UDHR, the International Pact of Civil and Political Rights in 1979, and CEDAW in 1993. CEDAW is one of the most important international legal instruments concerning the rights of women, including in the areas of nationality and citizenship. Article 9 in CEDAW asserts:

1 States Parties shall grant women equal rights with men to acquire, change or retain their nationality. They shall ensure in particular that neither marriage to an alien nor change of nationality by the husband during marriage shall automatically change the nationality of the wife, render her stateless or force upon her the nationality of the husband.
2 States Parties shall grant women equal rights with men with respect to the nationality of their children.
(UN 1979)

While Morocco signed and ratified CEDAW, the state made a variety of reservations, including to Article 9,[8] making such a commitment null and void. The tendency of many states to invoke reservations to international human rights frameworks reduces their legitimacy, since the principles are not universal, but rather can be excepted based on political or religious preference (Mashour 2005). The Moroccan government and the King had announced plans to lift reservations on a number of occasions since 2008. In mid-2011, they formally lifted reservations to CEDAW and ratified the optional protocol.

The Moroccan campaign for the right to transmit mothers' nationality to their children

Building on the momentum gained through the Moudawana reform campaign, Moroccan nationality reform activities were initiated in the early 2000s along with the regional efforts. The campaign mobilization strategy consisted of: (1) establishing a working group that included women experiencing nationality discriminations; (2) designing tools and action research to analyse the current state of nationality laws and studying the public's awareness of the discrimination that women faced under the current law; (3) creating alliances between national women's organizations, human rights NGOs, political parties, and other actors in civil society; and (4) lobbying and mobilizing support at the political and grassroots levels.

First, ADFM led an extensive research effort to better understand nationality laws in relation to constitutional and international law. In 2002, the organization held meetings throughout the year to listen to the accounts and experiences of women affected by the nationality law. ADFM then sent these testimonies to 22 media outlets to generate empathy for the social and familial issues involved with the unequal nationality law and to call for its reform. Activists at ADFM also commissioned a variety of studies, including one led by Amina Lemrini and Rabéa Naciri, about women married to non-nationals.

This study, the first of its kind in Morocco, helped to highlight three challenging and interesting issues. First, an analysis of marriage records in the Rabat courts showed that the number of Moroccan women married to foreigners was much higher than Moroccan men married to foreigners. This phenomenon, which had not been measured in the past, generated media interest and showed that far from being a marginal phenomenon, hundreds of thousands of Moroccan women were in this situation across all socio-economic strata. Second, the majority of women in the sample, regardless of their educational level, were not initially aware of the consequences of being married to a non-national; and only learned of their citizenship status after marriage or after giving birth to their first child. The study showed the deep extent of discrimination and deprivation that children in such marriages faced (especially those whose fathers were not European or Western). The women were deeply affected by the fact that certain rights and freedoms, including the most basic, interfered with their children's access and freedom to travel (Lemrini 2006). The research gave activists the important demographic and personal information with which they could develop a more in-depth communication and awareness-raising strategy. ADFM and other women's associations built on the recommendations of the women who participated in the study in order to formulate a broader mobilization plan for the nationality campaign (Idrissi 2008).

The process of identifying and gathering affected women was a particularly difficult part of the campaign. After sustained outreach and personal contact, ADFM was able to organize a collective of women directly affected by the problems (*ibid.*). However, since many of these women had not participated in the women's movement, it was difficult to impress upon them that their struggle would only succeed if the group shared a collective vision and sense of solidarity. This went beyond the issues specific to each woman and her family to the need to construct coherent and comprehensive legal claims. The tragedies faced by many members of this group (and their families and children) made this an uneven and difficult process. Many women came with the expectation that, upon their joining the collective, ADFM would provide individual and specific support to each woman and family. ADFM worked extensively with the collective in developing a common vision and in drawing out their unique experiences and struggles in supporting how the campaign was messaged. From ADFM's perspective, by involving women whose lives had been ruptured by the nationality law, activists were able to engage in participatory organizing processes that strengthened voices and demands for equality, deepening campaign legitimacy.

The first public debate on the Moroccan Nationality Code reform took place in April 2004 and was followed by a press conference in October 2004. It was during these public debates and discussions that activists learned they had the support not only of the left-inclined parliamentary parties, including the Socialist Union of Popular Forces (USFP) and the Progress and Socialism Party (PPS), but also of the ruling Islamist Justice and Development Party (PJD). Support was expected from the USFP as, in 2002, the party had filed a legislative proposal to change Article 6 of the Nationality Code. However, support from the PJD was quite surprising (Nafaa 2008; Idrissi 2008), and this was particularly the case given their strong opposition to the Moudawana reform. In this instance, the Islamists noted there was no precedent in Islamic law regarding citizenship and women's status. As such, there was nothing to bar women from passing their nationality on to their children, with the condition that foreign spouses were Muslim.[9] The unexpected support offered activists an important lesson on the way in which loyalties can shift depending on the campaign topic, the frame and the underpinning ideologies involved in the campaign issues. Spaces were opening up for NGO activists to leverage the momentum and political opportunities,[10] particularly those brought about through the increased national dialogue on women's rights in the country.

The activists' demands for reform were bolstered by King Mohamed VI on the sixth anniversary of his ascension to the throne in 2005, when he asserted that in his role as 'commander of the faithful' he had decided that the nationality law must be reformed so that a mother's nationality could be passed onto her child (HM King Mohamed VI of Morocco 2005). The King called for a democratic process of law reform in alignment with the principles in the new Moudawana. Following his statement, the Ministry of Justice created a commission to reform the nationality law and passed their recommendations on to Parliament (Lemrini 2006). Saïda Idrissi (2008), vice-president of ADFM, remarks: 'The political will was there for the reform. Except that it took a lot of time ... the law against terrorism slowed the process down.... Everything started well, but with the Casablanca attacks and the promulgation of the anti-terrorism law, there was a lot for everyone to think about.'

Two factors contributed to the delay in the reform. The first was related to the question of the Moroccan community in those European countries that prohibited dual citizenship. In Morocco, the law does not allow for the forfeiture of Moroccan nationality, which is acquired for life. Negotiating how this would work out in practice took time. The second, and more substantive concern, involved the nationality of foreign male spouses in Morocco. The authorities had established a close link between international *jihadi* groups and the acquisition of Moroccan nationality through marriage. The feminist movement was demanding that foreign husbands should benefit from the same procedures applied to foreign wives (provisions related to the acquisition of nationality by marriage), making it easier for them to acquire citizenship. This made the issue more contentious. Given these setbacks, activists continued their efforts to stimulate public debate on citizenship and nationality, holding a series of public debates and meetings in Rabat, including a roundtable held with the Science Faculty, which the Minister of Justice attended. However, this was a time of uncertainty. There had been strong political support for the Nationality Code reform, but no action had been taken. Idrissi (2008) describes this time period:

> There was total silence after the King's speech in 2005 … without any information on the code, on the reform. Nothing. The Commission, who worked on the Nationality Code reform process, they had no information on it, they were not answering their telephones…. And with this, there were rumours … they are going to reform … they are not going to reform.

In 2006, Moroccan activists seized upon an opportunity after months of silence from legislators. In March of that year, Morocco became a candidate for entrance to the Council of Human Rights in Geneva.[11] In order to gain membership, the state needed to make progress in complying with important human rights declarations. Women's rights activists seized this opportunity to bring attention to the fact that there were still reservations attached to CEDAW and that this affected women's equality as citizens. Feminists stressed the need for cohesion between international and domestic law in order to support the Moroccan candidacy (Lemrini 2006). To maximize the impact of their intervention, activists continued high-level political lobbying and also organized a series of sit-ins in public spaces, notably in front of Parliament and at the headquarters of the Ministry of Justice in order to pressure the state and Parliament. Before the mobilizations, ADFM contacted all the major Moroccan and foreign media outlets, such as Al Jazeera, Alarabia, Almanar and Radio Monte Carlo. This ensured heightened visibility and kept the issue of reform in the forefront of the public mind. As with the Moudawana reform, activists focused on a multi-layered discourse of women's citizenship as a political issue. The activists drew on the framing of the nationality issue elsewhere in the region and focused attention on the political arena, through lobbying and media-related events, where arguments to align the current constitutional and international law would have greater impact. Moreover, they strategically leveraged national consensus on issues already settled in constitutional law as a means to justify further reform.

However, as these mobilizations evolved, the campaign strategy began to shift. According to information received from inside the leadership circle, the government was totally opposed to granting Moroccan citizenship to foreign husbands for reasons that included security issues. Given this political entrenchment, ADFM and its partners felt it would be best to limit their demands to the revision of Article 6 in the Nationality Code, the right to pass nationality on to children. This strategy was justified based on an assessment of the Moroccan social and political context and the opening already present in the current code, which allowed a foreign wife to acquire Moroccan nationality through marriage, provided they had two years of residence. Making the strategic trade-off to focus only on the child did not lessen the political impact and underlying message of the reform efforts.[12] Indeed, as Rabéa Naciri (2007b), former president of ADFM, asserts:

> The revision of Article 6 [Nationality Code] comes to supplement the Moudawana. It has a great range in so far as this article puts the father and the mother on equal footing. The identity of the child can be defined by his mother or father. In this sense, it is a significant blow to the patriarchal status and to the 'primacy' of men to women.

This strategic realignment proved a successful way to negotiate the shifting political climate. After extensive mobilization, political lobbying, and public awareness raising, in February 2007 Parliament ratified the Nationality Code. The new code is retroactive and states that a Moroccan is any child born to a Moroccan father or mother. After the success of the campaign, ADFM initiated a number of follow-up activities to monitor the reforms, coordinated by the Anaruz Network and the Nejma Centre. The

Anaruz Network is monitoring the Ministry of Justice to ensure new juridical regulations for applying for citizenship are respected. ADFM has been offering a variety of workshops, training affected women in their new rights, and conducting public awareness-raising events. In 2007, ADFM activists began documenting the legal reform process in a guide (Idrissi 2008; Oueldammou 2008) that provides advice to other groups interested in implementing nationality reforms in different countries, and offers suggestions for communication and mobilization strategies.

In the Moroccan case, even though the political context was ripe for feminist voice and strategy to be channelled and well received at the highest political levels, reform was not an immediate outcome, complicating the picture of pathways to reform.[13] Instead, a more complex set of political factors stalled reform efforts until political timing combined with activists' strategic retooling could bring about a positive outcome. Reflecting on the process and success of the nationality campaign, Rachida Nafaa (2008) credits the Moroccan success to the political context, leadership and solidarity. Moreover, in Morocco the politically favourable reform context was undergirded by a relatively homogeneous religious and ethnic state. Nafaa (2008) notes that in other countries such as Lebanon and Bahrain, where there are multiple religious sects and more diverse coalitional politics, reform becomes a much more complicated endeavour.

The importance of political process in the nationality reform

In comparison, the Lebanese campaign process has been deeply affected by religious and ethnic factionalism, political instability, and conflict. In 2006, the Lebanese nationality campaign seemed to be close to achieving successful reform until the July war with Israel broke out,[14] which had long-lasting social and political consequences (Abou-Habib 2008; Afkhami 2009). Among the direct campaign challenges, the Lebanese activists met fierce resistance to nationality reform from politicians. Lina Abou-Habib (2008) notes:

We didn't have the opposition from where we expected it. But I think we were foolish, because we underestimated the opposition and I think that there is a myth that you have in your mind that bad guys are only located in one place. But, actually they are not; they are all over the place. And so, the most rabid opposition came from politicians, from political groups, which had various political agendas and quite a bit of religious racism....

The politicians argued that given the significant population of Palestinian refugees in Lebanon (over 400,000 or 10 per cent of the population), changes in nationality law would interfere with the Palestinian right to return and tax Lebanese resources, social services, and social and economic infrastructures (Hayek 2008; CRTD.A 2004). Political arguments against reform referenced the implications of shifting the political demographic in the country, implying that with reform Sunni Muslims would then form a majority, upsetting the delicate sectarian balance. Lebanese nationality campaign activists countered that this line of argumentation was merely loosely veiled socio-religious discrimination, particularly given that only 2 per cent of Lebanese women are actually married to Palestinian men.[15]

Mobilization was further stalled in the aftermath of the presidential election of 2007, when lack of parliamentarian consensus left the country without a head of state for a protracted period of time. During the political instability, the campaign essentially went into abeyance, having laid the strategic groundwork for the right political moment. After months of political impasse, the new president, General Michel Suleiman, was elected in May 2008. More favourable political conditions for the women's movement began to arise when a former lawyer, Ziyad Baroud, legal expert for the nationality campaign, was appointed Interior Minister in July 2008, creating a new direct political pathway for channelling feminist demands for reform (Hayek 2008). Lebanese campaign partners spearheaded a process of strategic reflection during these extensive periods of political uncertainty and war. CRTD.A emerged with a targeted strategy and a list of demands that included fully implementing CEDAW by lifting reservations, particularly on Article 9 (2) (to which Egypt and Morocco had committed); and initiating a 35 per cent gender quota for parliamentary elections to be held in 2009. The campaign has yet to secure reforms, however, and experienced some significant setbacks in 2010 and 2011.

An important development in the Lebanese context was the strategic lobbying of jurists. This approach has also been used by other campaign partners – Egyptian feminists, for example, have taken nearly a dozen cases to court to challenge discrimination against Palestinians and have pressed the Minister of Interior to recognize the inequalities (Abou-Habib 2010a). In Lebanon in June 2009, a court decision created a precedent for a Lebanese woman married to an Egyptian man, who was deceased, to transmit her nationality to her four children (WLP 2009a). However, while jurist lobbying led to an initial victory, the landmark ruling was eventually reversed under appeal on 18 May 2010. In order to protest the unjust reversal of rights and highlight the public outcry, the Lebanese nationality campaign members held a high-profile 'Popular Mock Court for Women's Right to Nationality'. The event used popular theatre techniques, including actors as judges, complete with symbols of 'blind justice'. The actors engaged with protesters, dramatizing stories of injustice resulting from the unequal nationality laws (Abou-Habib 2010b). Although the event made public the growing national and international attention focused on unjust nationality laws, the government has continued to sidestep the issue through partial solutions, such as the recent decree granting Lebanese women married to foreign nationals the ability to gain three-year residency permits. This is not acceptable from the perspective of establishing true equality, and campaign activists continue to push for full immediate reforms (Abou-Habib 2010b). Activists are still countering the influence of the opposition's arguments that reform of the nationality law will effectively naturalize thousands of Palestinian men and children and upset the delicate sectarian balance in politics.

In 2011 a new development posed a significant challenge to campaign activists when the cabinet approved a draft bill in Parliament that would allow dual citizenship for expatriates with a Lebanese grandfather or father, but not a mother or grandmother. This draft bill was strongly rejected by members of the Nationality Campaign for its blatant violation of women's human and citizenship rights, as well the inherent bias and restriction of citizenship lineage to a patriarchal frame.[16] As Lina Abou-Habib reflected (2011a), 'I think this time they've gone too far in saying that basically this is a country for men and in ignoring that citizenship is a right for women … Despite evidence and testimonies, they have ignored the economic hardships faced by many Lebanese women who live here. And now on top of this they have proposed a new law which doesn't recognize women' (*Daily Star* 2011). Considerable challenges lay ahead for the campaign if the law was to be ratified by Parliament, and activists have been organizing a torrent of protest, showing their extreme dissatisfaction with the bill and underscoring its implications for women's nationality and rights.

For example, CRTD.A organized a sit-in in front of the Ministry of Interior in late December 2011, which filtered the outrage and opposition in unique ways. Media, the public, and a variety of NGOs, including non-feminist organizations, showed up in greater numbers than previous protests. Most importantly, the public demands were infused with the more nuanced messages that the feminists had been developing in the nationality campaign over the past decade – the recognition of the patriarchal nature of the law and the necessity of women's full citizenship to ensure women's rights. This deeper understanding of the issues at stake had never been recognized quite in this way before. A symbolic blood donation centre was erected and celebrated by participants as 'despite what the Lebanese state says and thinks, we have blood, same as men!' (Abou-Habib 2011b). CRTD.A saw the event as a turning point and transformation of the landscape of protest around nationality reform, as feminist demands began to be internalized across a broader sector of Lebanese society. What became most prominent was the impact of the careful research, lobbying, organizing of grassroots women and organizations over time. Throughout the years of the campaign, change incrementally began bearing the fruits of its efforts, as affected women became empowered and organized to make a difference, and as the reach of their calls multiplied and deepened in diverse communities and the broader public through media (Abou-Habib 2011b). While there have yet to be changes to the law, protests continue and demands for women's rights reverberate louder than ever.

The politics of negotiating international funding

Beyond local political opposition and contention, funding challenges can also become sites of struggle. NGOs operating in the MENA often face a variety of domestic and international constraints. For example, domestic social norms around philanthropic giving typically are routed to charity through social service providers or religious institutions. Additionally, some states complicate or even prevent NGOs from receiving funds from foreign sources. For example in Jordan in 2008 the Law of Societies Bill was passed, which among other things effectively barred the free transfer of foreign funds to local NGOs. All fund transfers require governmental approval. In Egypt, additional regulations and scrutiny exist, with the registering and foreign funding of NGOs. Under Mubarak human rights NGOs in particular were subject to intense scrutiny and their activities could be suspended without reason (see Tadros in this volume). This presents significant challenges since advocacy NGOs often rely on international funding given domestic fundraising constraints.

International donors, of course, have their own political agendas and requirements. Most relevant for the MENA region is the growing use of and mandatory compliance with the 'terrorist clause'. Internationally, the US government passed a new law related to international fund disbursement, known as the 'terrorist clause', which requires public and private foundations and government agencies to abide by the law in which grantees sign a disclosure agreement. This compliance mechanism creates a donor–NGO relationship built on power imbalances and characterized by parochial relations, which many NGOs in the region refuse to accept (WLP 2006).

In order to minimize donor-driven agendas, the regional nationality campaign partners were very selective in their donor partnerships (Abou-Habib 2010a; Afkhami 2009). The International Development Research Center (IDRC) in Canada supported initial stages of the nationality campaign research in 2001 and 2002, and has promoted the innovative research and advocacy work of the campaign, by creating a high-profile publicity event demonstrating the positive role that donors can have in supporting gender equality and reform. The UNDP Programme on Governance in the Arab Region (POGAR) initiative was a conduit for disseminating the IDRC-funded analysis and case studies on nationality. The Heinrich Böll Foundation has also been a strong supporter of the campaign. By ensuring that the campaign has deep and mutually respectful relationships with donors, activists circumvent potential problems associated with donor-driven agendas and instead ensure partnerships of mutual respect and support.

The power of networks in stimulating collective change and raising the visibility of nationality issues has also played an important role in the nationality campaign. Five years after the regional campaign was established, campaign partners began discussing different ways to leverage the international impact of the campaign and amplify campaign voices. Members of the nationality coalition believed an international campaign would effectively highlight the unequal citizenship laws across a broader range of constituents and policy makers across the Global North and South (Abou-Habib 2008). In 2006 the Women's Learning Partnership (WLP), an international network of women's rights organizations (of which ADFM and CRTD.A is a part), launched the international campaign, 'Claiming Equal Citizenship: The Campaign for Arab Women's Right to Nationality' (WLP, no date). WLP has been an effective partner, in its bridging and coordinating role, thanks to its extensive connections to and leverage with the international policy community, civic NGOs, international funders, and government officials in the Global North and South.

Even with such positive donor and network partnerships, challenges have arisen. In 2008, CRTD.A received a project document from a UN donor (Abou-Habib 2008, 2010a). Despite the political instability in Lebanon's leadership, the donor felt a new campaign strategy was necessary since reform had not occurred. In putting forward this different tack, the donor had mistakenly copied Lina Abou-Habib into their communications with other recipients of a significant grant to fund nationality rights. The funder had, in effect, asked another organization in Lebanon to replicate the exact steps and strategies that CRTD.A had already successfully implemented over the past seven years. Lina Abou-Habib (2008) notes the irony as 'before [the funder request for a parallel nationality campaign] there was absolutely no doubt that the nationality campaign was "indigenous" and led by local groups'. However, now there was significant interference with local activism on the ground, disconnected from the history of nationality as a political issue in Lebanon and inattentive to the existing activist and grassroots networks that had been forged over the past decades. These realities highlight the need for less replication and more collaboration on the ground, as well as a greater understanding of the local context and of the actors working toward gender equality and justice. Donors must understand that deep transformative changes to gender equality, such as changes in legal or social norms, take time – that change may be incremental, have stagnant phases, or even face reversals in the path toward change. That means the way that we assess success must take a longer-term view, be flexible, and account not only for the actors and outcomes of reform, but also for the external factors that shape opportunities and constraints to reform (Batliwala and Pittman 2010). Indeed, transforming existing power structures, institutions, and relationships takes time, and change trajectories take various paths depending on the context, as well as the unique point in time in a particular country's history.

The current state of campaign progress

To date, three of the six countries involved in the regional nationality campaign – Algeria, Egypt, and Morocco – have reformed nationality laws and granted women the right to pass their nationality on to their children. In the post-revolution period in Egypt in 2011, nationality rights were extended to women married to Palestinian nationals, thus including all ethnic groups. Yet, even though laws exist, problems have arisen for Egyptian children born before the 2004 reform passed in terms of gaining retrospective citizenship. A study conducted by the Forum for Women in Development, found that:

> almost a million sons and daughters of Egyptian women married to foreign men born before the amendment have been disadvantaged because the law does not grant them the right to automatic naturalization. Even though the law does allow them to apply for citizenship, the requirements, stipulations, fees, and procedures are in fact the same as those required of foreign adults applying for Egyptian citizenship. Monitoring and documentation have revealed that the number of cases that have succeeded in obtaining citizenship through this conditional, complicated, and costly procedure is in fact very limited. (WLP 2009b)

The 2005 reform in Algeria granted women married to non-nationals permission to pass their nationality on to their spouses and their children. The Algerian reform is among the most comprehensive to date and remains a model for many of the nationality coalition members. As described, the 2007 reform in Morocco allows women married to non-nationals to pass their nationality on to their children. In Bahrain, in 2009, some progress was made: the state removed non-national fees, including, health and education, for children with Bahrainian mothers married to foreign husbands. Further progress was made in late 2011, with the King granting nationality to children born to women married to non-nationals. However, BWS argues that the changes do not go far enough in ensuring women's equality and must be inscribed into law. Activists demand the full reform of Article 4, extending women equal rights as citizens in compliance with international conventions signed and ratified by Bahrain. In Jordan, Syria and Lebanon, activists are still campaigning for reform.

Conclusion

This case study has demonstrated how voice has been channelled in diverse and powerful ways within the nationality campaign. Two central lessons for campaign development and the role of voice are highlighted in the conclusion: the way in which networks helped to diversify and amplify voice, leading to the cross-fertilization of campaign strategies; and the use of voices to humanize campaign demands in the public sphere.

Diversifying and amplifying voice through networks

Central to the dynamic reform process in each country was the varied use of political alignments, opportunities and constraints, and the salience of diverse ethnic and religious identities in politics. Transnational coalition building broadened and diversified feminist voices for reform beyond national boundaries. NGO activists strategically used transnational bonds as mechanisms to expand demands for reform. Keck and Sikkink (1998) argue that this process occurs through the 'boomerang pattern of influence' where transnational actors, such as NGOs, put pressure on states to make policy or law changes in alignment with their rights commitments. The transfer of these localized movement strategies back to transnational spheres of influence also augments the literature and furthers our understanding of how trans-border campaigns evolve (Alvarez 2000; Friedman 1999).

Research by Sonia Alvarez (2000: 3) suggests two primary reasons that NGOs seek out transnational connections: solidarity and leverage. NGO activists find strength in 'transnational contacts as a means to (re)construct or reaffirm subaltern or politically marginalized identities and to establish personal and strategic bonds of solidarity with others who share locally stigmatized values'. Ultimately, a third factor can be added to these: transnational connections serve movement learning purposes (Pittman 2009). In the case of the nationality campaign, it was a critical component – coalition activists created a regional system of collaboration, knowledge sharing, critical reflection and feedback that is normally only developed at a national or organizational level. By sharing these adaptive strategies, the activists contributed to stronger movement-building practices that can be replicated elsewhere. Moreover, when activists track, monitor and publicize the progress of reform in each country, as the Forum for Women in Development did in Egypt, states across the region are symbolically implicated (or 'named and shamed'), if not practically held accountable to regional and local practices in the nationality code.

The case study also shows deeper cross-fertilization of learning strategies and the growing transnationalization of women's movements in the region (Moghadam 2005; Alvarez 2000). As NGOs work together on a variety of social change efforts, the diverse sets of strategies and lessons learned from the sharing of experiences can be drawn on for future campaign development. Specifically, through inter-movement communication and diverse coalition building, lessons from the nationality campaign advocacy model have been transferred to other campaigns and women's rights movements.

Using voices to humanize demands

Another primary strategy in the regional campaign was to involve women and children affected by nationality laws in the campaign planning and implementation process. In this way, the voices of affected women shaped the national voice and humanized the nature of the reform demands. In fact, the testimony of women and their children (through television and radio) aimed to generate a deep emotional reaction in the public: beyond supporting the claims of justice for equal citizenship, many people came to understand that discriminatory laws can take a serious, and sometimes tragic, social toll on children and their families. The very process of organizing affected women catalyzed an important reflective and consciousness-raising process. NGOs acted as interlocutors between the grassroots and political and civil society, translating affected women's concerns into actionable strategy. The positioning of seasoned activists as recognized actors in the political sphere was further used to leverage campaign voice.

Of course, all these campaign efforts have been engulfed in a larger process of democratic and political protests and uprisings, some quite violent, since early 2011. Even though we have seen the fruits of democratic revolution and protest in some regions, a backlash against the claiming of women's rights has also emerged with the election of political Islamists to power. Rollbacks on important legal advances are being called for or are under way in many different countries – Tunisia, Egypt, Morocco. In Morocco, where the the Islamist PJD was elected with a clear parliamentary majority in 2011, the status of revolutionary legal advances in women's rights since 2005 has been placed under question. Moroccan feminists are organizing strongly against a possible rollback. In Egypt, while women were key and equal participants in political protests, requests for gender equality and equal representation in the transition were sidelined and they have been largely excluded from political processes.[17] Indeed, counter-movements have even tried to link feminists and women's rights activists to the authoritarian Mubarak regime and the political reform projects of Suzanne Mubarak as a means to further discredit their agenda. Events across the MENA will continue to shift given the energy and organizing power of different challengers to the state. The respect accorded to women's rights and gender equality within any new political structures that emerge will be the central litmus test for true transformative and equitable change, built on inclusive citizenship rights.

Indeed, the reform of nationality laws will have broad socio-political implications on gender equality and women's empowerment in the MENA: 'For in reality, what is being disputed here is the future nature of the socio-political structure in the Arab world. More specifically, it is the core of the social and cultural fabric of the Arab world that is being re-drawn' (CRTD.A 2004: 9). The regional nationality campaign and the local adaptations give us a better sense of key trends and strategies being employed in liberal feminist movements in the MENA. The campaign also highlights the tension and inequalities mandated by the state, which limits women's full public participation (CRTD.A 2004; Joseph 2000). Once the notion of a universal male-headed household is discredited and the family is no longer seen as the arbiter of citizenship, a profound shift will occur in the meaning and practice of citizenship. Women's autonomous citizenship, defined outside the kinship model, will then fundamentally challenge the core assumptions of family relations as encoded in personal status codes across the region (Joseph 2000). In aiming to deconstruct male privilege and appropriate women's autonomy and right to citizenship, fundamental notions of patriarchy are being challenged and rewritten, offering significant potential and possibilities for future reforms, and ultimately for gender equality.

Acknowledgement

Warm thanks to Dounia Loudiyi who translated this case study into French.

Notes

1   The term 'feminist' is used in this case as the activists self-identify as such. It is important to note that there is a wide range of feminist positionings. The shorthand use of feminist is not meant to obscure the diversities that exist with this identity; rather, it is used for the sake of brevity.
2   Framing is one component of effective movement strategy, where activists 'assign meaning to and interpret relevant events and conditions in ways that are intended to mobilize potential adherents and constituents' (Snow and Benford 1988: 198).
3   For an interesting comparison of the liberal and Islamist feminists' framing of the family, see Zakia Salime (2007). Salime describes how Islamist feminists made demands to the state to 'take the mosques back', focusing on bringing women into positions of leadership and

power in the mosque through preaching. They also highlighted the moderate goals of a politicized version of motherhood while calling for gender-equitable progress within religious institutions.

4   Politically, Morocco is a constitutional monarchy with a democratically elected bicameral Parliament following the 1996 constitutional reforms. The King is also the religious authority in his role as 'commander of the faithful' (Amir al-Mu'minin). The country's move toward more openly democratic structures in the 1990s created the space for civil society groups to flourish, particularly women's rights associations. During this time, King Hassan II began a gradual process of political liberalization through constitutional reforms. More recent constitutional reforms were stimulated by the wave of Arab Spring protests, and changes were voted on by the public and passed in July 2011. The reforms place some restrictions on the King's power, and while some pro-democracy critics believe the reforms were not far-reaching enough, many women's rights activists are applauding the institutionalization of important aspects of gender equality and human rights in the law (Abou-Habib 2011a; ADFM 2011). However, when the Islamist PJD won the 2011 elections with a parliamentary majority, these advances around women's rights began to be called into question.

5   The inheritance share given to a male descendant is equal to twice the share of a female descendant. In the absence of male descendants, the widow and her daughters only receive one-eighth and two-thirds respectively. The rest of the inheritance is given to *acebs* (relatives on the male side). Religious disparity is also a cause of inheritance discrepancies. A non-Muslim woman is excluded from the inheritance of a Muslim (wife, mother).

6   For a more detailed and nuanced description of political positions and events, see Buskens (2003) for the main legal debates, Salime (2005) for an analysis of how political positions and ideologies interacted in the reform context, and Pittman and Naciri (2007, 2010) for a description of the reform effort from the Moroccan liberal feminist perspective.

7   See official 1996 constitution in French, http://www.maroc.ma/NR/rdonlyres/B6B37F23-9F5D-4B46-B679-B43DDA6DD125/0/Constitution.pdf.

8   For past Moroccan reservations as well as other countries' reservations to CEDAW, see http://www.un.org/womenwatch/daw/cedaw/reservations-country.htm.

9   This condition was not an ideological assertion that Moroccan Muslims have no rights to marry non-Muslims.

10 Political process theory (PPT) highlights the central role of political opportunities in creating the conditions for social movement mobilization (Tarrow 1998). Political opportunities can have an influence on the tactics activists select and influence how they react to shifts in the movement context. See Meyer and Minkoff (2004) for a cogent review of the literature on PPT and areas for further development, and Goodwin and Jasper (2004) for a critique. Paying attention to the normative dimensions of law, we explore the role of cultural or ideational forms of movement persuasion (Cress and Snow 2000).

11 Morocco was appointed to the Council of Human Rights later in 2006. See www.unog.ch/80256EDD006B9C2E/(httpNews By Year_en)/C5BF0606F91D8B7FC125713000376A2E?OpenDocument.

12 For further work on the issue of strategic trade-offs, see Sultan and Nazneen in this volume.

13 A long line of research has shown that political contexts and opportunities are critical levers to reform, including research by Amenta *et al.* (1992, 2005), or political process theorists like Tarrow (1998) and, more recently, Gaventa and McGee (2010).

14 On 12 July 2006, Hezbollah fighters began shooting rockets into Israeli border towns. Fighting ensued between Israeli soldiers and Hezbollah. Israel widened the conflict by bombing civilian and military targets and infrastructure in Beirut and initiating a ground invasion in Southern Lebanon. The war lasted from 12 July to 14 August when a UN ceasefire agreement was signed. There was heavy damage and the humanitarian crisis was significant, with over a thousand Lebanese deaths and over one million Lebanese civilians displaced.

15 In total, the nationality law affects over 80,000 people and 18,000 are Lebanese women married to non-Lebanese men (UNDP 2009).

16 Press communiqué by the Arab Women's Right to Nationality Campaign, 'Lebanon, a Country of Men and for Men … Only', 14 December 2011, http://www.learningpartnership.org/lib/lebanese-cabinet-issues-draft-law-reinstate-lebanese-nationality-descendants-lebanese-fathers-an.

17 See http://www.learningpartnership.org/blog/2011/11/women-democracy-egypt/ (accessed 4 January 2012).

References

Abou-Habib, L. (2008) Personal interview, 3 September 2008, Maryland, USA.

—— (2010a) Personal interview, 2 February 2010.

—— (2010b) 'In Lebanon, Gender Justice for the People, by the People', blog, 30 June, www.learningpartnership.org/blog/2010/06/lebanon-equality-campaign/ (accessed 11 November 2011).

—— (2011a) 'Reaping the Results of Three Decades of Feminist Activism: Constitutional Reforms in Morocco Set Precedent of Institutionalizing Gender Equality', http://www.learningpartnership.org/lib/reaping-results-three-decades-feminist-activism-constitutional-reforms-morocco-set-precedent-ins (accessed 14 December 2011).

—— (2011b) 'The Journey toward Women's Citizenship Rights: Getting There One Step at a Time', http://www.learningpartnership.org/blog/2012/01/the-journey-toward-women%E2%80%99s-citizenship-rights-getting-there-one-step-at-a-time/ (accessed 16 January 2012).

ADFM (2011) 'Women's Rights in the Constitution Draft', press release, http://www.adfm.ma/spip.php?article1596&lang=en (accessed 14 December 2011).

Afkhami, M. (2009) Personal interview, founder and President of WLP, 3 February 2009 and 26 March 2009, USA.

Ahmed, L. (1992) *Women and Gender in Islam*, Yale University Press, New Haven, CT and London.

Alvarez, S. (2000) 'Translating the Global: Effects of Transnational Organizing on Local Feminist Discourses and Practices in Latin America', *Cadernos de Pesquisa*, No. 22, www.sociologia.ufsc.br/cadernos/Cadernos%20PPGSP%2022.pdf (accessed 3 November 2007).

Amenta, E., B. G. Carruthers and Y. Zylan (1992) 'A Hero for the Aged? The Townsend Movement, the Political Mediation Model, and US Old-Age Policy, 1934–1950', *American Journal of Sociology*, Vol. 98, No. 2, pp. 308–39.

Amenta, E., N. Caren and S. J. Olasky (2005) 'Age for Leisure? Political Mediation and the Impact of the Pension Movement on US Old-Age Policy', *American Sociological Review*, Vol. 70, No. 3, pp. 516–38.

Batliwala, S. and A. Pittman (2010) 'Capturing Change in Women's Realities: The Challenges of Monitoring and Evaluating Our Work', http://www.awid.org/About-AWID/AWID-News/Capturing-Change-in-Women-s-Realities (accessed 15 December 2011).

Bessis, S. and S. Belhassen (1992) *Femmes du Maghreb: l'Enjeu*, JC Lattés, Paris.

Buskens, L. (2003) 'Recent Debates on the Reform of Family Law in

Morocco: Islamic Law as Politics in an Emerging Public Sphere', *Islamic Law and Society*, Vol. 10, No. 1, pp. 70–131.

—— (2008) 'Sharia and National Law in Morocco', paper presented at the Law and Society Conference, Montreal, Canada, 29 May 2008.

Charrad, M. (2001) *States and Women's Rights: The Making of Postcolonial Tunisia, Algeria, and Morocco,* University of California Press, Berkeley, CA.

Cress, D. M. and D. A. Snow (2000) 'The Outcomes of Homeless Mobilization: The Influence of Organization, Disruption, Political Mediation, and Framing', *American Journal of Sociology*, Vol. 105, No. 4, pp. 1063–104.

CRTD.A (2004) 'Denial of Nationality: The Case of Arab Women', www.pogar.org/publications/gender/nationality/CRTDAesum.pdf, Collective for Research and Training on Development Action (accessed 14 March 2007).

Daily Star (2011) 'Dual Nationality Draft Law Sparks Praise and Ire', http://www.dailystar.com.lb/News/Local-News/2011/Dec-14/156829-dual-nationality-draft-law-sparks-praise-and-ire.ashx#ixzz1gVpVjuyu (accessed 14 December 2011).

Friedman, E. (1999) 'The Effects of 'Transnationalism Reversed', in 'Venezuela: Assessing the Impact of UN Global Conferences on the Women's Movement', *International Feminist Journal of Politics*, Vol. 1, No. 3, pp. 357–81.

Gaventa, J. and R. McGee (2010) *Citizen Action and National Policy Reform: Making Change Happen*, Zed Books, London.

Goodwin, J. and J. M. Jasper (2004) 'Caught in a Winding Snarling Vine: The Structural Bias of Political Process Theory', in J. Goodwin and J. M Jasper (eds), *Rethinking Social Movements: Structure, Meaning, and Emotion*, Rowman and Littlefield Publishers, Oxford.

Goyal, R. (2009) Personal interview, Executive Director of WLP, 3 February 2009 and 26 March 2009, USA.

Hayek, V. (2008) Personal interview, coordinator of the regional nationality campaign, 2 September 2008, Maryland, USA.

HM King Mohamed VI of Morocco (2005) speech made on Throne Day, 30 July, www.maroc.ma/NR/exeres/55901BD3-ED0A-4907-A86F-D145 (accessed May 2011).

Idrissi, S. (2008) Personal interview, vice-president of ADFM, 12 September 2008, Rabat, Morocco.

Joseph, S. (2000) 'Gendering Citizenship in the Middle East', in S. Joseph (ed.), *Gender and Citizenship in the Middle East* (with a foreword by Deniz Kandiyoti), Syracuse University Press, Syracuse and New York, NY.

Kandiyoti, D. (1991) *Women, Islam and the State*, Macmillan, Basingstoke.

Keck, M. and K. Sikkink (1998) *Activists Beyond Borders: Advocacy Networks in International Politics*, Cornell University Press, Ithaca, NY.

Khorasani, N. A. (2009) *Iranian Women's One Million Signatures: Campaign for Equality – The Inside Story*, Women's Learning Partnership, Bethesda, MD.

King, L. (2007) 'Charting a Discursive Field: Environmentalists for US Population Stabilization', *Sociological Inquiry*, Vol. 77, No. 3, pp. 301–25.

Lemrini, A. (2005) Personal interview, founder of ADFM, 27 April 2005, Rabat, Morocco.

—— (2006) 'Moroccan Nationality Campaign. Women as Equal Citizens: Advocating for Change in Muslim-Majority Societies', address, Johns Hopkins University, Baltimore, MD, 6 September.

Mashour, A. (2005) 'Islamic Law and Gender Equality: Could There be a Common Ground?: A Study of Divorce and Polygamy in Sharia Law and Contemporary Legislation in Tunisia and Egypt', *Human Rights Quarterly*, Vol. 27, No. 2, pp. 562–96.

Merry, S. E. (2003) 'Constructing a Global Law: Violence against Women and the Human Rights System', *Law and Social Inquiry*, Vol. 28, No. 4, pp. 941–79.

Meyer, D. S. and D. C. Minkoff (2004) 'Conceptualizing Political Opportunity', *Social Forces*, Vol. 82, No. 4, pp. 1457–92.

Moghadam, V. (2003) *Modernizing Women: Gender and Social Change in the Middle East*, second edition, Lynne Rienner Publishers, Boulder, CO.

—— (2005) *Globalizing Women: Transnational Feminist Networks*, John Hopkins University Press, Baltimore, MD.

Naciri, R. (2007a) Personal interview, 14 February 2007, Rabat, Morocco.

—— (2007b) 'What's Next for the Moroccan Campaign: Interview with Rabéa Naciri' (President of ADFM), www.learningpartnership.org/citizenship/2007/02/morocco-bill-naciri-interview/ (accessed 6 August 2008).

Nafaa, R. (2008) Personal interview, ADFM board member and Dean at Hassan II University-Mohamedia, 13 September 2008.

Oueldammou, K. (2008) Personal interview, member of Nationality Campaign committee, Rabat, Morocco, 12 September 2008.

Pittman, A. (2009) 'Transforming Constraint: Transnational Feminist Movement Building in the Middle East and North Africa', unpublished PhD thesis, Boston College.

Pittman, A. and R. Naciri (2007) 'Cultural Adaptations: The Moroccan Women's Campaign to Change the Moudawana', Institute for Development Studies, Brighton, www.ids.ac.uk/ids/Part/proj/pnp.html (accessed 1 November 2007).

—— (2010) 'Winning Women's Rights in Morocco: Cultural Adaptations and the Moroccan Campaign to Change the Moudawana', in J. Gaventa and R. McGee (eds), *Citizen Action and National Policy. Making Change from Below*, Zed Books, London.

Rachid, A. M. (1985) *La Condition de la Femme au Maroc*, unpublished PhD thesis, Université Mohamed V, Rabat.

Sadiqi, F. (2008) 'The Central Role of the Family Law in the Moroccan Feminist Movement', *British Society of Middle Eastern Studies*, Vol. 35, No. 3, pp. 325–37.

Salime, Z. (2005) 'Between Islam and Feminism: New Political Transformations and Movements in Morocco', unpublished PhD thesis, University of Illinois at Urbana-Champaign.

—— (2007) 'The War on Terrorism: Appropriation and Subversion by Moroccan Women', *Signs*, Vol. 33, No. 1, pp. 1–24.

Snow, D. A. and R. D. Benford (1988) 'Ideology, Frame Resonance, and Participant Mobilization', *International Social Movement Research*, No. 1, pp. 197–217.

Sonbol, A. (2003) '"The Woman Follows the Nationality of Her Husband": Guardianship, Citizenship and Gender', *Hawaa*, Vol. 1, No. 1, pp. 86–117.

Spillman, L. (1995) 'Culture, Social Structures, and Discursive Fields', *Current Perspectives in Social Theory*, Vol. 15, pp. 129–54.

Tarrow, S. (1998) *Power in Movement: Social Movements, Collective Action, and Politics*, Cambridge University Press, New York, NY.

UN (1979) 'Convention on the Elimination of All Forms of Discrimination against Women: Article 9', www.un.org/womenwatch/daw/cedaw/text/econvention.htm#article9 (accessed 11 November 2011).

UNDP (2009) 'Towards Reforming the Nationality Law in Lebanon', UNDP, New York, NY.

WLP (2006) 'Women's Learning Partnership Transnational Partners Meeting', Potomac, MD, 3–6 September 2006.

—— (2009a) 'Fighting for Citizenship in Lebanon', Women's Learning Partnership, 30 August, www.learningpartnership.org/lib/fighting-citizenship-lebanon (accessed 11 November 2011).

—— (2009b) 'Egypt: Discrimination Continues Despite Law Reform', Women's Learning Partnership, 15 September, www.learningpartnership.org/lib/egypt-discrimination-continues-despite-law-reform (accessed 11 November 2011).

—— (no date) 'Claiming Equal Citizenship' campaign website, Women's Learning Partnership, www.learningpartnership.org/citizenship/ (accessed 11 November 2011).

5

Motivated by Dictatorship, Muted by Democracy
Articulating Women's Rights in Pakistan

Afiya Shehrbano Zia

A cursory reading of the literature on women's activism in Pakistan[1] gives the impression of a negative correlation between women's meaningful democratic rights and the various military regimes, due to the limitations routinely imposed by the latter. Democracy is often idealistically contrasted with the highly masculinized traits displayed by military rule in its various seizures of state power in Pakistan. However, regardless of the nature of civilian or military leadership, the experience of women activists has forced them to acknowledge that notions of *state* security, whether envisaged by military or civilian rulers, have consistently been opposed to and prioritized at the expense of *social* security, especially for women.

Similarly, there is no differentiation between military and civilian policies that equally strip communities of protection from public/state violence, and accept the privatized structures of governance run by the male elites of communities and tribes. State judicial systems, during periods of civilian democracy, are equally misogynistic in their views, especially with reference to policing women's sexuality, and community justice continues to dispense sexual punishment for women regularly, as part of restoring and upholding the sanctity of 'honour' codes. These and other discriminatory policies continue to concur and persist as challenges, regardless of whether control over the centralized and localized political state contexts is in civilian or military hands. Even the idiom of religion and 'saving Islam'

152

is a political tool used by military and liberal-civilian governments alike.

There is a general consensus among women's rights activists that, during every regime, multiple layers of patriarchal interests have colluded, in varying degrees, in campaigns against women representatives (political or activists). At the very least, male-dominant state policies maintained the impunity for those who chose to exploit it. While conservative or Islamist political parties are obviously patriarchal in their policies and governance, it is the contradictions experienced under liberal dictatorships or liberal-civilian governments – promising and then reneging on rights for women – that raise wider dilemmas for women's groups.

This is especially so as Pakistan, in the last decade, has arguably experienced its highest level of intra-state conflict and insecurity (only the splitting of the eastern wing of Pakistan into an independent Bangladesh in 1971 offers a close comparison). The presence of militant Islam at the north-western border is a massive threat to social security in itself, but as a source of disruption it is matched by the boost it gives to local religious conservatism, violently expressed in systematic bigotry against women and religious minorities. A fragile, uncertain and nebulous democratic government today strives to maintain its rule without ruffling the politically ambitious feathers of the Pakistan army, or upsetting the landlords who wield electoral power and form the traditional power base of their government. Both are compelling centres of patriarchal control.

Given the variety of political experiments and disappointments emanating from liberal, political sources, the collective task ahead for women activists lies in framing a new vision and policy approach for women's equal rights. How can this be inclusive of all voices and actors without compromising the progress they have achieved so far? What should the process be, and how are those legitimate voices to be determined, given that the very vocabulary of women's rights is constantly being contested?

This chapter discusses two related themes. The first section outlines the interplay of democratic and dictatorial regimes in terms of their influence on women's movements. It does not try to capture the historical trajectory of each political period, but instead highlights the variety of contracts and negotiations that women embarked upon to further the rights agenda. The main focus is the complexity and difficulty of forging a consistent and permanent relationship with democratic state processes, when military coups and dictatorships regularly abort such efforts. The argument is that many activists have succumbed to the pragmatic project of engaging with dictatorial regimes, assuming that a women's rights agenda may continue uninterrupted and be taken forward despite the absence of democratic norms.

The second half of the chapter attempts to answer the thematic question that links all the other contributions in this publication. What is the role of 'voice' within women's movements? This chapter argues that on the one hand women's rights activists in Pakistan wrestled with civilian democratic governments that would not open or pursue the agenda for women's rights as much as activists would have liked. On the other hand, dictatorial regimes were either sufficiently oppressive to motivate a radical resistance that, in retrospect, gained considerable success; or, as in the case of General Musharraf's 'liberal' dictatorship, co-opted all progressive forces to gain credibility and, as a by-product, enabled considerable progress for women's rights. Outside of this larger discourse, and within the fissures of such political developments, the voice of Islamists gained considerable 'carry' in the country. The voice of Islamist women[2] reached Parliament for the first time under General Musharraf's mechanized elections of 2002, and the social impact of such influences are discussed in this chapter. A part of this section also examines the work of a generation of post-modernist scholars, who support the notion that religion (already dominant in all public spaces) must be further accommodated within the public sphere while they critique liberal, secular feminist activism.

The chapter concludes that – regardless of the surge in women's rights activism that resisted General Zia's Islamization, or the achievements for women's rights during General Musharraf's enlightened moderation – ultimately it is only democratic politics that can ensure meaningful and sustained progress for women and, possibly, localized resistance to fundamentalist forces. Activists who adhere to this principled stand continue to support the increasing induction of women representatives to advocate on women's issues, at all tiers of government. The dependence on political parties that are increasingly succumbing to political pressure by Islamist forces, however, has made the project of enlisting larger numbers of independent feminist and secular political actors both more difficult and more imperative. However, what activists have not resolved is the increasing theocratization of social and public spaces – and this is, perhaps, the most dangerous challenge that the country will face for some time to come.

The Ayub Khan years (1958–69): a promising start?

Many of the women's rights activists who were instrumental in the pro-democracy movements in Pakistan in the 1980s clearly attribute the downward slide for women's rights to General Zia-ul-Haq's military 'Islamic' dictatorship (1977–88).[3]

General Zia's Islamization policies[4] were a rude shock for the liberal middle classes and, particularly, the established bourgeoisie of Pakistan, especially when compared to the previous benevolent dictatorship of General Ayub Khan (1958–69). It was during Ayub's era that the first wave of Pakistani women's rights activists, particularly the All Pakistan Women's Association (APWA) campaigned for critical reforms to the Family Laws. From the platform of the Commission on Marriage and Family Laws (1955), these influential upper-class women recommended reforms in the inheritance and divorce rights of women, and restrictions on polygamy. In 1961 the Commission's recommendations influenced the Family Laws Ordinance, which was later passed by Parliament and duly implemented.

For many amongst the older generation of activists, this still remains the 'golden era' in women's progress, despite the overall non-democratic nature of the Ayub Khan regime. Significant inroads and influences led to the reform of laws and policies for women's equal status in the 1960s. In retrospect, such contributions were symbolic in distinguishing Pakistani women's rights and identities quite distinctly from those prevailing in Arab Muslim-majority countries.[5]

The Zulfiqar Ali Bhutto years (1971–7): constitutional rights for women

The years of Prime Minister Zulfiqar Ali Bhutto's civilian rule (1971–7) saw administrative reform, within an overall improved legal status as enshrined in stated equal rights in the amended constitution of 1973. Discrimination was countered through reserved seats in the legislature, and overall progressive and liberal gender policies informed the newly formed Women's Rights Commission of 1976. The appointment of women in key positions such as the governor of Sindh, a university vice-chancellor, and a deputy speaker of parliament, are some examples (Ali 2000). The 1975 UN World Conference on Women gave a further fillip to women's rights campaigning and added momentum to it when a strong delegation from Pakistan participated and committed to many universal rights for women, including maternity rights and making crèches for women working in the public sector.

Several commentators, however, note that it was the secular Bhutto who authored the manipulation of political Islam when, as a gesture of appeasement to the Islamist political forces who refuse to recognize the minority Ahemdias as 'Muslim', he passed policy measures that officially ex-communicated the Ahmedia sect. This legacy persists: the state today continues to demand that all Pakistani citizens declare Ahmedias to be non-Muslim (all Pakistanis who apply for passports have to take a signed oath that they do not recognize the Ahmedias as Muslims). However, the contrast between this discriminatory policy and a fully fledged programme to theocratize the state became clear when General Zia ul Haq undertook his Islamization campaign. The severe and long-term setbacks for women's rights during his regime (1977–88) have been well-documented by activists, who note that its effects still impede women's progress today.

Motivated by General Zia's dictatorship (1977–88): the birth of women's NGOs

A number of activists who had founded women's rights groups and had led street resistance against General Zia's dictatorship carried their experiences over into the new post-Zia era and documented these as part of an effort to build a body of feminist literature in the country. This period coincided with a global agenda that was looking to fund 'women and development projects' outside the government sector. As a result, several advocacy-oriented women's organizations were set up in the 1980s.

Since many of the women's rights activists were now involved in development work, they soon realized that baseline and empirical data for developing gender policies simply did not exist. The contribution of these liberal feminists includes many foundational texts and policies, legal reviews, revisions of international and national literature, reclamations and translations. They published a considerable body of feminist literature (although comparatively smaller than the impressive output in Iran or India), more than generations before or after have produced.

Also, during and despite the regressive policies of General Zia, members of the Women's Action Forum co-operated with the newly established Women's Division of the time to draft a special report for the Sixth Five Year Plan for the Planning Commission (Jalal 1991). Ironically, as military rule became increasingly retrogressive, civil society organizations and women's groups developed some of their most crucial research, applied outreach programmes, and extended support mechanisms that assisted women directly, as well as influencing policy (particularly on development) in the years to come.

A radical, direct-action street activism had helped to forge an alliance of women's groups across the ideological spectrum. It could be argued that the military dictatorship galvanized a dynamic women's movement in Pakistan. There was a dialectical reflection within urban women's groups, which debated whether they were representative, socially relevant, feminist, or secular enough. Islamist women also joined street demonstrations, bringing about frequent convergences of secular, liberal and Islamist women's groups, especially on rape cases – but not to contest the principle of Islamization of the state.

That women were targeted during the regressive Zia regime, and were on the receiving end of misogynist and discriminatory legal, social and economic policies, has been fairly well documented (Ali 2000; Jahangir and Jilani 1990; Zia 1994). A military-mullah masculinist nexus, dominating state discourse, is held to be the main historic cause for the persistence of women's low position on all current socio-economic indices.

The limitations of such analysis in the contemporary context is discussed later in the chapter, but first I shall examine the trajectory of collaboration between women's rights groups and governments or state machineries. It was a process that sustained itself during the unlikely (as to some of its outcomes), anti-women and inimical dictatorship of General Zia. The introduction of international funding invited the process of what is known in developmental language as 'gender mainstreaming' and it encouraged women's groups, now registered as NGOs, to act as the natural catalysts between state, development and women's rights.[6]

Notably, several women politicians who served in General Zia's Parliament (Majlis-e-Shura) reinvented their political careers in ways that enabled them to remain politically relevant through civilian and military rule. Several women who were a part of General Zia's government continued to serve in subsequent democratic governments; they went on to be members of the political party that collaborated with and supported the most recent military rule of General Musharraf; and tenaciously they continue to sit in the current civilian democratic government.

They serve on women's committees and influence legal debates, and are reminders of how chequered, fluid and disconnected the relationship between state ideology and representing women's concerns is in Pakistan.

Women's muted voices in democracies (1988–99)[7]

Although the democratic period from 1988 to 1999 turned out to be an uneasy one, this period also invited much optimism on the part of the women's movement. Many of these women's rights activists had been a part of the Movement for the Restoration of Democracy through the 1980s, too, with Women's Action Forum (WAF)[8] as a lead organization, although other human rights organizations had been hesitant to raise any anti-Zia and anti-military slogans. This resulted in a consciously feminist politics that understood democratic representation to be the most promising channel for advocating women's rights. During this time the first woman Prime Minister of the Muslim world, Benazir Bhutto, was also elected into power (in 1988) after a decade-long military dictatorship. However, the Pakistan's People Party (PPP), which she led, was dominated by political confrontations, as democratic parties were attempting to establish themselves and define a new culture of democratic relations. PPP did not command a majority in the Parliament to realize their electoral promise of reversing discriminatory Islamic laws such as the Zina Ordinance. It also had no sustained policy with which to roll back conservative social trends, even as the new military-mullah nexus loomed threateningly in the background.

Several women activists have reflected on the compelling necessity of political or democratic compromise on women's rights, especially since any corrective measure towards achieving women's rights requires the restructuring of all the social, political, economic and personal benefits and privileges that patriarchal norms extend to male-dominated political parties.

However, it was during the two tenures of the late Prime Minister Benazir Bhutto that some tangible outcomes were seen.

These included women's police stations, the first women's bank, women judges, and women's studies centres at universities. The twenty-year plan for the Beijing Plan of Action was developed; many women's NGOs were funded; and, in 1996, during her second tenure, CEDAW was ratified by her government. The most important lesson here was that gendered policy carries the potential to be effective when leadership understands its importance and is committed to it.

The spirit of co-operation between women activists and Benazir's government was at its peak during the Fourth UN World Conference on Women in 1995. Government reports were drafted with inputs from social activists, joint efforts marked the UN regional and international meetings, and women-friendly policies were initiated. While the impact of substantial efforts and policies are harder to measure as Benazir's rule ended abruptly, women activists were visible and influential during her leadership. However, activists have often expressed, in internal meetings, their criticism and disappointment about the failure to roll back Islamization policies during this period. But these complaints were toned down in public.

During the second term of the conservative government of the Pakistan Muslim League (PML) led by Nawaz Sharif (1997–9), women's groups found themselves losing ground to political conservatism, as well as religious revivalism in both social and political arenas. Between 1997 and 1999, under Nawaz Sharif's leadership, the government launched a series of campaigns to impose the Shari'a. For example, the Council of Islamic Ideology in its annual report of 1997 recommended the obligatory wearing of the *hijab* (veil) (Rashid 2006: 147); the Punjab government announced a ban on cultural activities in girls' schools and colleges, directing them to abide by the Islamic dress code; and in 1998 dance performances by women were banned. NGOs came under criticism and suspicion from the conservative government, which attempted to regulate their activism – or what it called the 'spreading [of] vulgarity, immorality and obscenity in the name of human rights' (*ibid.*).

Enlightened dictatorship (1999–2008)

The military coup led by General Pervez Musharraf in 1999 brought in Pakistan's fourth period of army rule. By this time Islamist forces had gained ground the most from the atrophying of the two main democratic parties (whose leaders – Bhutto and Sharif – were forced into exile). During Musharraf's rule, Islamist parties managed to align religious and political policies to their advantage, and pave the way for extremist militancy in Khyber Pukhtunkhwa (formerly the North-West Frontier Province), which they governed for five years.

Meanwhile, many who otherwise supported liberal democratic values, including many members of 'pro-democracy' NGOs, welcomed, supported and even joined the 'enlightened and moderate' government of General Musharraf. However, the contradictions and tensions of this period ultimately made it arguably the most challenging for the women's movement.

General Musharraf's very first speech assured the Pakistani people that his was not an obscurantist religious agenda. The liberals were relieved not to have another uniformed, faith-based, moral crusader in power. The enlightened moderation theme of General Musharraf's rule became the *raison d'etre* which helped him to continue at the helm of state affairs rather than calling for elections and reverting to total civilian governance. The reason there was no concerted serious protest movement against this was that liberals saw him as a bulwark against the conservative ambitions of the previous government. During Musharraf's rule (1999–2008), women were being inducted into public services as a matter of policy. Examples of this include the appointment of the first woman state bank governor, official female guards to Mohammad Ali Jinnah's mausoleum, women pilots in the coast guard and in the armed forces, and women in senior positions in the cabinet and bureaucracy.

However, in Khyber Pukhtunkhwa, the provincial Muthahida Majlis Amal (MMA) government (a coalition of religious parties that won the 2002 elections in a post-9/11 fervour) launched a systematic drive to remove any signs of womanhood in the public sphere. For example, battered women's shelters/refuges were accused of being Western-inspired initiatives that encouraged adultery and obscenity, and were attacked and shut down. In fact, the youth wing of the religious alliance of the MMA conducted a vicious anti-obscenity campaign whereby billboards and hoardings of women in advertisements were blackened with paint and torn down. The most symbolic act was the provincial government's order that all mannequins must be removed from shops as they represented the (disembodied) female form in public. All forms of femaleness had to be relegated to the private, domestic realm of the family. Women leaders and activists of the religious parties were at the forefront and complicit in such campaigns, as well as in efforts that actively prevented women from exercising their vote in local government elections. However, the leaders of the progressive PPP and the ANP (the Awami National Party, a nationalist, secular party with its political base in the province) were not averse to striking similar deals with the PML-N and the MMA to exclude women from the electoral right to vote at the district level.

However, an honest appraisal of the relationship between women's rights groups and General Musharraf's regime[9] reveals that his liberal attitude encouraged key women activists and accommodated several progressive policies and laws. An important policy move under his leadership was to induct prominent women's rights activists into his cabinet and key government posts. This commitment to women's progress may even have been motivated in response to a general policy hubris over the years. Therefore, women served as the driving symbols of Musharraf's 'enlightened moderation' theme.

It is to the credit of these key appointees that there was a visible result and progress at policy and implementation levels. Examples include some official policies such as the establishment of a National Commission on the Status of Women in 2000, a National Policy for Development and Empowerment of Women in 2002, Pakistan's Population Policy (2002), the National

Health Policy (2001), unprecedented reservation of seats for women at local government, parliamentary and senate levels, the Citizenship Act (2000), the Ministry of Women's Development Family Protection Project, the Human Trafficking Ordinance (2002), the Gender Reform Action Plan, the Women's Political Participation Project, the Beijing Plus Ten process, and laws such as the Honour Killings Act and the Women's Protection Act. At provincial levels too, several gender-related policies were introduced to tackle honour crimes, and women were appointed to the national guard and in the armed forces, as part of the policy approach of the Musharraf government.

Arguably the most important policy was the substantial increase in seats reserved for women at all tiers of legislature, introduced by General Musharraf through a constitutional amendment. The issue of formal political representation as a vehicle for including women's voices within state structures, and particularly the legislature, serves as a useful benchmark for any comparative analysis between dictatorial and civilian governments in Pakistan.

Under the 1956 constitution, ten national seats were reserved for women in the general elections, based on women's votes. This constitution was abrogated in 1958 and general elections were banned by General Ayub Khan. The 1973 constitution provided for 10 reserved seats to women, indirectly elected at the national level, and this was increased to 20 in 1984. This lapsed (since ordinances have to be ratified within a specified timeframe) after the 1988 elections, and there were only two women in the 1990–3 and four in the 1993–7 national assemblies, who were elected through direct voting. In 2002, General Musharraf passed the Legal Framework Order, which made constitutional changes to increase the number of overall seats in the legislature, as well as substantially raising the quota of seats reserved for women. Apart from the 12 directly elected women, an unprecedented 60 seats were reserved for women in the National Assembly and 17 in the Senate. Some 30,000 women councillors were mobilized and trained to serve on Union Councils throughout the country.

Several bills for women's rights were introduced by the then opposition party – the PPP. Its leader Benazir Bhutto was in political exile but PPP's party members included several women who were active and effective as lobbyists and parliamentarians in 2002–8. Equally vocal in the National Assembly were the Islamist women.[10]

While the benefits and shortcomings of these policies are still being debated, the central concerns of activists through this decade are to do with the contradictions invoked by this military-led rule. Thus, policies were double-edged. Liberal policies were countered by the overall oppressive control that resulted in unsustainable policy and limited progress. What was missing from General Musharraf's 'progressive' agenda, which increased the visibility of women in state machinery, was the lack of sustained and assimilative policy for women. Another contradiction played out during this period was that, while women had increased public and political mobility (and lip service was paid to their freedom of expression) under the liberal policies of Musharraf's government, they were also directly attacked, censored and obstructed in their practical progress across the entire country by the religious parties (such as MMA) that were the government's allies. For this reason, many of the practical benefits of progressive policies for women launched in this era have in fact been difficult to realize.

An example of one such contradiction is the well-known case of rape survivor Mukhtaran Mai. In an interview with a US newspaper in 2005, General Musharraf was quoted as suggesting that Mai's was a case in point of women who cry 'rape' every time they want to gain visa or asylum rights in Canada. He also banned her from travelling to the US to prevent the tarnishing of Pakistan's image abroad (*Al Jazeera* 2005). Another prominent case was that of the Tourism Minister of the party that supported the government (PML-Q), Nilofar Bakhtiar. In 2007, she was forced to resign after clerics passed a *fatwa* against her when newspapers carried a photograph of her hugging the male instructor after a parachuting stint in France as part of a media call. She was neither defended nor supported by her party or the President.

Voice and representation

The definition of 'a women's movement' in Pakistan has also been the subject of debate. It has been challenged as it has often primarily referred to the WAF in historical documentation of women's activism in Pakistan.[11] Since its inception in 1983, members of this urban-based national forum were primarily from the upper and middle classes. Despite the presence of trade unionists, professional women and students in its membership, concerns about its class base have led to several debates regarding what constitutes a 'feminist' as distinct from a 'women's' movement. Although WAF members work with, and have primarily targeted issues and cases of marginalized groups of women and religious minorities, its own membership base has made it a target for a right-wing backlash. WAF is accused of being 'Westernized', upper-class and, even, a promoter of promiscuity. Often, such allegations have been received from liberal men and politicians, too.

However, WAF remains symbolic of the professional, upper-class but political women's movement, and has retained its credibility over the years. Its relevance was first recognized when it spearheaded street activism at a time when it was virtually impossible and dangerous to hold political demonstrations. More recently, its commitment to remaining a non-funded activist forum rather than a donor-supported, project-based, advocacy organization has brought a respectful acknowledgement from political and civil society.

The structure, nature and relevance of WAF has been debated and discussed at some length, mainly because its members include theorists, academics and development practitioners who have the skills to theorize and whose careers depend on analysing women's issues.[12] The different perspectives on what direction women's activism should take, and within which frame, are often contested, resisted and criticized by some of WAF's members. Such discussions are seen as being too 'reflective and not active enough'. Most often, interactive dialogue on these issues is left incomplete because documenting debates on women's issues is considered by several of its members as an 'academic' and not developmental or empirical concern. This chapter acknowledges that the women's movement, however defined, is splintering into interesting, new and non-linear directions. However, it argues that many of the new directions are in contrast to the historical experiences of an activism against an oppressive Islamization period and, therefore, often tangential to the aims and experiences of women's activism between the 1980s and 1990s.

How this shift in the nature of women's activism will affect the relationship with state and democracy in the future is difficult to predict. This chapter evaluates some of the recent experiences of women's activism under dictatorships and democratic governments in order to examine whether this is a useful distinction when measuring expectations on progressive rights for women.

The strategy of strengthening women's engagement with the state and increasing their representation within state machineries and structures also needs fresh scrutiny. Does 'working from within' fundamentally challenge or simply validate oppressive patriarchal state discourses? Is the barter of some pro-women policies enough, in exchange for the legitimacy women's rights activists lend the state and military in its attempts to modernize its own image as a progressive alternative to fundamentalist politics and/or corrupt civilian governments?

Democracy or dictatorship?

Today, many of the activists who were part of pro-democracy and women's rights groups lead prominent NGOs, while some are a part of state institutions and yet others have entered mainstream political parties formally. There is consensual agreement among those who suffered censure during the dictatorship years that the current insidious spirit of intolerance and politicized religion are products of Zia's years of false Islamization. Seasoned activists, who now head some of these NGOs, interpret much of the suspicion and backlash that they face from right-wing political actors as a response to their own roles in resisting the conservative political forces spawned by General Zia's regime.

The narratives, analyses and images of women's struggles for their rights, as documented by the activists mentioned above, are important contributions towards recording women's histories, especially in relation to the state and the insidious placement of religious conservatism within all state machineries, social relations and popular discourse.

However, hinging the trajectory of the women's movement almost exclusively to this historical period is problematic for two main reasons. The first is the assumption that contemporary religious identities and faith-led consciousness are a direct, sequential legacy of General Zia's period. This defies the entire body of work that interrogates the contemporary post-colonial experience of identity construction, whereby it is argued that figures and actors in post-colonial states have confounded the received definition of tradition and modernity in order to resource, engineer and restage new religious and political identities (Bhabha 1990). Therefore, the insistence on grouping all current religious identities as products of Zia's Islamization has also led to what Amina Jamal (2005) and a host of other scholars are drawing attention to – the denial of the agency and autonomy of right-wing Islamist forces, and especially of women who belong to such movements.

Second, this suggestion of a linear downward slide of women's rights ignores the hybridity of counter-cultural expressions found amongst a new generation of post-feminist commentators, particularly those in the new media and in academia. This is a generation for whom the metaphor of General Zia's oppressive Islamization is underwhelming in comparison to their conscious anger over Western Islamophobia, which they associate with Anglo-American persecution of Muslims globally. The militant attacks on the state of Pakistan by the Taliban over the last decade have led many younger Pakistanis to re-examine the presumed fundamentalism of religious parties, revise concepts of rights within an Islamic framework, and negotiate for increasing spaces for religion in the public sphere. They are not sympathizers with Zia's politicization of Islam, but neither do they see it as significantly linked to the current challenges that confront Pakistan.[13]

Some believe that women's groups, especially women's NGOs, are reactionary products of the era. One such view disputes the characterization of women's NGOs as 'either pro-feminist or anti-feminist, progressive or regressive, pro-state or anti-state', and goes on to argue that the 'actions and agendas of women's NGOs in Pakistan are largely a response to Islamic fundamentalism' (Jafar 2007: 257).

These are some of the extraneous debates that challenge the totalizing experience of the oppressive post-Zia Islamist backlash chronicled by women activists of WAF. Partially, such analysis is inherently problematic because it undermines the agency of many who were active in the left political movements, as well as several members who carried feminist consciousness prior to their resistance to the dictatorship and Islamization campaign of General Zia. Yet, the related point it raises is worth exploring. In directing its energies towards resisting the Islamization of the state, critical as this challenge was, did the women's movement lose ground on the sociological developments that were becoming widely diffused throughout society and popular culture?

While some of the growing militancy over the last decade is obviously traceable to the material and ideological continuation of the Zia state, new religious identities were being produced under other and various influences. This included an increasing 'Arabization' of local cultures through the transmigration of labour to Gulf Arab countries and the growth of women's piety groups and privatized religious practices and rituals.[14]

Few paid attention to the new faith-based identities that were germinating under their watch – developing, morphing and turning the 'ideology of Pakistan' into an even more complex secular-religious minotaur than before.[15] This merely escalated later, in reaction to US occupations of Iraq and Afghanistan, and in an era of globalized Islamophobia in the new millennium. However, more than any other source, the nascent and growing local conservatism – engineered, cultivated and unchecked, spreading through steady grassroots-level social work and piety movements – has contributed most effectively to this dangerous cocktail of sectarianism and religious fascism in Pakistan.

This chapter argues (Zia 2009a, 2009b) that by investing hope in the potential of an imagined women's 'resistance theology', some members completely misread and underestimated the hegemonic religious ideology that was propagated by women's piety movements such as the Al-Huda movement (Ahmed 2009). This was developing around the same time as the liberal women's movement was attempting to institutionalize its own programme for women's progressive and equal rights. These cleavages between and amongst women activists opened the door for a bolder, emergent Islamist movement which focused on women as signifiers, not necessarily as 'oppressed subjects' but as agentive Muslim women with a political voice.

Increasing Islamist influences

From the perspective of the liberal feminists from Zia's era, Islam was a strategic threshold: its cultural relevance opened up an entry point into communities for women's rights activists to promote feminist ideals and practices. Culturally appropriate methods and messages necessitated, in their minds, references to Islam and feminist interpretations of Islamic rights for Muslim women.[16] Arabic feminist literature became their guide as they sought to fuse and connect, as well as excavate, an 'indigenous' feminism.

The political agency of Islamists, however, has moved far beyond mere attitudes or misinterpretation of religion. The movement has genuine grassroots support in many cases and it is precisely through their methods of service delivery, empowerment and provision of social justice that they have successfully institutionalized their cause. The norms that govern the framework of this revived religiosity are consistently gender-discriminatory and anti-minorities. This is not to say that these are always expressed in overtly violent forms, but that they are insidiously introduced through charity work. Some banned extremist outfits adopt aliases and conduct charity work in poor communities as part of their social reform agenda. This assists them to develop successful patron–client relationships and gains them credibility with the people.

The full veil, for example, was a rare practice observed by a minority of women in select parts of urban Pakistan. Over the last decade, in what used to be a very gender-assimilated campus in the liberal environment of Karachi University, the full veil has now become a norm: women students say they wear it as a 'social uniform', not necessarily under any compulsion imposed by the university (personal interviews with MPhil women students, 2010). Voluntary groups such as Islamic Relief and other faith-based NGOs are proliferating, and are particularly active after natural disasters when monitoring volunteer activity is virtually impossible.

One analysis suggests that

> the need to counter-balance the image of NGOs as Western agents, as well as the desire to promote an indigenous solution to women's issues [and] also simultaneously challenge[s] the negative stereotypes of Muslims in the West, also pushes women's NGOs and activists in the direction of religion. Because of these desires, scholars, activists, and NGO workers are forced to stay within a religious and nationalistic framework whether they are themselves believers or not. (Jafar 2007: 270)

However, this analysis does not see any inherent contradiction in this effort but goes on to rationalize this 'reality' by suggesting that

> It is thus too simplistic to assert that NGOs inevitably sap the efforts of feminism or undermine a 'feminist agenda', or that it is the 'NGO-ization' of the women's movement that has weakened its political drive by not addressing women's long-term strategic interests. It is not the NGOs, but the cultural and political environments that NGOs

are forced to operate within, that has forced feminist compromises in Pakistan. Feminists and [the] women's movement … if they wish to take part in something more than just an intellectual exercise, if they wish to make a 'real' difference … soon realize the inevitability of compromise. (*Ibid.*: 271)

Reductive, pragmatic conclusions such as these enable a simplistic connection between the social forces during Zia's years and the current Islamist resurgence. This essentialist rationale presumes that Pakistan's culture is a homogeneous entity that demands adherence to a presumed logical, naturally progressive, linear connection to 'Islamic identity'. It also implies that there is some invisible border whereby polluted culture can be pried away from pure religion, that the resultant expression will thus be uncontested, and that the fruition of such a project will result in harmony.[17]

Such analyses deny all the bases of social relations that conflict and compete across class, ethnic, and gender identities. They also offer a naïve objection to those opportunistic secular leaders who use religion as a tool, just as Islamists do. Such a view considers Islam to be some neutral tool that does not lend its power to politics but merely to the personal; or that its precepts are not in accordance with a prescribed hierarchy; or, indeed, that it is not meant to be engaged in matters of state or law. It is due to the limitations of such analyses, and in the face of a revived Islamist movement that claims to be the authentic arbiter in seeking women's (unequal) rights as explicated within the religious discourse, that the influence of a secular women's movement has retreated considerably over recent years.

It remains for the liberal progressives either to confront and challenge such a structural take-over through convincing alternatives or to be absorbed by this larger force. Anything in between, such as reinterpreting religion and using cultural/ religious practices as tools for empowerment, is likely to fail, or merely be co-opted by the very sophisticated and nuanced Islamist movement which includes radical women within its cadres.

Can democracy deliver?

The above challenges, which include reneging on women's equal rights; increasing violence against women; and Islamism as a determinant of social and public policy in the informal and formal sector, make it easier to understand why many women activists invest their hopes in increasing women's political participation at all levels. The notion of working from within the 'state system' encourages women to turn to political representation as the most effective interventionist strategy.

Although donor agencies have assisted women's political empowerment through programmes, such as devolution and training of women councillors at local government levels, when the democratically elected PPP dismantled local governments in 2008, these programmes collapsed. Thus, women activists (rightly) tend to consider women's parliamentary presence as the only permanent and independent democratic option for ensuring women's legal and political rights.

However, the question of alliances, too, has become complicated. With regard to the performance of the highest number of women in Parliament under General Musharraf's presidency, activist Farzana Bari observes:

> Women parliamentarians … showed a high level of oppositional gender consciousness.… Many women parliamentarians who had no history of working with women's rights groups or civil society organizations, now actively reached out to women's rights groups and organizations and tried to champion the cause of women's rights, in order to build themselves a constituency and legitimize themselves by championing political causes. (Bari 2010)

However, under the current civilian government, ruled by PPP which is headed by the late Benazir's husband as president, there are very serious concerns over how the women's movement should strengthen alliances with these very women representatives who have often, symbolically and politically, succumbed to patriarchal norms and become submissive supporters of male leadership in Parliament. This used to be the criticism levelled at women in right-wing political parties, but today it has become the accommodative behaviour of women in 'liberal' parties too. If these women disempower themselves under the patriarchal compulsions of male-stream politics, what should be expected of them as champions of social change?

Under the current civilian democratic government alliance, formed between the liberal PPP and the ANP, several political casualties (in the sense of actual terminations of the right to life) have exposed the government's contradictions and vacillations on women's issues. Just a few of these are summarized here.

One of first steps taken by the PPP leadership was to dissolve the local government structure that had enabled the training, consciousness raising and direct inclusion of nearly 30,000 women councillors at the grassroots political union levels, in districts across Pakistan. Then, in 2009, the liberal civilian government signed a 'peace for Shari'a' treaty (the Nizam-e-Adl Regulation) that aimed to impose Shari'a laws in the Swat Valley, which was then occupied by the militant Taliban in the North-West Frontier Province of Pakistan. The peace deal was brokered by Sufi Muhammed, leader of the Tehreek-e-Nafaz-e-Shariat-e-Mohammadi (TNSM), an Islamist group, which has conducted the active reversal of women's basic freedoms and rights in the region. The appointment of two politicians, Senator Israrullah Zehri and Hazar Khan Bijarani, to the federal cabinet in 2008, met with protests from human rights and women's rights groups. Both men, along with other male representatives, had defended the brutal murder of several women for allegedly refusing their customary arranged marriages. These male politicians claimed the reprisal to be an appropriate traditional norm. They maintained that any criticism of tribal practices against women was an affront to the tribal honour of their constituencies (*The Nation* 2008). Both were inducted into the PPP cabinet. The official religious court, the Federal Shariat Court, in early 2011 reversed the Women's Protection Act (2006) that had amended the more blatantly discriminatory aspects of the Zina Ordinance. Yet the current government has refused to file an appeal against this reversal in the apex court despite pressure from activists (*Daily Times* 2011).[18] At the end of 2010, the Governor of Punjab, Salmaan Taseer, a veteran PPP member, was murdered by his own guard for defending the cause of a poor Christian woman who had been accused of blasphemy and accordingly sentenced to death by a lower court. The late Governor's cause was completely disowned by the ruling party for fear of political fall-out in the aftermath of a brief uprising by Islamist groups who demonstrated against any amendment to the blasphemy law. Subsequently, the Minister for Minorities, Shabaz Bhatti, was murdered in the capital outside his mother's house. Still, the democratically elected leadership remained silent. The ruling party backtracked on any possibility of amending procedural lacunae within the law itself, when this was proposed by yet another prominent member of their party and woman Member of Parliament, Sherry Rehman. She received death threats and legal cases of blasphemy were registered against her as acts of intimidation, yet her own party has refused to support or protect her stance.

Clearly, the environment for furthering liberal and secular causes has become increasingly vaporous in Pakistan. Yet, the fear and refusal to defend women's and human rights, when they are specifically and directly threatened and targeted, only serves the narrow cause of Islamists and further reverses basic rights for the majority. It contradicts every principle that liberal parties pay lip service to when showcasing themselves as viable or relevant alternatives to parochial Islamist politics at international levels. In reality, the gap between the attitudes of liberals and religious chauvinists has become incredibly narrow, as demonstrated in male political bearing in recent years.

For women activists, progressive possibilities still hinge on the idea of increasing women's representation in Parliament and pushing through legislation against domestic violence, acid throwing and the economic rights of home-based women workers. However, activists who are successfully lobbying for such ends will soon have to reflect on what happens after several pro-women laws are enacted, yet the social environment is resistant to women's rights as being culturally and religiously inappropriate.

Post-feminist activist voices and their challenge

In recent years, new voices have emerged via blogs, social networking, and in random coffee-shop consciousness-raising sessions. In various degrees of seriousness, they are arguing, debating and theorizing on Pakistan's politics and social issues. This 'cyber generation' also expresses strains that in form, ideology and politics, can only be termed post-modernist. The young women (and men) discussing such issues are not always located in Pakistan and tend to be self-styled academic experts, by which I mean they have degrees from or are located at foreign universities, though they are not always immersed directly in Pakistan's political processes. Some dip in and out of Pakistan when there is a disaster such as the massive earthquake of 2005 or the recent devastating floods (2010) that displaced and affected an estimated 20 million people. The more experienced activists refer to such visits somewhat cynically as 'disaster/development/ PhD tourism'. In any case, these tours and their academic qualifications, despite a political disconnect, seem to have given a younger generation of diasporic 'activists' an authoritative voice that is sometimes bolder and more confident than that of the older generation of development workers and activists based in Pakistan.

These young post-modernists (a few of them feminists) are well-versed in Western philosophy and, at the same time, shaped by a post-9/11 consciousness that encourages them to question the moral authority of post-colonial, Western universalism, particularly with reference to notions of human rights and women's rights. They respond unapologetically to Islamophobic attitudes in the West (at least in writing, one is not sure of direct action methods) and often accuse Pakistani liberals of being under undue influence from the same source.

With regard to Pakistani feminism, some challenge what they

characterize as the latter's 'secular, liberal' ideological base.[19] The presumptive base for this challenge is unfortunate, in that it falls into the same category of critique that *used* to emerge from fundamentalist groups. The central flaw in this critique is the assumption that the only self-identified feminists in Pakistan are the more visible, urbane, articulate activists, and that they are the only ones who advocate for a liberal, secular state and society. The post-modernist critique considers the Pakistani women's movement to be redundant or, at the very least, they question the credence of secularism as a viable feminist ideological base in contemporary Pakistan – which in their world-view means post-9/11 Pakistan.

This is not to suggest that there is a face-off between or amongst these feminist circles or any conscious debate, nor even that they necessarily know of each other. In fact, the parallel paths of these floating ideologies are so wide apart that it is interesting to observe that there is practically no understanding or knowledge of each other's work. The younger women have an idea of the historical ideological leanings of the women's movement of the 1980s and 1990s, whereby the Islamization project of Zia's state was the main nemesis of women's rights. However, the post-modernists are critical of these WAF feminists for remaining stuck in their statist politics and, more importantly, blinded by their secular compulsions which make them anti-Islam and willing dupes of Western/universal liberalism. This criticism of the liberal feminists' project suggests that their historical resistance to Islamization translates into a secular, de-contextualized and elitist affront to religion, particularly Islam.

Straddling these two generations, the perspective of this chapter argues a different understanding of the secularist feminists' failure to plug the growth and spread of Islamist influences at state and private levels.[20] The argument offered here is that the secular feminists have never been secular enough, troubled as they were by their own personal Muslim identities in the early years of the struggle. Later on, the opportunism afforded by the focus of development projects and research on religio-identity politics, upgraded many of them to become experts on issues of women and religion.[21] It also afforded them the expertise that catapulted several into international forums as special rapporteurs and enabled them to become intermediaries for progressive Muslim women's rights via the route of integrating the more universalist agendas of various international organizations in New York, Geneva and Bangkok. The Ministry for Women's Development has historically depended on the input of these knowledgeable experts and often contracts them to advise on national government programmes, even as they run their non-governmental programmes simultaneously. This issue of the 'multiple hats' that feminists wear has also raised side-debates on the ethical boundaries of activism and careerism. Ironically, today the post-feminists also receive a similar reception within Western academia for their ethnographic and anthropological recovery of the 'agency' of the Islamist woman subject, and for their critique of liberal feminist projects in Muslim majority contexts.

From the perspective of this chapter, the pragmatic, rationalizing project of approaching women's rights exclusively from within an Islamic framework limits the realm of social scientific analyses offered. It ignores all the non-religious, secular expressions and activism that quite routinely function in rural and urban contexts. These range from strategies evoked by women survivors of violence, in struggles for personal autonomy and other grassroots movements, such as the nation-wide campaign launched by women health workers for regularizing their status and higher pay. An entire gamut of diverse (class) struggles work effectively outside the limits of religious props and relief. To reduce all possibilities to a pragmatic communitarian logic of Islam is to defeat the very tangible strategies, as well as universalist principles of equality, that women do carve out, engage in and mine from unceasingly, without succumbing to using religion as a tool of resistance.[22]

If one were to offer a comparative definition of these two variant strains of women's rights activism, it could be said that the liberal (secular) feminists continue to follow their activist route to policy influence and developmental reform in the liberal framework. They often achieve some limited success but their activism tends to be well-crafted within an internationally defined framework or reference. This is not to suggest that it is not informed by, or relevant to the local concerns for which their projects and policies are developed. However, their faithful adherence to the international framework of universal rights, Beijing Plans of Action and discriminatory laws and Islamic extremism keeps them blinkered from challenges emerging from within a newly developed, indigenous and more influential discourse with reference to women's political expression.

An emergent new challenge is the faith-based women's movement and the supporting scholarship offered by post-modernist academics. The insistence of some liberal feminists that it is the patriarchal compulsions of religion, or the opportunist state that exploits religion and/or the male Islamists' undue influence and coercion of women that politicizes and manipulates women's faith, is an outright denial of the agency of women in faith-based movements in Pakistan (Jamal 2005).

The reason for this narrow analysis by the earlier generation of liberal feminists may be an outcome of the reflexivity from this second wave of women's rights activists, who after years of strategizing, resisting state patriarchy and following the community of internationally defined sisterhood, do not consider this new activism by religious actors as viable. The strategic approach of women's rights groups heading the NGO sector could also be a result of the single-minded dedication required to change governance structures. This includes the struggle to integrate women and their agendas at formal levels, such as Parliament and the criminal justice systems, as well as interventions required at informal levels and to counter power structures such as *jirgas*[23] and domestic crimes against women. In the process, the creeping changes in structure, content and direction of the emergent political identities of women within Islamist organizations and movements, may have been considered a peripheral issue. To date, some liberal feminists acknowledge the growing influence of piety movements but deny their independent political aspirations or, indeed, viable agentive ability to displace the feminist agenda in Pakistan.

In some ways, the comparative approaches of liberal feminist and post-feminist women's activism also help to contrast broader differences in Pakistan's social activism. Both claim they are anti-imperialist and culturally indigenous, but the former accommodates the economic rationale of Western aid through the 'NGO-ization' of their activism, while the latter leans almost exclusively towards cultural and technological, online social networks such as Facebook, which is casually referred to as 'cyber activism'.

Future challenges

The stark contrast in political activism is splitting feminist agendas along a generational line. The influence of cyber feminism is more fluid and remains virtual rather than real, but the growth of new media gives many young people access to opinion columns and an opportunity to contribute to television soundbites. This is despite their limited, direct experience of working within people's movements, or any political engagement with the state. Further, the neo-orientalist interest in the Muslim woman subject, post-9/11, has led to the launch of a growing number of international research projects in Pakistan. This in turn, has led to joint ventures between international and Pakistani aspiring academics. This has lent neophyte women a certain authoritative voice within foreign academia, which may very well be lacking reference points for or representation of the concerns or experiences of women activists within Pakistan.[24]

Meanwhile, leading women activists and NGO leaders in Pakistan have, after years of direct involvement in the field and interaction with the state departments, cultivated a social relationship with liberal politicians, bureaucrats, diplomats and donors. These activist leaders have social access to sympathetic parliamentarians whom they lobby in the comfort of their offices and private spaces. Such practices have resulted in the relinquishment of public spaces where collective pressure tactics or activism used to be enacted. Instead, the liberals' public discourse has now been replaced by 'Track 2', parallel, confidential agreements and recommendations for changes to laws and policies.

Liberal activists do seem to have lost their appetite for debate or critique. They remain hopelessly defensive about the only self-acclaimed liberal hope for Pakistan, at least in theory, in the form of the late Benazir Bhutto's political party, the PPP. The leadership's isolation of members such as Sherry Rehman, who represent some kind of continuity with Benazir Bhutto's liberal vision, has disappointed some die-hard apologists. However, there remains a reluctance to pressurize for plugging the fast-haemorrhaging liberalism of the PPP leadership and an increasingly acquiescent alliance.

It is no longer the fear that 'NGO-ization' will dilute the sharpness of the direct action strategies and commitment to causes that poses the challenge facing the women's movement. Even faith-based organizations are registered as NGOs and several politicians have set up not-for-profit organizations in their constituencies. The real challenge within the social fabric comes from the dual sources of cultural and religious patriarchal collusions.

Until recently, Pakistan was one of the few countries which had both a Permanent National Commission on the Status of Women and a Ministry of Women's Development, and ranked one of the highest in the world in terms of reserved seats in the National and Provincial Assemblies and at the local level. It also hosts one of the most dynamic and high-profile civil society movements that addresses women's rights at the national and local level. A woman holds the position of Speaker of the Parliament and has stood in as President at least once since 2008. Additional demands regarding increased pro-women legislation and the inclusion of offices of women ombudsmen and judges at superior courts are consistently on the agenda of women activists.

Conclusion

This chapter has attempted to outline the variations in voice and tones within the urban women's movement in Pakistan and its experiences through dictatorial and democratic rules. It has noted the main contributions and limitations of a generation of activists that rose to strength in resistance against General Zia's dictatorial Islamization programme, as well as the more accommodative political engagements by activists who saw promise in General Musharraf's enlightened moderation (which was his attempt at reinventing his dictatorship and therefore, his relevance). In 2008, General Musharraf was ousted by a new democratic government as well as a renewed surge of popular consciousness, led essentially by the Lawyer's Movement to which pro-democracy forces, including the women's movement, lent their support. At the time, there was a clear understanding that the real threat to Pakistan's state and society was coming from Islamic militancy both externally, as well as from the conservative fundamentalist organizations within the country. Subsequently, an unspoken consensus gained momentum, which is that sustained resistance to the attacks on the state and the country's socio-political fabric can only come in the form of egalitarian democratic representation.

Three years on, the initial optimism has become muted with the performance of the current government and its seeming inability to offer liberal resistance and alternatives, as outlined above. Still, according to many activists, the increased number of women political actors at provincial and national legislatures is a promising sign for the advancement of democratic norms. However, the caution is that unless these can counter the social forces that germinate and resurge at critical points to fulfil conservative Islamist agendas, women's rights issues may become casualties of yet another round of democratic governance. If the progressive movements in the country do not chart a clear vision of the form and substance of such a secular resistance, then – ushered forward by the post-modernist, post-feminist analysis mentioned above, and that which often finds its way into international think-tank reports and donor agency projects[25] – it is highly likely that the anti-secularist, anti-democratic and conservative forces will quickly gain a louder voice than any other, and will thwart women's democratic rights.

Notes

1   I refer to the women's movement through a more inclusive definition which recognizes women activists across the board regardless of their ideological location in the political spectrum. In general, the activists with a consciously feminist orientation and involved in human rights based work are referred to (by the media, analysts, and in development literature) as 'progressives' and 'liberals' while the more right-wing women activists, usually associated with religious political parties, are perceived as 'radical' and 'conservative'.

2   The term 'Islamist women' is used here not as a binary distinction from 'Muslim women' but rather in recognition of the former's political persuasion, consciousness or activism. It includes those women who lead and associate with pietist or mosque movements, in recognition of their self-defined subjectivity or agency, which I consider political.

3   A compilation of such analysis can be found in Khan (2004).

4   Of particular concern to women and human rights activists have been the Hudood Ordinances, which comprised laws that were passed in 1979 as part of General Zia-ul-Haq's Islamization policy. The Zina Ordinance made adultery a crime against the state punishable by death, and blurred the line between rape and consensual intercourse. Many hundreds of women have been victimized and jailed under this law. It was amended in 2006–07 under the Women's Protection Act.

5   It may be noted that this was the time when Pakistan identified with the Western/US bloc in the Cold War and scoffed at the idea of non-alignment (NAM) led by Nasser, Nehru and Sukarno; Arab oil/petro dollars and Arab Islam did not yet hold the attraction that they hold today; this influence dates from the mid-1970s.

6   The registration of NGOs was one of the functions of the newly formed Women's Ministry.

7   For an overview of the complex relations between women's activism and new democracies, see Kandiyoti (2009; 2011).

8   WAF is a women's rights organization founded in 1981 and has a presence in several cities in Pakistan. It is a non-partisan, non-

hierarchical, non-funded, secular organization. It lobbies on all aspects of women's rights and related issues, irrespective of political affiliations, belief system or ethnicity. It was the lead organization that took to the streets in protest against the promulgation of discriminatory Islamic laws during the military dictatorship of General Zia-ul-Haq.

9 For a deeper analysis of the effect and relationship between the state and women during Musharraf's regime see Zia (2009a).

10 Some of these debates and interjections are documented in Mirza and Wagha (2008). For analysis of the Islamist women members' interventions see Zia (2009a).

11 For an analysis of debates within WAF see Khan (2004), Sumar (2002) and Shaheed (2002).

12 For a similar discussion on instrumentalization of feminist activism, see de Alwis (2009) and with reference to peace activism in Sri Lanka, and for an overall perspective on instrumentalism and gendered activism see Kandiyoti (2009, 2011).

13 Many such debates are not formally documented; rather, they exist in virtual space and in the form of cyber debates. One such series of debates circulated on Google Group by the name of the People's Resistance, which became an umbrella forum for activists from different existing groups and organized itself in alliance with the Lawyers' Movement against General Musharraf's regime in 2007. This included several younger, first-time recruits. Another group of cross-generational membership can be found on the Socialist Pakistan Network (SPN), where such identity issues are regularly debated.

14 Examples are *dars* and *khatums*. *Dars* are piety lessons or informal study groups for discussions of the Qur'an and Islam, and *khatums* are literally 'the end' prayers usually held at funerals followed by sermons. Some liberal feminists (Shaheed 2002) defended these rituals as personal empowerment strategies for women, but some of these practices have empowered women's groups into serious movements that advocate and reinforce patriarchal norms and nationalist chauvinism.

15 The constitution of Pakistan has gone through several ideological revisions. Some lobbies have pressurized for further 'Islamizing' it, while critics have pointed out that this is against the original intent and vision of the founding father, Mohammad Ali Jinnah.

16 Some of the earlier proponents of such a view include US-based Pakistani scholar Riffat Hasan and Farida Shaheed, who represents the South Asian chapter of the Women Living

Under Muslim Laws network (WLUML), but subsequently the phenomenon of Islamic feminism has increased its supporters globally, as the movement seeks the possibility of mining rights for Muslim women within a reinterpreted and feminist reading of the Qur'an and Shari'a.

17 For a host of other examples of such scholarship, see Bano (2010), Aziz and Cheema (2007), and Cheema and Rahman (2007). See also Ahmad (2007), Iqtidar (2011), and Mushtaq (2007).

18 At the time of going to press there are reports by the watchdog body, the National Commission on the Status of Women, that the government has lodged an appeal over this under pressure from activists.

19 See note 12.

20 For a more historical discussion on this see Zia (2009b).

21 See note 15.

22 For an incisive and wide spanning discussion on this topic see Tadros (2011).

23 Parallel legal systems comprising of male elders (communities or tribal collectives) who are empowered to dispense local justice.

24 For a brief outline of such projects see Zia (2011).

25 For a discussion of some of these projects see Zia (2011).

References

Ahmad, I. (2007) 'Cracks in the 'Mightiest Fortress': Jamaat-e-Islami's Changing Discourse on Women', *Modern Asian Studies*, Vol. 42, pp. 549–75.

Ahmed, S. (2009) *Transforming Faith: The Story of Al-Huda and Islamic Revivalism Among Urban Pakistani Women*, Syracuse University Press, New York, NY.

Ali, S. S. (2000) 'Law, Islam and the Women's Movement in Pakistan', in S. Rai (ed.), *International Perspectives on Gender and Democratization*, Macmillan, Basingstoke and London.

Al Jazeera (2005) http://english.aljazeera.net/archive/2005/09/ 200841011 2050342208.html.

Aziz, S. and Cheema, M. (2007) 'Beyond Petition and Redress: Mixed Legality and Consent in Marriage for Women in Pakistan', paper presented at the Third Social Sciences Annual Conference, Lahore University of Management Sciences, December.

Bano, M. (2010) 'Female Madrasas in Pakistan: A Response to Modernity', Working Paper 45, Religions and Research Development Programme,

Birmingham, DfID, http://www.religionsanddevelopment.org/files/resourcesmodule/@random454f80f60b3f4/1280142650_working_paper_45___complete_for_web.pdf.

Bari, F. (2010) 'Women Parliamentarians: Challenging the Frontiers of Politics', unpublished paper.

Bhabha, H. (1990) *Nation and Narration*, Routledge, New York, NY.

Cheema, M. and A. Rahman (2007) 'From Hudood Ordinances to the Women's Protection Act', paper presented at the Third Social Sciences Annual Conference, Lahore University of Management Sciences, December.

Daily Times (2011) http://www.dailytimes.com.pk/default.asp?page=2011%5C04%5C27%5Cstory_27-4-2011_pg7_29.

de Alwis, M. (2009) 'Interrogating the 'Political': Feminist Peace Activism in Sri Lanka', *Feminist Review*, Vol. 91, pp. 81–93.

Iqtidar, H. (2011) *Secularizing Islamists? Jamaat-i-Islami and Jama'at-ud-Da'wa in Urban Pakistan*, Chicago University Press, Chicago.

Jafar, A. (2007) 'Engaging Fundamentalism: The Case of Women's NGOs in Pakistan', *Social Problems*, Vol. 54, No. 3, pp. 256–73.

Jahangir, A. and H. Jillani (1990) *The Hudood Ordinances; A Divine Sanction?*, Rohtas Books, Lahore.

Jalal, A. (1991) 'The Convenience of Subservience: Women and the State of Pakistan', in D. Kandiyoti (ed.), *Women, Islam and the State*, Macmillan, London.

Jamal, A. (2005) 'Feminist "Selves" and Feminism's "Others"; Feminist Representations of Jamaat-e-Islami Women in Pakistan', *Feminist Review*, No. 81, pp. 52–73.

Kandiyoti, D. (2009) 'Gender in Afghanistan: Pragmatic Activism', *Open Democracy*, http://www.opendemocracy.net/deniz-kandiyoti/gender-in-afghanistan-pragmatic-activism.

—— (2011) 'Promise and Peril: Women and the 'Arab Spring', *Open Democracy*, http://www.opendemocracy.net/5050/deniz-kandiyoti/promise-and-peril-women-and-%E2%80%98arab-spring%E2%80%99.

Khan, N. S. (ed.) (2004) *Up Against the State*, ASR Publications, Lahore.

Mirza, N. and Wagha, W. (2008) 'A Five Year Report on Performance of Women Parliamentarians in the 12th National Assembly (2002–2007)', Aurat Foundation Publication, Islamabad.

Mushtaq, F. (2007) 'Al-Huda: New Forms of Islamic Education', paper presented at Miskeen Study Group, Karachi.

Rashid, T. (2006) *Contested Representation: Punjabi Women in Feminist Debate in Pakistan*, Oxford University Press, Karachi.

Shaheed, F. (2002) 'Women's Experiences of Identity, Religion and Activism in Pakistan', in K. Nadvi and S. M. Naseem (eds), *The Post-*

Colonial State and Social Transformation in India and Pakistan, Oxford University Press, Karachi.

Sumar, S. (2002) 'Women's Movement in Pakistan: Problems and Prospects', in K. Nadvi and S. M. Naseem (eds), *The Post-Colonial State and Social Transformation in India and Pakistan*, Oxford University Press, Karachi.

Tadros, M. (ed.) (2011) 'Gender, Rights and Religion at the Crossroads', *IDS Bulletin*, Vol. 42, No. 1.

The Nation (2008) 'Induction of Bijarani Zehri into Federal Cabinet Slammed', http://nation.com.pk/pakistan-news-newspaper-daily-english-online/Regional/Karachi/14-Nov-2008/Induction-of-Bijarani-Zehri-into-Federal-cabinet-slammed.

Zia, A. S. (1994) *Sex Crime in the Islamic Context; Rape, Class and Gender in Pakistan*, ASR Publications, Lahore.

—— (2009a) 'The Reinvention of Feminism in Pakistan', *Feminist Review*, No. 91, pp. 2946.

—— (2009b) 'Faith-based Politics, Enlightened Moderation and the Pakistani Women's Movement', *Journal of International Women's Studies*, Vol. 11, No. 1, pp. 225–44.

—— (2011) 'Donor-driven Islam?: The Politics of Research on Gender and Religion in Pakistan', *Open Democracy*, http://www.opendemocracy.net/5050/afiya-shehrbano-zia/donor-driven-islam.

6

Feminist Voices and the Regulation, Islamization and Quango-ization of Women's Activism in Mubarak's Egypt

Mariz Tadros

This chapter was researched and written between September 2009 and August 2010, before the Egyptian people's uprising of 25 January 2011 that led to the ousting of Mubarak from power and the subsequent revolt against President Morsi's brief regime that took place on 30 June 2013. However, the state of feminist activism prior to the revolution has had an impact on organized women's groups' ability to take advantage of political opportunities afforded by the regime changes. The historical dynamics discussed in this chapter are critical for understanding why Egyptian feminist mobilization was so limited in its influence in the first few months after Mubarak's demise.

Feminist literature suggests that the nature of women's collective action prior to regime change plays an important role in influencing the extent to which the processes and outcomes recognize gender equality (Waylen 1994; Viterna and Fallon 2008; Zulu 2000). Viterna and Fallon's study of four countries that have experienced regime change (South Africa, Argentina, Ghana and El Salvador) argues that among the key factors in a positive outcome for integrating gender equality in new political orders are a cohesive coalition within the women's movement and a legacy of women's activism that legitimates present–day feminist demands (2008: 669). Lindiwe Zulu, a member of the African National Congress who served as MP in the South African Parliament, also highlights a number of factors that put pressure on the post-apartheid regime to adopt gender-inclusive policies (2000). These include the level of feminist mobilization during the national liberation period and the ability of these 'graduates' to join forces and coalesce around a common agenda through the formation of the Women's National Coalition (WNC). Zulu also stresses the power of numbers: the WNC was comprised of 90 women's organizations, with a constituency of two million women.

Outcomes of regime change never rest on one main factor. Instead a constellation of factors will include dynamics flowing from the agents, such as the nature of feminist organization; or context-specific factors, such as the new regime's ideological openness to gender equality, the extent to which there are genuine political openings for democratic mobilization, and the role of internal actors in supporting an enabling environment for inclusive political order. While the post-Mubarak environment (state-sponsored ideology, political parties, role of international actors) created a deeply hostile environment for attempts to promote women's rights, nevertheless, it is argued here, a number of characteristics associated with feminist mobilizing during Mubarak's era helped to sideline women's equality issues after the demise of the regime. These include the absence of a unified women's movement – which meant that women activists could not agree on a common set of leaders and a common agenda through which they could mediate their political demands; the absence of a constituency for women's rights at a time when street politics bore political weight – so that women activists did not have the power of numbers that would grant legitimacy to their demands and force the power holders to take them seriously; and the tainted reputation of the national women's machineries formerly led by the First Lady (Mubarak's wife) – a connection used by opponents to discredit the women's equality agenda altogether, rejecting it as an element of the former regime's corrupt rule. The historic and context-specific dynamics that explain the emergence of these factors are discussed in the chapter that follows.

I argue that women's activism in Egypt thrived in a context in which, politically, an authoritarian regime controlled citizen space; ideologically, religion had become the normative framework for public engagement; and organizationally, the national women's machineries claimed representation of Egyptian women's voices and interests. The rise and salience of these forces emanated from a historical trajectory involving a complex power struggle between local, national and global actors. The outcome has severely undermined prospects of influencing the critical juncture in which new configurations of power are being forged. Politically, the reproduction of highly authoritarian relations after the 25 January revolution has meant that while new political spaces for mobilization opened up, those invited to the negotiating table were still a small elite group that denied representation from actors who would endorse the rights of youth, women and religious minorities. Ideologically, Islamist political forces' ascendancy to formal power through majority representation in Parliament and the Muslim Brotherhood's assumption of the presidency through their nominee, Mohamed Morsi, led to the instrumentalization of religion by highly conservative leaders in order to constrain women's choices, both in the legal sphere and in their public and private lives. Moreover, as we have seen, the revolt against Mubarak meant that the national women's machineries formerly led by the First Lady were deeply discredited as the product of a corrupt and illegitimate regime. The challenge of building legitimacy for the national women's machinery in the eyes of the public and the intelligentsia is immense.

During the last twenty years of Mubarak's regime, religious values became increasingly pervasive in government policy, and the political struggle between the government and Islamist opposition groups over who most faithfully represents Islam intensified. For women activists in Egypt openly to contest an increasingly conservative and religionized gender regime would incur high costs to their legitimacy, manoeuvring space and the ability to engage a grassroots Muslim constituency. The costs of articulating an openly feminist voice – one that uses a human rights standpoint to advocate for women's rights – are particularly high. Accordingly, an increasing number of secular feminist voices are being framed in religious terms to accommodate the Islamization of society, challenging the conventional secular vs Muslim/Islamist dichotomy. The space for engaging policy and practice for women's activisms, in particular secular feminist voices, is also shrinking as national women's machineries are established and assert their claim to represent women's interests in Egypt. I argue that since 2000 there has been a Quango-ization of women's activism through the national women's machineries, which have also become the new donor darlings.

In this chapter I will examine feminist voice in the light of the shifts in representing and framing gender equality rights by women's NGOs; the emergence of collective forms of mobilization around bread and butter issues by women workers, civil servants and citizens; and the increasing political activism of women Islamist movement members. However, the chapter also cautions against conflating feminist voice with power and influence, or using voice as a proxy for activism. In Egypt, feminist voice is not the voice around which the largest numbers of women mobilize, neither does it wield the greatest influence at the policy level. It is therefore significant to understand feminist voice in relation to women's activisms and the agendas they champion.

This chapter draws on qualitative data collected in 2000–10 through both formal and informal interviews, undertaken with feminist and women activists belonging to the Muslim Brotherhood as well as an analysis of the Egyptian press, complemented by a literature review. I am both an insider and an outsider. I have been deeply engaged in feminist circles in Egypt for more than 15 years, participating in the growth of several feminist campaigns and coalitions, as well as being organizationally affiliated as a board member of the Centre for Egyptian Women's Legal Assistance, a feminist organization engaged in human rights and development in Cairo. On the other hand, I am an outsider in so far as I have always worked on the fringes and have been peripheral to the central decision-making core within Egyptian feminist groups. Writing about women's activisms in Egypt carries certain biases stemming from my feminist standpoint, which informs the narrative. This is not necessarily shared by all women who are currently engaged in various forms of activism.

The chapter is divided as follows: the first part highlights the historical, socio-economic and political dynamics that have influenced the trajectory of different forms of women's activism in contemporary Egypt. The usefulness of deploying 'voice' for analysing women's activism is explored, and the extent to which it is relevant for understanding different forms and strategies of activism is questioned. The second part addresses the forces of regulation, Islamization and Quango-ization in relation to women's activism, and the way in which their hegemonic impact is resisted as well as accommodated.

Women's feminist activism in Egypt

It is impossible to do justice to the diverse and complex forms of women's struggles that have emerged in Egypt.[1] The focus here is on the emergence of organized feminist activism since the late nineteenth century. While women and men in Egypt have struggled for centuries to address gender inequalities, the founding of the Egyptian Feminist Union by Huda Shaa'rawi in 1923 generally marks the beginning of the organized feminist movement. The movement's membership mainly comprised upper- and middle-class women who organized around a multiplicity of causes, from family law reform to the implementation of nation-wide social service programmes. With the rise of Islamist groups in the 1930s, parallel women's organizations premised on a commitment to an Islamic cultural and political project were also established.

The repression of civil society organizations in the 1950s under the Nasserite government led to the silencing of both the feminist movement and Islamist women's organizations. Instead, the Nasserite government supported its own version of state feminism, which extended a set of political, economic and social rights for women as part of its modernization strategy. In effect, this meant that women's organizations could no longer hold the government to account for its performance, nor for its failure to reform the personal status legislation, which regulates family matters and continued to serve as a source of patriarchal subordination of women (Hatem 1986; Tadros 2004).

The Sadat government in the late 1960s adopted economic liberalization policies, followed by very limited political liberalization initiatives that chiefly benefited the Islamists with whom Sadat had made a pact. They were to thwart leftist groups in return for increased political space. It was in this context that the Islamization of society gradually began – and direct attacks on feminist groups became more conspicuous.

The 1990s witnessed the government's increased adoption of a welfare pluralist policy and the continued growth of NGOs. A notable expansion was seen in religious organizations extending charity to the poor, a significant proportion of whom were women. As with other contexts in which economic liberalization policies were pursued in tandem with the promotion of welfare pluralism, the NGO-ization of the Egyptian women's movement occurred in response to the donors' increased interest in promoting civil society. NGO-ization led to a proliferation of organizations representing different political perspectives but also to the creation of a large set of 'boutiques'[2] working on gender issues. Competition for foreign funding became more acute from the mid-1990s in particular, as donor funding for women's NGOs increased, making it more difficult for organizations to work together through coalitions, let alone unified movements.

However, women activists did mobilize at opportune political moments. For example, the International Conference for Population and Development (ICPD) in 1994 saw the collective organization of NGOs present a unified voice on reproductive health. Following the ICPD, a coalition to address female circumcision in Egypt (the FGM Taskforce) was established and lasted six years before eventually dissolving. Women affiliated with Islamist movements organized counter-campaigns against the ICPD agenda, arguing that it sought to impose values, ideas and frameworks that were anathema to the religious and moral values of Muslims.

The political context changed significantly from the mid-2000s onwards, compared to a decade earlier: the government allows protests, sit-ins and demonstrations to take place, although this political space is not free and is heavily controlled by the security apparatus. Different actors have seized this space and engaged with it in different ways. Large numbers of female workers, civil servants and low-income employees have taken to the street, usually in partnership with men to protest their meagre wages, lack of rights, as well as challenging rising prices. This is set against a context in which a sustained economic liberalization programme has taken its toll on the poor. The state has increasingly privatized its welfare services (by expanding the scope and burden of cost recovery measures) together with its state-owned enterprises, and, as social inequities widen, inflation rises and deprivation increases.

Another important development is the marked salience of religion in every aspect of life in Egypt. Religion has come to represent a normative framework for engaging with all kinds of public and private issues. This reflects the rise of political opposition movements such as the Muslim Brotherhood but also the state's active encouragement of the infiltration of religion in media and society, as well as its competition with the Islamist movements in demonstrating observance of ritual reqirements and deference towards Islam. This has influenced women's agency in two significant ways. First, women belonging to the Islamist movements, in particular the Muslim Brotherhood, have increasingly claimed public space to advocate for an Islamist platform. While their numbers are not as large as the women workers, they have nevertheless used diverse spaces – universities, mosques, and the street – to articulate their demands for the application of their movement's agenda and vision.

Second, the increasing prevalence of the Islamist framework has influenced how women activists engage with the socio-cultural environment, in which religion plays such a critical role. The literature on women activists in the Middle East that has emerged in the past decade tended to distinguish between secular activists, who advocated an approach to gender equality based on human rights, and those who advocated for the advancement of gender rights within the parameters of a religious framework. In the early 1990s, Azza Karam classified women activists as secular feminists, Muslim feminists and Islamist feminists. Islamist feminists reject gender equality but do recognize women's oppression as part of the wider order of socio-political injustice. Muslim feminists aim to show that 'the discourses of total equality between men and women are Islamically valid'. They believe that 'a feminism that does not justify itself within Islam is bound to be resisted by the rest of society and is therefore, self-defeating' (Karam 1997: 22). Karam contrasted Muslim and Islamist feminists with secular feminists who 'firmly believe in grounding their discourse outside the realm of any religion and place it instead within the international human rights discourses.... Religion is respected as a private matter but is totally rejected as a basis from which to formulate any agendas on women's emancipation' (*ibid.*: 24).

The above dichotomy between the secular and religious platforms for advancing gender equality in Egypt does not represent the contemporary context. Virtually all organizations that work with a constituency, the media, the government (or any other non-Western, non-academic party) engage in discussions about the compatibility of their platforms with Islam. This fundamental shift in strategy of engagement is a direct consequence of the increasing Islamization of space, politics and social norms, a theme to which I shall return later. It is also significant that the Egyptian government itself, when seeking to advocate gender reforms, is keen to frame its calls as deriving from Islam and supported by Muslim scholars.[3] Interviews with activists in August 2010 have indicated that individual leaders feel that without framing ideas and agendas in terms of their conformity to Islam, they do not stand a chance of winning campaigns or constituency support. The extent to which this fundamental shift in engagement represents an ideological shift in personal belief systems is impossible to decipher. However, what is significant is that religious frameworks have become the 'natural' pathway of advocating for social change on gender matters.

The continued proliferation of donor funding for gender and development initiatives also spawned a number of important phenomena. First, the continued growth of the 'boutique', which encourages women activists to keep up with the latest development fads rather than the changes in needs on the ground, has further deepened the disconnect between the grassroots and the elites who run the organizations. Second, as large funds are earmarked for promoting gender equality by multilateral and bilateral donors, the national machineries become the new donor darlings. Vast amounts have been channelled for nation-wide programmes to implement services that more conventionally would have been offered by local NGOs. The implication has been that NGOs are not only competing with each other, but also with the national machineries for funds. Against this backdrop of the religionization and professionalization of women's activisms, the voices of those championing a feminist agenda have become increasingly marginalized, as I shall discuss below.

The limitations of voice as a proxy for feminist agency

There are several limitations to using voice as a proxy for agency, which in turn undermines its relevance to the discussion of activism. First, what is 'voiced' is not necessarily an articulation of the underlying agenda. For example, both the government and women NGO activists who use religious framing may often voice their agendas in terms of 'protecting the family', when in fact their underlying motive is the advancement of women's rights without giving the Islamist opposition an opportunity to attack them. Hence, an analysis of their agency in terms of the agendas they voice would be highly problematic, in that we do not know whether the use of religious framing is a matter of political pragmatism or ideological standpoint.

The assumption that voice can be equated with power is also misleading. Marnia Lazreg is critical of the association between women's voice and empowerment in postmodernist feminist thought. While Lazreg is specifically engaging with the idea that giving poor women voice is an act of empowerment, her critiques are also relevant to examining voice and activism. Lazreg suggests that to assume women's voice is empowering through their representation is 'a feminist romantic act of creationism' (Lazreg 2004).

The assumption that power is mediated through the expression of voice is reductionist, as actors may choose to exercise their agency in multiple ways, sometimes speaking out through voice, but sometimes deliberately withholding voice as a means of exercising their power not to participate, share or engage.

However, voice can also signify presence. And voice as an articulation of an idea or objection, even if marginalized or of minimal influence, is still of political importance. Voice as used here is contextually bound, time-bound and relational. In this chapter, feminist voice refers to the advocacy of a women's rights agenda which is by default secular because it uses universal human rights as its reference point. The use of feminist voice to refer to those who advocate an overtly feminist agenda does not preclude the possibility that other voices that express their agendas in terms of economic interests or religious framings can be feminist too. The significance of this feminist voice is in representing an alternative reading, approach and perspective on gender justice in a context where government, women NGOs and the Islamist opposition are often inclined to resort to religious framings to rationalize their positions. The very presence of feminist voice(s) manifest in the alternative vision it articulates is noteworthy, because the political and social odds against articulating such an agenda are so high.

In Egypt, most forms of female activism do not articulate a feminist voice as defined above. Feminist voice is expressed by a small group of women activists who tend to come from a professional background, work through NGOs, and are engaged in many struggles (against authoritarianism and a range of other social constraints). They have been active in launching advocacy campaigns to challenge gender-discriminatory practices such as sexual harassment and domestic violence. While they do not have a significant constituency to champion their causes, they have often been successful in ensuring that their voice is present in the media, and have succeeded in highlighting issues for debate amongst the public. There are both ideological and class ruptures behind the divisions between the minority secular feminist voices and the majority of women's activist voices. Ideological rifts have emerged between secular feminists who refuse to adopt a religious framework and women activists working through NGOs who have increasingly embraced a more conciliatory approach towards integrating 'progressive' religious discourses in their work. The dispute over whether to defend a leading religious authority in his decision to prohibit the use of the face veil (*niqab*) in school as symbolic of the growing power of conservative religion, or whether to oppose it on the premise of its denial of women's rights to choice is a case in point (see next section).

The nature of the interests that are being advocated, and on whose behalf claims are made, limits mobilization behind feminist voice. Feminist voice in the contemporary Egyptian context has generally focused on campaigning for strategic gender interests, 'those involving claims to transform social relations in order to enhance women's position and to secure a more lasting repositioning of women within the gender order and within society at large' (Molyneux 2003: 153). Examples include feminist critiques of gender stereotypes in education and the media. However, in practice, women workers and civil servants have organized around practical gender interests, 'those based on the satisfaction of needs arising from women's placement within the sexual division of labour' (*ibid.*). Rowbotham argues that there is a need to recognize that engaging with women's autonomy and gender relations cannot be abstracted from material circumstances (1992: 306). This reflects the dilemma facing those voicing a feminist agenda: intellectually, they are engaged with gender in relation to practical issues, however, in practice, the necessary links with a constituency that can lead on the advocacy campaigns and research work are absent. This disconnect between feminist activists and the wider female constituency is partly due to limitations on freedom of association, inexperience in engaging grassroots communities, and the elitist background of some of the activists. The following section further analyses the political constraints influencing the spaces in which women's activism occurs.

The visible and hidden regulation of women's activism

The political situation in Egypt is volatile, subject to both internal and external factors of influence. The authoritarian regime has come under pressure to democratize at various times (most recently during 2004–6 under the Bush administration's democracy promotion initiative in the Middle East) and has subsequently allowed controlled democratic spaces to emerge in order to maintain the status quo whilst appeasing calls for democratization. A variety of strategies are deployed in engaging with activisms. For example, a thriving independent press that has emerged in Egypt in the past five or six years has had to exercise a certain level of self-censorship. Yet, hand-in-hand with the tolerance of controlled democratic spaces has gone the continued use of repression by security forces and plain-clothes police.

The establishment of associations is highly controlled and is one of the most effective ways of inhibiting voice. Women NGOs, like other forms of NGOs registered with the government, are regulated by a highly restrictive NGO law overseen by the Ministry of Social Solidarity (formerly the Ministry of Social Affairs) (Tadros 2004). In addition to these formal powers, there is the real informal power exercised by the Ministry of Interior through its State Security Investigations apparatus, commonly referred to as the state security or domestic intelligence agency. Any organization, irrespective of its ideological orientation or mission, is surveyed by the state security.

In some cases, state security has openly blocked the activity of organizations, including feminist ones such as the New Woman Foundation, which has been active since the 1980s. Previously known as the New Woman Center and registered as a non-profit civil company in order to evade the NGO Law and the Ministry of Social Affairs' heavy-handed bureaucracy, it was eventually forced to apply for registration in conformity with the new Law 84, which prohibited non-profit organizations from registering under any other umbrella. When the New Woman Foundation submitted its registration papers to the Ministry of Social Solidarity, its application was rejected by state security on security grounds. It was closed for many months before the court ruled in its favour, and during this time its status was in limbo, forcing a rupture in communication with its stakeholders.

State Security Investigations has also intimidated individual women activists. Since the emergency law allows for citizens to be detained without charge, activists face the threat of being suddenly detained for unknown periods of time.

Both secular and Islamist women activists have an ambiguous relationship with the state apparatus. They find themselves compelled to negotiate engagement between their constituency and wider society with state security. However, the situation varies greatly from one activist, one organization, and one political moment to another. The level of compromise on the part of women's organizations and activists when dealing with state security is partly attributable to their own negotiating power (deriving from their social and political positioning).

Women mobilizing around bread and pay

Women activists of all political and ideological orientations are vulnerable to becoming a state security apparatus 'target' on account of being seen as threatening to the regime. Yet in spite of this highly repressive and unpredictable political environment, women are openly contesting government policies, organizing, mobilizing, and leading marches and demonstrations.

In the past decade, as part of the Mubarak government's strategy to appear to tolerate political opposition, some protests and demonstrations have been allowed within a highly securitized and controlled space. The key question is: who has been capitalizing on this controlled space to organize and mobilize people into open political forms of activism? Some women have participated in the emerging opposition groups (such as *Kefaya*! Enough!) and protested Mubarak's never-ending presidency and the possible succession of his son, Gamal Mubarak; yet their representation in leadership positions has been negligible. However, where we have witnessed strong women's leadership and participation en masse is by two groups of women organizing for two very different causes: women workers organizing around everyday issues; and women who belong to the Islamist movements.

By far the largest numbers of women engaging in collective political activism have been the women workers mobilizing around livelihood issues such as poor wages, delays or cancellation in bonuses and fringe benefits (already a substitute means of refusing or delaying the raising of salaries). These women are not organized within formal trade unions, given that they are government-controlled and often take a position against workers' rights; instead they mobilize around specific local contexts: a particular factory at risk of shedding labour as a consequence of privatization, a public-owned enterprise failing to give workers their wages for months on end. In response to the increasing deprivation and fall in the standard of living, women have been at the core of the groups who have organized protests, sit-ins and appeals for their rights. They have organized, however, not as women but as fellow workers and employees. They have assumed leadership positions, earned through the support of both men and women, to speak out against the injustices and negotiate with the ruling powers over the terms of any compromises reached. In doing so, they have broken many social taboos regarding the appropriate spaces for women to occupy as well as socially prescribed curfews on when to be at home (sleeping in tents on the streets and sleeping in factories during sit-ins).

In many cases, these women and their families have succeeded in arriving at deals that secure their rights. In December 2007, hundreds of property tax workers, a significant proportion of whom were women, staged a peaceful sit-in which lasted over 11 days. Finding it increasingly difficult to cope with the rising cost of living, they demanded fair pay commensurate with those of other workers on the Finance Ministry's payroll. Women brought their children and their belongings and set up tents in the streets of central downtown Cairo. The image of these white-collar women, some with their entire families, sitting in tents in some of the city's most vibrant streets elicited sympathy from the public and represented a major embarrassment to the Egyptian government. The negotiations that followed culminated in a 330 per cent increase in their pay. The success of this incident prompted many other groups to consider sit-ins and strikes as a means of making remuneration demands (*Al-Ahram Weekly* 2009).

Women activists participating in these contentious forms of politics organized others in their thousands and had a powerful influence on determining the outcome of the struggle to secure minimal economic and social rights from the government or the business owners in question. Their activism was not sustained after deals were reached, however, and so far has not been transformed into larger movements supporting further-reaching agendas. There are many possible explanations for this: one is that activists have found their campaigns more successful in eliciting public support and government interest when they are around a very specific set of concrete demands (rather than structural demands, such as freedom of association or expression). A second is that these activists are at a stage where livelihood concerns predominate and they neither feel ready nor wish to embark on larger, broader agendas. A third is that negotiating on pay and other compensations may be as far as state security will allow them to go.

Women mobilizing around Islamist ideology

The second group of women who have organized as activists are members of the Islamist movements in Egypt. By far the most populist of these movements is the Muslim Brotherhood, officially outlawed by the Egyptian government but in practice tolerated (albeit vulnerable to sporadic waves of violent repression involving their incarceration in large numbers). Women members of the Muslim Brotherhood have consistently expressed the party line, which has tended for the most part to be in defence of the Islamist political project and its activists in their broadest meanings.[4] The voice of these women activists is highly complex in relation to feminist voice and in relation to the government and wider society.

There has been an ideological struggle between Islamists, who see women's equality as achievable only in the context of a just Islamic state, and feminist activists who are critical of the Islamist view. On the street, the struggle has been won by the Islamists.[5] Politically, there is consensus on the Muslim Brotherhood's ideological positions on some issues, such as the necessity of veiling. Central to the Muslim Brotherhood women activists' strategic use of voice to mobilize has been their nation-wide access to mosques, which provide spaces where they can recruit and mobilize adherents. The mosque space is closed to secular feminists as long as they do not conform to ideas about religiously prescribed appropriate female behaviour, discourse and attire (this varies from one mosque to the next). Thus they are excluded from a key space for dialogue, mobilization and collective action with women who regularly visit the mosque.

The competition between the Muslim Brotherhood and the Egyptian government (as well as the ruling National Democratic Party) to show who is more committed to Islam adds another layer of complexity to interpreting the increasing Islamization of public life in Egypt in the past three decades. This complexity was brought to the fore recently through two incidents: in one the Minister of Culture openly criticized the veil; in the second, the Minister of Education prohibited the wearing of the *niqab* during examinations.[6] In the first incident in 2006, both the Muslim Brotherhood and the government took the same position in response to an off-guard statement made by the Minister of Culture about the veil. Both political forces, normally in opposition, were united in their call for the Minister's resignation. In the second incident, in 2009, the Minister of Education's position on the *niqab* drew open protest from the Muslim Brotherhood, while different elements in the Egyptian government voiced more subtle critiques. While both incidents are controversial, more significant is what the responses reveal about the pervasive political culture and the space allowed for deviant voices.

The first incident involved an unofficial conversation between Farouk Hosni, the Minister of Culture, and a female journalist, in which he spoke out against veiling and attributed its popularity in Egypt to the *Wahabi* Islamist influence. He also lamented that Egypt was going backwards compared to Bahrain and Qatar, where 'women are starting to remove the face veil, *niqab*, while in Egypt people are taking it up' (*Al Masry Al Youm* 2006a). Mr Hosni later insisted that the statements were an expression of his personal opinion and were not made in his official capacity. However, the resultant storm was sustained for weeks, with many female Muslim Brotherhood members participating in public protests, while in Parliament the Muslim Brotherhood led the campaign, with ruling National Democratic Party MPs chiming in, calling for Mr Hosni's resignation. This was presented as the only appropriate action to be taken in response to his inappropriate comments, which were interpreted as an attack on Islam itself (*Al Masry Al Youm* 2006b). In a context in which the overwhelming majority of Muslim women don the veil, the government statements struck a chord with public opinion.

The significance of the Muslim Brotherhood and government reactions was far-reaching for secular feminist activists and others who hold various ideological positions on women's veiling. It is noteworthy that Mr Hosni's statement was not made from the perspective of women's right to choose (not to wear the veil), but from the negative implications of the pervasiveness of an imported political Islam. Yet what is significant is the normative framework in which the discussions were taking place, one which ostracized voices that expressed alternative standpoints. Part of this normative framework was to pit veiled women as righteous against non-veiled women whose morals were questioned. Another important element of this normative framework was the presentation of religious dogma in absolutist terms, thus obstructing the possibility for engagement with multiple interpretations and perspectives on the position of Islam on veiling. What was clear was that conforming to mainstream conceptions of religion became the norm, and any deviation from this norm was increasingly met with opposition and hostility.

The second incident occurred in 2009 in response to a policy adopted by Sheikh Mohammed Tantawy, the head of Al-Azhar University, to ban students from wearing the *niqab* (face veil) in all-women classes tutored by an all-women faculty. Tantawy explained that the *niqab* is a habit and not a religious obligation (*ada*, not *'ebada*). A conversation between Tantawy and a preparatory female student wearing the *niqab*, in which he obliged her to remove the face veil, insisting that this was not required by Islam, was criticized as disrespectful. It is worth noting that there is complete gender segregation between students at all levels of education in Egypt. While the content of the conversation remains controversial in terms of interpretation, the Minister of Higher Education subsequently issued a policy banning women donning the *niqab* from university student accommodation. The anti-*niqab* stance catalyzed a series of protests and demonstrations by Muslim Brotherhood women activists on account of its violation of the right of freedom of attire. Feminist activists were divided. Some lauded the voice of moderate Islam expressed by Tantawy, while others asserted the right of choice.

Irrespective of how the incident is interpreted, the debates that followed showed the extent to which the prevailing social climate was constrained. Sheikh Safwat Hegazy, in a public address extolling the *niqab* wearers, compared them to those whom he criticized for immodest attire and labelled prostitutes. It is estimated that 17 per cent of Egyptian women wear the *niqab*, a trend that is believed to be on the rise. A recent study also suggests that it is mostly young women who opt for the *niqab* after frequenting certain mosques controlled by *salafi*[7] movements, which strongly encourage women to switch from wearing the headscarf to the 'legitimate form of veiling', namely the *niqab* (*Al Distour* newspaper, 1 July 2009). Socially, there is very little tolerance of views considered antithetical to prevailing interpretations of Islam. This is significant for feminist voices who choose to work outside this normative framework, and who find their positions being de-legitimized.

Women mobilizing through Quangos

In Egypt, the national women's machinery is constituted by the National Council for Women (NCW), a para-state entity established in 2000, answerable to the Prime Minister and presided over by the First Lady; and the National Council for Childhood and Motherhood (NCCM), established in 1988 and also led by the First Lady.

These organizations are a hybrid between a Quango (quasi-non-governmental organization) and a Gongo (government-organized non-governmental organization) (Fowler 1997). Institutionally, they typify Fowler's definition of a Quango, namely, a para-state body set up by government as an NGO, often to enable better conditions of service or create political distance. They enjoy the status of autonomous organizations and are neither considered part of the executive arm of the government nor accountable to any governmental ministry.

They have their own budgets, board and internal governance structure. However, in terms of function, national women's machineries serve as Gongos, since they are used to capture or redirect non-profit funds allocated by the official aid system. Both the NCCM and NCW have received extensive funding from foreign donors, which has increased their capacity to implement women's programmes on a national scale. There is some duplication of the work undertaken by women's NGOs and national machineries; however, many donors have chosen to channel funds via the latter because of their ability to implement programmes at a national level. The implications are that donors have strengthened the national machineries' visibility and claims of representation of the gender agenda in Egypt.[8]

If the Islamists' sphere of influence on gender issues is populist, the overriding influence on gender issues in the policy arena is claimed by the activism of women within or close to the regime's political entourage. Women who are affiliated to the national women's machineries tend to be able to exert direct influence on the policy-making process, whereas Muslim Brotherhood women activists and feminist voices have indirect influence at best. The national machineries' legitimacy derives from the political will of the ruling regime, which in turn allows them political proximity as well as political autonomy.

The increasing visibility of the national machineries (based on their claims to represent Egyptian women's needs) and the expansion of their role in policy work and development contributes to making gender equality issues more explicit in the public domain. Yet it has also meant appropriating feminist voices in civil society.

Like national women's machineries elsewhere, the NCW and NCCM are not homogeneous institutions; they encompass actors who represent the voices of feminists and other committed activists, as well as apolitical government bureaucrats. Thus the exercise of their agency is not singular and the relationships forged are very diverse.

Yet by and large, women's machineries' internal governance

structures leave very little room for the inclusion of feminist voices from within civil society. The nature of the leadership is heavily influenced by the will of the First Lady and the Secretary-General (whom the First Lady appoints). In the case of the NCW, the First Lady has the mandate to appoint one third of the board of members and change them every three years, while the Secretary-General has the mandate to appoint all 27 heads of branches. A significant number of those occupying governance positions are also members of the ruling National Democratic Party, and the machineries are accountable directly to the Prime Minister, which limits the potential to influence them given the absence of downward accountability.

Moreover, national machineries capitalize on their political proximity to the 'powers that be' to effect change on gender issues, thereby transforming policies and decrees, without trans-forming the closed channels through which change is affected. By the nature of this policy arena, national machineries are better positioned than most NGOs to influence the majority national democratic party, and have access to government-controlled public media. Yet the focus on influencing the policy-making arena has meant that little attention is paid to the process of creating consensus around the policy (who participated, whose voice, whose agenda?) or the impact of the policy on more marginalized groups.

In authoritarian regimes where the policy-making arena is restricted to a closed circle of elites, political openings for the wider citizenry to influence policy sometimes do exist, but they are few and far between.[9] In effect, most policy reforms in Egypt have been achieved without widespread participation from those on whose behalf reforms are being made. In 2001 for example, the ministerial decree which prohibited women from giving their nationality to their children (commonly referred to as the nationality law) was changed, largely through the efforts of a few key organizations and activists who were able to influence public opinion and reach out to policy makers. They used case studies of women whose children's rights were denied as a consequence of the existing law, but these were used to support their campaign rather than lead it.

Consequently, the greater the access feminists have to the circle of highly connected people affiliated to the national machineries, the greater the potential for influence. For feminists this poses a dilemma. On the one hand, if they want to influence the government strategically, engaging with senior members within the national machineries may be an effective way of acquiring political buy-in for the cause being advocated. Some feminists have found this productive, especially in terms of the visibility and impact of events done in partnership with national machineries or under the auspices of the First Lady. For these feminists, what is most important is to effect change on the ground. If it means partnering with national women's machineries, so be it. On the other hand, some feminists have found that the long-term impact of such a strategy is the appropriation of their demands and struggles.

While national machineries do play a highly influential role in eliciting legislative reform, they often claim sole credit for policy changes. The decades-long contribution of civil society organizations in documenting women's problems, raising consciousness on the implications of discriminatory structures, and transforming cases of injustice into public opinion issues does not feature in the official narrative of how change happened. In her assessment of the national machineries of Egypt, Khafagy notes that 'the NWM in Egypt succeeded, through lobbying with the Parliament, to change the nationality law, the pension law, the tax exemption law, the alimony fund law and introduce the khul' law and the family court law' (Khafagy 2007: 8). Extensive lobbying by women NGOs and activists to elicit change, and their role in publicizing gender issues and getting them debated, is not acknowledged. In the case of the nationality law, when Parliament discussed the change to the ministerial decree, MPs made no mention of the role of civil activism – many years of lobbying by women's NGOs and feminist activists – in bringing this change to the table. Rather, one MP after another stood up to thank the First Lady for her benevolence towards Egyptian women.

In authoritarian contexts where, in order to strengthen the regime, governments wish to appear as benevolent patrons who change policy in response to their recognition of the people's needs, there is a further disincentive to recognize the role of civil society organizations. Hence, who can claim policy change as an outcome of their role becomes highly problematic where different parties are involved in adversarial rather than backdoor forms of advocacy.

Similarly, the NCCM claimed to be the principal force behind criminalizing female genital mutilation (FGM) in 2008 under the rubric of the child law, which ingenuously provided the appropriate framing to minimize opposition (likely to occur when anything is framed under women's or human rights). While the NCCM was the one to negotiate with the powers that be and push the law forward in Parliament, it was really thanks to the earlier work of feminist and women activists that the issue was brought to the fore – among the first contributions being the advocacy efforts of prominent (secular) feminist Nawal el Saadawi, as well as the sustained work of the FGM Taskforce (a coalition of NGOs and activists led by veteran feminist, grassroots activist and development worker Marie Assaad). This pathbreaking work introduced appropriate ways of engaging on the issue to elicit culturally sensitive social change on the ground, as well as encouraging public debate on religious and health perspectives.

When Nawal el Saadawi was asked recently about the promulgation of the new legislation against FGM, she said that the law came as a consequence of struggles by the Egyptian population of which she had been a part. She suffered a great deal as a result of her participation – losing her job and her reputation, and being castigated by religious men and doctors for campaigning on the issue. However, when the law was finally issued, her contribution was ignored and she wasn't mentioned. Instead the recognition for the achievement went to Suzanne Mubarak as First Lady.

The political significance of who gets credit is not about who gets gratitude but whose contributions are seen as worthy of recognition and therefore political influence. As the national machineries become increasingly hegemonic in claiming to represent Egyptian women's interests, feminist activists' contribution to civil society is increasingly downplayed, and in this way their voices are marginalized.

Conclusion

This chapter sought to examine the predicament of a feminist voice that articulates a women's rights agenda in contemporary Egypt within the current socio-political context and historical trajectory. The choice of examining who, how and why this agenda is being vocalized was not based on the size of its constituency, its 'newness' or its political weight and ability to influence. In terms of collective strength, women members of the Islamist movements outnumber by far the small number of organizations and women who express a feminist voice. Also, women workers and civil servants represent the largest collective mobilization of women (as well as the newest) that Egypt has witnessed in half a century. The increasing religionization of the work of women's NGOs that were conventionally secular also represents a relatively new phenomenon that is worthy of its own focus and study. As for the two bodies that made up the national women's machinery, they could justifiably claim to yield the most significant political weight and ability to influence policy agendas – led as they were by the First Lady, with proximity to decision makers in government.

Accordingly, on the surface the study of feminist voice as it has been defined here may appear to divert attention from other more prominent voices that are neither secular nor necessarily championing gender strategic interests. Admittedly, the secular feminist voice is politically marginal and is not propped up by a strong constituency. However, it is the very marginalization of the secular, feminist, agenda in particular in the past ten years that is in and of itself politically very significant. The fact that the women's NGOs that are now increasingly turning to religious frameworks to work with the masses and connect with policy makers are the very same organizations who ten years ago engaged through a human rights framework testifies to the installation of religion as the normative route to change. Their strategic choice of engagement through religious framings is a direct consequence of the increasing Islamization of politics and culture, a phenomenon that has been supported both by the Islamist movements and by governments. In such a context, while adherence to a secular, human rights framework may appear to some to be a misguided strategy, its importance lies in its articulation of a counter-hegemonic narrative.

Feminist voices have expressed alternative agendas to the predominantly religious-inspired ones in a context where multiple limitations are placed on feminist organizing, mobilization and advocacy. The manipulation of political space by the state security apparatus, alongside the co-option of the gender agenda by elites in close collaboration with the government, have contributed to a disabling environment. Concurrently, the increasing salience of Islamist women's 'voices' indicates women's increased articulation of their beliefs. However, such voices ultimately serve to undermine women's empowerment, as they deny one of its fundamental tenets: the freedom of choice, and the right to exercise it to contest and oppose religious ideology. It is not that they voice a particular ideological agenda, but that – as their protests against the Minister of Culture's views on veiling suggest – they see their agenda as the only possible and legitimate one for society at large. It is in this context that feminist presence and articulation of alternative agendas and frameworks demonstrate that, against all odds, they continue to be a voice that refuses silence.

Postscript (written 1 September 2013)

Egypt has been in the throes of tumultuous political change, having witnessed two regime overthrows in the space of thirty months (President Mubarak's nearly thirty-year reign ended in January 2011, and President Morsi's one-year tenure on 30 June 2013). During those thirty months, Egypt witnessed two important phenomena: a regression in its commitment to gender equality in public policy, and the surge of resistance against the violation of women's rights through women-led protests that can only be paralleled in scope with the uprisings against British colonialist rule in 1919, almost a hundred years earlier.

The political restrictions inhibiting feminist activism during Mubarak's era certainly undermined outreach opportunities, particularly as state security officers and their informants shadowed activists wherever they went. However, with political restrictions out of the way after the demise of Mubarak's regime, feminist organizations in Egypt faced a major challenge in building a constituency. The absence of a constituency among the poor, the working class or even the middle class could be explained earlier as a consequence of authoritarianism, but after Mubarak feminists came under even greater pressure to demonstrate a support base committed to their cause, or at the very least testifying to the legitimacy of speaking on their behalf. In order to make up for the absence of a political constituency that provides sustained support for gender equality, feminist activists forged alliances and coalitions with youth revolutionary movements and newly formed political parties. Such alliance building made a difference to their mobilizational power: whereas in 2011 the number of citizens who participated in the stand-in in Tahrir Square to mark International Women's Day on 8 March was dismal, the numbers were dramatically higher on the same occasion the year after, when youth revolutionary coalitions and non-Islamist political parties joined forces.

The context in which feminist activists strive in post-Mubarak Egypt is a vicious and systematic backlash against women. This backlash has been led by several actors. By far the most insidious attacks have come from the Islamists, in particular the Muslim Brotherhood and the ultra-radical Salafi movement. The Islamization of public life described in this chapter provides some insight into the Islamists' ability to mobilize people in the name of defending Islam (for practical examples see Tadros 2012c). While the Islamist groups would have launched an attack on laws favouring women's rights irrespective of who instituted them, the fact that Suzanne Mubarak, head of the National Council for Women in Egypt, was the principal instigator certainly gave those opposed to women's emancipation the opportunity to mobilize – not around the content of the laws, but on their very association with a much-loathed figure. This raises important policy implications for women's rights advocates who choose to play by the rules of the games instituted by authoritarian regimes – seeking the support of First Ladies, or their equivalents, without having any constituency or alliances to support their campaigns. It also sounds alarm bells for international donors who choose to support the national women's machineries of undemocratic regimes on the premise that they can use their political proximity to the powers that be to elicit policy change. Once those in power are removed, the legitimacy of their causes comes into question.

The great backlash against women's rights during Egypt's transition has been led not only by the Islamists, but also by the interim government. Musharraf's government responded to reactionary voices to have the Family Law reviewed, and revoked the Quota Law allocating women 64 seats in Egypt's 544 seat parliament – leading to a drop in women's parliamentary representation from 13 per cent in 2010 to 2 per cent in 2011 (Tadros 2012a). Women's representation in the 100-member constituent assembly formed to write Egypt's new constitution comprised no more than 6 per cent. Most of these women constituent members had no record of promoting gender justice. The constitution approved in 2012 included new articles that potentially could be used to curb women's rights in both the public and private sphere (Tadros 2012b). A high-ranking official within the Ministry of Population mentioned that they had been given instructions to disband their campaign against female genital mutilation (which had achieved success among Egypt's rural communities) immediately, and put a halt to the family planning awareness efforts and anti-smoking campaign. While ceasing the first two campaigns could be interpreted as acquiescence to some of the more radical Islamist agendas, the latter, on smoking, is driven by a desire not to 'antagonize' the Egyptian population at a time when it is going through extreme socio-economic hardship.

The uprising that Egypt witnessed on 30 June 2013 against President Morsi's government was far greater than the tumult the country experienced two years earlier against President Mubarak. The proportion of women who joined in the 30 June revolt in 2013 was higher than in 2011; they also enjoyed greater diversity (more working-class women, women from Upper Egypt and women from rural areas) (Tadros 2013a). Having learnt from the first uprising that participation in revolutions does not translate into power sharing, feminist activists immediately mobilized to influence the policies of the new interim government formed in the aftermath of the demise of Morsi's regime. The extent to which feminist attempts to build alliances and coalitions will translate into a reconfiguration of power in the formal political sphere remains to be seen, as does the existence of a political will to pursue an inclusive democracy that involves the representation of women, youth and religious minorities, and entails the adoption of gender-just agendas. What is certain is that street politics will continue to play a key role in this revolutionary phase in the country's history – it has already spawned gender-just movements comprised of men and women who advocate for a more humane society that is free from sexual harassment and encroachment on women in public space (Tadros 2013b). Whether there will be a reconciliation of the women's agenda setting from above with gender justice movements from below will in part depend on the kind of political order that will unfold in the years to come. The signals three months after the 30 June uprising are mixed. On the one hand the composition of the constituent assembly entrusted with the task of arriving at a new constitution for Egypt is far more gender-friendly; it includes some women and men who have track records of championing social and gender justice. On the other hand, the representation of women in the 50 member constituent assembly is only 10 per cent, which represents an insignificant improvement on the women's representation in the 100-member constituent assembly under the Muslim Brothers (7 per cent, though in that case the ideological disposition was mostly anti-women's rights).

However, the meagre representation of women in the constituent assembly formed after 30 June attests to a disturbing reality that we have witnessed over and over again globally every time a regime is overturned through people power: women's participation in revolutions does not translate into power sharing in the new political order. Living in the shadows of the Brothers certainly blocked the path to gender justice, but their overthrow does not automatically pave the way for an inclusive, socially just political order.

Acknowledgements

I am deeply indebted to Professor Deniz Kandiyoti for the very constructive feedback to an earlier draft of this paper, as well as the very useful comments provided by Sohela Nazneen, Maheen Sultan and participants at the Bellagio workshop in November 2009. All disclaimers apply.

Notes

1 There are some excellent historical books about the Egyptian women's movement, including Ahmed (1992), Badran (1995), Karam (1998) and Al-Ali (2000).
2 I am grateful to Akram Habib for coining the word, in reference to individuals who have established organizations primarily for self-profit, under the guise of NGOs.
3 For example, in 2000, on introducing *Khul,* the government was keen to emphasize that it was advancing this as part of its commitment to the implementation of the Shari'a, rather than advancing gender equality (see Al-Sharmani 2009).
4 For example, Muslim Brotherhood women activists participated in their thousands in the protests against the Israeli strikes on Gaza. Such protests were driven by a political and ideological commitment on

the part of the Muslim Brotherhood to liberate the Muslim Ummah (in Palestine) from occupation.

5   For an excellent summary of the increasing Islamization of public space and of Egyptians, as well as the rise of the more fundamentalist Salafi movement in the past five years, see Rashwan (2009).

6   Please note that these debates must not be 'read' in the same light as those taking place in France, which are clearly racist and Islamophobic (from the author's point of view). In Egypt, the government has been implicitly endorsing the Islamization of public space for at least four decades, including the active promotion of veiling. Hence, the historical-cultural-political context is very different.

7   The literal meaning of *salafi* is someone or something that can be attributed to salaf, followers of a movement that take as their model the early followers of Sunni Islam. However, politically, the term is used to refer to a conservative Sunni movement that promotes a traditional Islam, often rejecting many of the modernist elements of Muslims' lives.

8   At the time of writing (2009–10) it was also noticed that some of the most significant decision makers working for funding agencies also happened to be occupying various ranks within the ruling party or NCW hierarchy.

9   The alternative is for activists to seek international pressure to be put on national government, which is an important strategy, but which makes its initiators vulnerable to attacks questioning their allegiance.

References

Ahmed, L. (1992) *Women and Gender in Islam: Historical Roots of a Modern Debate*, Yale University Press, New Haven, CT and London.

Al-Ahram Weekly (2009) 'Dena Rashed: Strike for Now', features pages, 9–15 April, p. 942.

Al-Ali, N. (2000) *Secularism, Gender and the State in the Middle East*, Cambridge University Press, Cambridge.

Al Masry Al Youm (2006a) 'Hosni: Veiling is a Return Backwards … and We Are Now Listening to *Fatwas* Worth Three Millions', Fatheya al Dakhany, 16 November, front page.

—— (2006b) 'The Brotherhood Call upon the President to Remove Farouk Hosny', 18 November.

Al-Sharmani, M. (2009) 'Egyptian Family Courts: A Pathway of Women's Empowerment?', *Hawwa*, Vol. 7, No. 2, pp. 89–119.

Badran, M. (1995) *Feminists, Islam, and Nation: Gender and the Making of Modern Egypt*, Princeton University Press, Princeton, NJ.

Fowler, A. (1997) *Striking a Balance*, Earthscan, London.

Hatem, M. (1986) 'The Enduring Alliance of Nationalism and Patriarchy in Muslim Personal Status Laws: The Case of Modern Egypt', *Feminist Issues*, Vol. 6, No. 1, pp. 19–43.

Karam, A. (1997) 'Women, Islamisms and the State', in M. Afkhami and E. Friedl (eds), *Muslim Women and the Politics of Participation*, Syracuse University, Syracuse, NY.

—— (1998) *Women, Islamisms and State: Contemporary Feminisms in Egypt*, Macmillan and St Martin's Press, London and New York, NY.

Khafagy. F. (2007) 'Assessment of National Machineries in Egypt', Euromed Role of Women in Economic Life Programme, Cairo.

Lazreg, M. (2004) 'Development: Feminist Theory's Cul-de-Sac', in K. Saunders (ed.), *Feminist Post-Development Thought: Rethinking Modernity, Post-Colonialism and Representation*, Zed Books, London.

Molyneux, M. (2003) *Women's Movements in International Perspective: Latin America and Beyond*, Institute of Latin American Studies, London.

Rashwan, D. (2009) 'On Features of the Islamist Phenomenon in Egypt', *Al-Shorouk*, 17 November, www.shorouknews.com/Columns/Column. aspx?id=155466 (accessed 2 February 2009).

Rowbotham, S. (1992) *Women in Movement: Feminism and Social Action*, Routledge, London.

Tadros, M. (2004) 'Food for Faith Welfare Provision in a Poor Urban Settlement of Cairo', Unpublished PhD thesis, University of Oxford.

—— (2012a) 'Bringing Gender Justice to the Egyptian Parliament', *In Focus* Policy Brief, Institute of Development Studies, Brighton, http:// www.ids.ac.uk/publication/bringing-gender-justice-to-the-egyptian- parliament.

—— (2012b) 'The Islamization of State Policy', *Open Democracy*, 8 January 2013, http://www.opendemocracy.net/5050/mariz-tadros/egypt- islamization-of-state-policy.

—— (2012c) 'Egyptian Women Have Had Enough of Being Told to Cover Up', 29 May 2012, *The Guardian*, http://www.guardian.co.uk/ commentisfree/2012/may/29/egypt-women-cover-up-coptic.

—— (2013a) 'Understanding the Politics and the Pulse of Egypt's Protests', Institute of Development Studies, Brighton, http://www.ids.ac.uk/ news/understanding-the-politics-and-pulse-of-egypt-s-protests.

—— (2013b) 'Real Time Insights into Gender Based Violence in Egypt', Institute of Development Studies, Brighton, http://www.ids.ac.uk/ news/real-time-insights-into-gender-based-violence-in-egypt.

Viterna, J. and K. Fallon (2008) 'Democratization, Women's Movements and Gender-Equitable States: A Framework for Comparison', *American Sociological Review*, Vol. 73 (August), pp. 668–89.

Waylen, G. (1994) 'Women and Democratization, Conceptualizing Gender Relations in Transition Politics', *World Politics*, Vol. 46, No. 3, pp. 327–54.

Zulu, L. (2000) 'South African Women's Participation in the Transition', in S. Rai (ed.), *International Perspectives on Gender and Democratisation*, Macmillan Press, Basingstoke.

7

The Many Faces of Feminism

Palestinian Women's Movements Finding a Voice

Eileen Kuttab

This chapter is not only a scholarly attempt to understand the different expressions of women's voice in Occupied Palestine, but also the record of an activist from inside the movement who has engaged with and participated in its different stages and who offers here some critical observations and conclusions that need to be shared with feminists and the current and future women's leadership. Understanding the transformation that took place in the women's movement and reflecting on the lessons learnt is an important task, because it contextualizes and theorizes women's experience and voice under colonial occupation.

Palestinian women's voices have been presented mostly by women outside the movement – researchers from local or international communities – or by men who have interpreted women's activism through their own interests and instrumentalist framework. Rarely have women activists conveyed their own experiences directly to wider audiences. This chapter aims to reclaim this space for activist voices in the hope of reflecting a genuine but critical view of women's activism – one which is often misrepresented or misinterpreted by those outside the experience. Although it reflects the power of the women's movement in Palestine in resisting the colonial occupation, the chapter also clarifies the transformation of the women's movements' agenda and focus in different political periods – changing from purely and primarily resisting occupation and addressing gender only partially and in terms of practical needs, to a movement that has prioritized gender equity by challenging discrimination against women while marginalizing national resistance. I also explore the volatile encounters between popular women's organizations and professional women's NGOs, noting the interactions and complex ties between the two movements in terms of relations between the global and the local, as well as conflicting secular and religious or fundamental perspectives in the broad context of class and gender analysis. Finally, I address the divisive factors and risks to the women's movement in the light of changing political realities.

Context: positioning the Palestinian women's movement

Reflecting on the work of scholars and feminists, particularly from Latin America and South Asia, represents a turning point in terms of situating and positioning women's movements on the map of international feminist scholarship. Although most of the existing literature on women's movements has focused on experiences from West Europe and the United States (Ray and Korteweg 1999), scholarly work on women's movements in the South, particularly the Middle East, and especially during the 1980s and 1990s, has revealed the power of the women's movements and encouraged further research from international and local scholars, enhancing the development of transnational comparative work (*ibid.*).

The growing activism amongst Arab women at the political and scholarly level also helped to conceptualize and bring to light the uniqueness of women's national and political activism in the region. An alternative image of women was highlighted that contested the stereotypical representation of Arab women as oppressed, passive, recipients of international aid – subjugated by their patriarchal culture and traditions. Conversely, Arab women were now seen as active agents of change and advocates of women's rights. Jayawardena's (1986) pioneering work, as a leading feminist and academic, focused on Third World feminism(s), and conceptualized the various incarnations of the movement as indigenous and unique to non-Western societies, rather than mere offshoots of Western feminism(s). Her work revealed the fact that women's movements in the South needed to be understood in the context of colonialism and national liberation struggles, as in the Palestinian context.

Mohanty's important critique (1991) of the Western feminist view, reflecting the stereotypical image of Middle Eastern women, reinforces the new alternative image (Ray and Korteweg 1999). She argues against the distorted image of women from the South by explaining that women were seen 'as not agents of their own destiny, but as victims', also as 'average Third World wom[e]n who essentially led curtailed lives, sexually constrained because of their gender; and labelled as "Third World" reflecting an image of ignorance, poverty, illiteracy, lack of education, tradition, domesticity and victimisation' (Mohanty 1991: 56). This image contradicts the reality of women from the South, who have a long heritage of participation in resistance (Ray and Korteweg 1999; Basu 1995), and have transformed their roles according to the course and requirements of the political and social context of the national struggle. In these experiences, women's roles have varied from participating in the national liberation struggles, democratizing authoritarian regimes, and addressing gender inequalities and human rights violations, a role that has linked them to national and social struggles.

Recent writings of scholars from the South have shed light on the circumstances that initiated the creation and development of the women's movements, showing that women's agency was generated in response to their own political and national contexts and addresses problems and issues relevant to their own conditions (Basu 2010; Fleischmann 2003; Jad 2000; Kuttab 1993; Jayawardena 1986). This work disproves the hypothesis that they were 'mechanical' products of external factors such as modernization or development programmes and projects. Although these movements were struggles against colonial oppression, they focused on gender equality and social justice, made claims for political and economic rights based on a critique of gender-based violence, and asserted gender identity (Basu 1995; Alvarez *et al.* 1988; Jayawardena 1986). These issues reflect the *necessity* to ensure a link between social emancipation and the national liberation struggles, and an *opportunity* to influence the processes of change dynamically. The discussion below highlights the various aspects of the Palestinian women's movement over time.

Internal and external factors marginalizing women

The emergence of the Palestinian Women's movement within the national struggle, since the beginning of the twentieth century, has extended women's experiences in the public sphere and expanded their political and social space (Fleischmann 2003; Jad 2000; Kuttab 1996, 1988). These experiences promoted a kind of consciousness that linked national liberation to social emancipation and provided an opening for women to raise their voices and challenge the social and political setting. Sayigh (1988) recognized that the contradictions between women's mobilization for national struggles and the failure to recognize socio-cultural constraints − which were structural obstacles that bound them to limited kinds of action within the struggle − had become more pronounced over time. This recognition has motivated and justified the inclusion of a clearer gender agenda over the past two decades to address socio-cultural challenges from within, and to expose the overlapping components of resistance against colonial occupation and patriarchy, in the form of gender discrimination and class exploitation.

While some aspects of gender discrimination have come to the forefront, the recognition of class conflict has been continuously undermined and subdued in the different stages of the Palestinian struggle, reflecting the inevitability of elements like 'national unity' and social cohesion in facing the Israeli occupation (Kuttab 1999). Subsequently, as the issues of class and gender became more pronounced, they emerged as divisive elements of the resistance, especially within the so-called 'state-building' or Oslo

Agreement[1] process – which eventually undermined collective solidarity and substituted it with an individualistic ethos in the make-believe 'state-building' stage as participants sought to position themselves within the new reality.

On another level, the Israeli policy of mobility restrictions and siege, combined with the construction of the 'Apartheid Wall', have resulted in physical segregation and community fragmentation, separating different villages and households and isolating women further at the social and political level, reframing their role within fixed 'humanitarian' parameters, and hijacking their agency and voice[2] (World Bank 2010).

By accepting a gendered electoral system designed to undermine political pluralism and gender, the Palestinian Authority (PA) has further entrenched traditional structures like the extended family and regional affiliation that further limit the representation of women through the legislative (parliamentary) elections. The minimal number of women elected to the legislative council in 2006 reflected their marginal position within both the family and the political party. Historically they are positioned at the bottom of the social and political pyramid, unrecognized as political actors and barely registered on the overall political map.

The few women candidates who were elected to the Parliament were neither the result of a general political commitment to gender equity nor an appreciative sign of women's active role in the national struggle. The endorsement of gender equity by the Central Election Committee in 2005 included a mandatory clause within the election legislation that the first woman candidate's name should be placed amongst the first three names on the electoral list, whilst if there were other women candidates in the list these should be listed consecutively along with the names of male candidates (a 'zipper' system) to ensure women's representation. However, even with these electoral procedures and despite the achievement of women's quota (the bare minimum) in the 2006 elections – a result of women's struggle for greater representation as a transitional option and an expression of affirmative action – it has been difficult to attain a proportionate number of women representatives. The explanation lies in the patriarchal and hierarchical structure of the society at large, including the political parties.

Women were further marginalized as a consequence of the current internal political conflict between the Fateh movement representing the PA and the Islamic movement (Hamas), who won the 2006 legislative council elections. The conflicting political interests of the parties destabilized the coherence and harmony within the community, and threatened the continuity of the struggle against colonial occupation. This was a blow to the social and political safety net, and the absence of a coordinating will among women, who were divided on political lines, narrowed the political space for institutionalizing women's voice. The political parties continued to frame women's role within the 'protectors of society' and 'preservers of family' parameters, rather than seeking to view them as equal partners in the political process. Even the democratic parties of the left, which historically played an important role in democratizing the national movement in the 1980s, failed to unite or to create an alternative political space where people's aspirations, and women's interests and voice, could be protected.

The transformation of the Palestinian women's movement

Since the beginning of the last century, Palestinian women's activism has been influenced by its relation to, and identification with, the national resistance (Kuttab 1993; Jad 2000). Here I offer a historical analysis that examines the shifts and transformation of the movement from the more revolutionary democratic phase to the more globalized, state-building stage.

The late 1970s, a democratic transformation phase from a central urban-based women's movement to more decentralized mass-based committees reaching rural areas and refugee camps, were a step towards embracing gender and class concerns within the national liberation struggle. Initiated and led by the educated middle- and lower-middle-class women, the new mass-based committees adopted a form of participatory democracy that created new channels for representing an alternative women's voice reflecting the interests of poorer and vulnerable women. This new voice was more radical, unlike the traditional voice of charitable organizations in urban centres, which followed a relief-and-welfare approach to service provision. The women's committees gave the majority of women a direct voice in matters that affected their lives, making their agendas and programmes more responsive, relevant and sensitive to women's priorities and needs (Johnson and Kuttab 2001; Kuttab 1993). Looking back at entries in the historical diary of that period one enters a golden age of women's activism, one which succeeded in building a democratic culture with democratic tools and tactics. Spaces for expression were expanded, the interests of ordinary women were prioritized, and strategies for coping with everyday conflict and crisis were enhanced, thus enlarging women's public roles (Kuttab 1993, 1990; Taraki 1991; Hiltermann 1991).

Although these changes brought women's role to the centre of the national struggle (Davis 1997; Jayawardena 1986), the temporary social space that they struggled for has also exposed the gender limitations. Gender equality and women's voice are not mechanical outcomes of participation in the struggle, as clarified in other experiences from the South (Kuttab 1993; Jayawardena 1986). They represent an entry point to a process that enhances and legitimizes women's public role and voice. For such a voice to become powerful, prerequisites must be satisfied – like having enough time, continuous effort, and an increase of freedom for social mobility with less familial control.

National roles expanding new social spaces

Although the first uprising of 1987[3] was a consequence of continuous national resistance and democratic struggle over many years, the leadership representing different sectors like women, youth and workers created a social and political space in which women could be heard and engage. Obviously enough, when resistance becomes comprehensive and engages all sectors of the society, women's roles expand and their voice is represented.

Positive changes, in terms of attitudes towards women, women's activists, and their social positions become a reality if resistance continues.

Palestinian women played different roles in the struggle, ranging from being members of the united national leadership that guided the *Intifada* (uprising), to being political party members, community leaders, development practitioners and leaders of popular committees. These roles overlapped with their continuing roles as mothers, sisters, wives of a militant or prisoner, and at times heads of households. The public–private dichotomy, therefore, dissolved as women engaged in the struggle. Resistance was reflected in social attitudes. For example, the family's position towards marriage, choice of partner, and bride price (once an obstacle to marriage) has changed. The *Intifada* period witnessed young and mixed marriages across religions and classes, a decrease in bride price, and unconventional marriages with limited ceremonies. However, this is not to say that the new practices were permanent, or have become rooted in the social system, or even had an impact on legal and religious formulations. Although women's roles changed significantly within the *Intifada*, the struggle was aborted long before it could lead to any structural and long-lasting change. Evidence from other developing countries shows that women's active involvement in national liberation struggles does not usually culminate in any fundamental transformation of women's social status, or their fuller integration in national political systems after independence (Jamal 2001). As the *Intifada* did not continue long enough to make any permanent change, many positive social practices did not last. Instability opens opportunities for women to introduce changes to their lives and to their communities (Jayawardena 1986), but these cease as countries become stable. Political stability enforces gender power relations that institutionalize women's marginalization. The question to be examined is how can changes become permanent, and what tools or dynamics are needed to make them so?

During national liberation struggles in the South, according to Jayawardena (1986) and Basu (2010), patriarchal control, exerted either by the colonial power or by the national regime, is weakened. However, deep-rooted conventions, traditions and values in a society cannot be shaken simply by women's participation in a liberation struggle – even if it is on a wide scale – especially if participation is periodic or limited, and is not embedded in an emerging social and political system. Although Palestinian women have always participated in the struggle against colonialism, the intensity and the seasonal nature of participation did not succeed in engendering a revolutionary political system, and hence did not bring any significant changes for women (Jamal 2001). The new political system that resulted has continued to be traditional, patriarchal and authoritarian; and continued to undermine women.

The second uprising – *Al Aqsa Intifada* – in 2000, being more militarized, exaggerated gender biases and affected further the gender dynamics. Women's popular and informal roles within the struggle were hijacked, and women's positions and roles in public life threatened (Johnson and Kuttab 2001). In this context two observations are of relevance: first, when power is institutionalized by a state or national movement, and there is an absence of gender equality as it is not internalized theoretically and practically by the constitution, women end up marginalized and their roles in political processes are weakened. This was the case in Algeria, where women engaged in the national liberation struggle against French colonialism but lost their voice and space after liberation had been achieved. Women's economic opportunities and social space in the form of *rights* and *entitlements*, achieved as a result of their active participation in the struggle, no longer get considered (Malley 1996; Gallagher 2002). Second, when resistance takes the form of military action, the colonial state's aggression escalates, and women become the scapegoats, as they lose their space and voice and most frequently go back to traditional roles in the domestic sphere or in the welfare and humanitarian spheres, which disempowers them further.

Obstacles to advancing women's demands

In addition to the impact of colonial occupation on women's livelihoods, discussed above, other internal elements played a role in blocking the enhancement of women.

The Islamic movement

The rise of the Islamic movement (Hamas) in the late 1980s was an important factor that weakened women's voice and limited its activity in the struggle. At the peak of the first *Intifada,* Hamas imposed the veil on women by force, which consequently weakened the scope of women's participation in public and political life. As Hammami (1990) observed, Hamas's active role in the first *Intifada* combined with their practice of enforcing the veil (aimed at separating men and women), negatively affected women's roles and position in political and public life. Hamas's practice of controlling women in the streets, through threat and intimidation, weakened their visibility, participation and continuity in the struggle. This period was a turning point in the women's movement's history and culture of resistance, as it affected its strategic approach and nature of engagement, and left a long-lasting influence.

The secular forces

The post-Oslo period saw the takeover of the mainstream party (Fateh) and the emergence of a new political culture that focused on peace negotiations instead of resistance as the only realistic option for liberation. The weakening of the *Intifada* resulted in the failure to promote a powerful political dialogue. Resistance not only declined but changed its course, weakening women's active role and voice. Forced to cope with the social pressures exerted by the imposition of the veil, at the same time as the political pressure of the new culture of peace that undermined resistance, women's roles were destabilized. This prepared the stage for some women activists to withdraw from the national struggle, citing the weakness of the secular forces that compromised women's claims and prioritized the national struggle over the social. In 1991, a few years into the first *Intifada,* a conference held in East Jerusalem by the Women Studies Committee of Bisan Center for Research and Development addressed social issues precipitated by political conditions. The conference aimed to contextualize and legitimize the integration of 'social issues' in the national agenda. Although the goal was to ensure that women's issues were legitimately adopted at the national level and gender interests promoted within the national struggle, the conference was also a demand by women engaged in popular struggle for continuous support to safeguard the women's movement's democratic achievements (Bisan 1991).

Although this period brought a new wave of women's agency, where social and national issues became more linked, women activists also felt apprehension regarding the national movement's position towards social issues, justified by the national leadership as an attempt to prevent divisions among people or a political internal conflict. Thus they asked women to wear the veil to facilitate their mobility and make their participation in the struggle more feasible – a compromise that women neither appreciated nor accepted. It semed to them that declarations on gender equality had been betrayed, and that women's issues had been relegated to a secondary level compared to the national interest. At the same time, the mainstream party (Fateh), which had become the main political player, was asking them to play along with a compromise on gender issues, so as to strike the balance it was seeking with the rival Islamic movement.

Other social and political issues such as early marriage, school drop-outs, women's representation in the Palestinian political system, women's subjugation to Islamic symbols (such as the veil), gendered patriarchal families, and women prisoners were also addressed at the conference. The aim was to force the national movement to take a clear position in terms of gender issues. Although the national movement condemned Islamic discourse and practice in undermining women's active participation in the struggle, the conference was also pressing for a recognition of the daily obstacles to which women at the grassroots are subjected.

The professionalization of women organizations: donor-driven agendas

A focus on women's issues in line with the phase of state building, with attention to both post-conflict and global themes, was typical of the agendas and programmes of the new women's professional organizations (Hammami and Kuttab 1998). As the national movement marginalized women's issues in the process of prioritizing national ones, several women activists (especially from the left-inclined political parties) were encouraged to withdraw from party politics and reorganize in a parallel movement within professional, specialized NGOs that had mushroomed in the early 1990s. It was a positive and active response through which they sought to regain women's voice and space – but it was also a turning point that weakened the mass-based women's struggle. The phenomenon was timely, but it amplified the structural delinking of women's issues from the national context, depoliticized the social, and at the same time decreased women's capacity to mobilize and organize other women (Kuttab 2008; Hammami and Kuttab 1999) – thereby broadening the gap between women's leadership and women at the grassroots. The issues chosen by these NGOs, and their timing, were initiated and nurtured by the donor community. Although the issues addressed a national-democratic struggle, the resulting process delinked and depoliticized these activists in national terms, and this was a strategic risk.

The outcome was to depoliticize the concept of gender, separating gender equity from the power-sharing process between state and male or female citizens (Hammami and Kuttab 1999), and from the broader pursuit of equality and social justice, concepts that had been live issues in pre-Oslo political discourse. Thus the role of the United Nations organizations like UNDP, UN Women and others, and of different UN conventions and international conferences such as Beijing 1995 – combined with the PA's absence of political will to maintain gender priorities –

was to transform local agendas. I argue that, in effect, local and global agendas were merged and mainstreamed (Kuttab 2008). A trickle-down approach from neo-liberal actors unified and generalized programmes at all levels, either through international conferences and workshops, or through their financing policies and conditions. In this way local agendas were realigned by co-opting global concerns. In a further outcome the shift in organizational tools and tactics, and the aborting of relations with the grassroots, created a new elite. For instance, and with considerable irony, addressing issues like violence against women or honour killings became problematic because they were delinked from the political and national context (Abdel Hadi 1998 ; Bisan 1991). The professionalization of women's work did not in itself transform the women's movement, but it added to a debilitating complication and fragmentation amidst the physical segregation and mobility restrictions caused by the occupation.

Where are we now? Women's unfinished liberation and state formation

The political division within the women's movement, specifically in terms of gender and governance, which has widened since the Palestinian quasi-state was formed, was an important determinant of how women's roles were shaped in contemporary political life. The Palestinian quasi-state – the PA – was formed after the 1993 Oslo Agreement on the basis of a limited control of the Palestinian land of 1967, and the return of outside leadership in exile. The governing system created a clientelist bureaucracy within which boundaries and the separation of powers were limited and vague. This allowed for a class of beneficiaries with personal interests who viewed the national project as an economic opportunity, and thereby also limited transparency and accountability (Hilal and Khan 2004). This reality further marginalized women from political power and economic resources that started to accumulate within the government. In this context, the PA centralized power in a non-representative political structure. It devised and expanded a bureaucratic system that limited women's political participation and silenced their voices – until women made the most of an opportunity to step in, create their own space, and instal mechanisms to reflect their interests (Kuttab 2008, 1993; Jad 2003). The peace process created a 'post-conflict environment', inevitably imposing a global agenda and thereby arresting and displacing the local agenda – consequently expanded the gap between the women's leadership and women at the grassroots.

The main questions that need to be raised now include: whose voice was represented in this political stage, and how was it represented? Did this stage represent a new movement that had gained legitimacy from and was accountable to women, or were there other actors outside the movement who had the capacity to voice women's welfare concerns without representing their strategic gender interests?

Mainstreaming women's rights: an easy fix?

Confronted by different political and cultural obstacles, reaching gender goals is not a simple process. While there have been some positive changes in the PA's attitude towards women's issues and women's rights, there were two reasons for this. First, pressure from the women's movements to create their own social and political space was what counted, rather than unprompted commitment by the PA to gender equality. Second, and more telling, was the demand from the international organizations and the donor community for the integration and mainstreaming of gender issues in the state-building stage. That donors imposed gender-sensitive agendas as a condition was most effective in imposing gender on the PA and ensuring its incorporation in the national agenda.

Consequently, different gender units were established within the different ministries, and the Ministry of Women's Affairs was created, in parallel with experiences in other Arab countries. Establishing these units, however, was just an easy fix to indicate commitment, though this was not serious enough to make the structural impact necessary to bridge the gender gap at the national level. Gender unit programmes were not reflected in national budgets, which revealed the marginal attention the PA actually paid to gender. Intensive efforts were initiated by UN organizations and the European community to integrate gender into planning through gender mainstreaming policies promoting issues like legal reform, action on gender-based violence, and micro-finance programmes to alleviate poverty. These programmes have been operational tools for women's organizations and different gender units for mainstreaming gender. Furthermore, new employment opportunities based on political affiliation were created for women as the public sector expanded. Other opportunities were open to highly educated women who were technically and professionally capable of becoming local experts on gender issues – while the majority of women continued to deal with everyday grievances due to the PA's weak performance with regard to expanding necessary services or work opportunities for unskilled and lower-class women (Kuttab 2006; Hammami 2001).

On the informal level, the Palestinian women's committees' insistence that women's rights and gender equality should continue to be an integral and organic component of the national agenda has not been easy to sustain through all stages of the struggle or across the different women's committees. This position was stronger among the left secular parties, which followed either Marxist-Leninist ideology or the social democratic approach, although their commitment to this was only partially successful. The importance of the link was realized after the Oslo Agreement, when women found themselves isolated and not represented in the new government. Women from the mainstream Fateh, who constituted the PA, and other activists from smaller political parties who accepted the Oslo Agreement as a base for a political solution, found jobs in the new government. These women became more involved in regular government work, and were co-opted by the different ministries and representative bodies of the political system. Some of them believed that being more involved with the government would enable them to integrate gender concerns and make the claim for women's rights within the state apparatus. The belief that instituting gender within the state's political culture (unrefined state feminism) could bring a quick fix to gender inequality has not been borne out – and will not be, as other experiences have shown. 'Femocrats' have now emerged as a class within the new political culture, and they have become more inclined to implement international and donor-driven agendas in a depoliticized manner (Jad 2010; Hammami and Kuttab 1998), without linking them to the structural context that shapes women's conditions, status and role.

In this context, the women's rights discourse, promoted by the international community, trickled down through the different United Nations agencies into local institutions. In other words this discourse was abstracted and manipulated within a political system that was under colonial occupation and had no sovereignty or control over its material and human resources – and was therefore unable to produce citizens. In the absence of 'citizen power' there was no political will to promote women's rights in a situation where patriarchy still prevails as an institution and political system (Kuttab 2008). Indeed, it is difficult to understand how women's rights *can* be promoted, in a situation where all human rights are violated under colonial occupation. Although Palestinian women may bear the brunt of the struggle, by defending and protecting their households, their rights as women cannot be realized without a legal environment that has the capacity to enforce rights and account for violations. The women's rights discourse and its practical expression within the different programmes of women's organizations is far from being concretely realized. I thus argue that the concept of women's rights should include citizenship rights for the future state, and that discussions around human rights should not be a means to distort the current reality and make people believe that women can fully enjoy human rights under colonial occupation, when the goal of a sovereign state has not been realized.

Theoretical issues in women's activism

Different theoretical issues become visible when one analyses the women's movements in the contexts of a national liberation and a need for social emancipation. Some of these issues are raised in the following discussion.

Universalism versus localism

The call of some sociologists for less universalistic claims about women's mobilization and organization in the South, and more attention to theorizing the local and particular, can be true only when accompanied by serious comparative work that discusses and focuses on specific movements rather than overall structural transformation (Ray and Korteweg 1999). This call for understanding the dilemma between 'particularism and universalism' is extremely relevant when discussing women's movements in colonial contexts, and does not delay or obstruct the opportunity for transnational feminism. On the contrary, by reflecting on the uniqueness of the movements, one can conceptualize their relevance at the international or transnational levels, and articulate local understandings of the varying contexts. This chapter responds to this call, as it reflects on the particular nature of the Palestinian women's movement while bringing out issues of wider interest and international relevance. Communicating the way local movements understand and express their experiences within their own contexts, and reflecting on the meanings and concepts of the local context, can unite different movements and/or struggles, as well as promoting a deeper understanding of resistance movements.

Local accommodation and global manipulation

Another important theme is the responsiveness and dynamism of the women's movement within a particular context. The Palestinian women's movement continuously responded to the needs and obligations of the struggle, either by introducing or adopting different structures or formations, or by developing tactics and agendas. This in itself indicates progress and maturity in the women's movement's experience and responsiveness to changes at the political and economic levels. Although this dynamism confirms the dialectical nature of the women's movement, it also indicates the different changes and setbacks of the national and political struggle. For instance, the new structures devised to create change by transforming centralized urban-based structures to decentralized outlying committees was a dynamic response to women's practical and strategic needs for outreach and mobilization. Similarly, using different tactics like political education, productive co-operatives, or nurseries to mobilize women represented a choice and application of new tools for mobilization. Yet, the disruption of this dialectic dynamism was also due to responsiveness on another front, in the unquestioning adoption of global issues on local agendas. This distorted the process of responsiveness in the Palestinian context, and worked against the advancement of the women's movement and the development of its core agenda that could have mobilized the masses. As this disruption has become structural, there is no possibility of redirecting the work unless there is a genuine commitment to grassroots engagement. Although there are a few women's committees and initiatives that have maintained a level of relevance to grassroots needs and have detached themselves from the mainstream movement, they seem to be marginal.

Homogeneity and sameness versus heterogeneity and plurality

The concepts of plurality, heterogeneity and homogeneity of the women's movements are other conceptual issues that need to be investigated, in the context of the overlap between national and social liberation struggles. There are different points of view regarding the impact of plurality on movements, as some believe that it can offer strength and continuity, while others contest this understanding. The assumption that heterogeneity and plurality necessarily enhance a coherent movement is seriously flawed, as they can also lead to the fragmentation of the women's leadership and the disempowerment of grassroots organizations.

Diversity can cause antagonism, manipulations, co-options and alienation. The potential for unity through diversity is often undermined by the ever-present asymmetries of power and agency (Moser 2004). Although women from differing socio-economic backgrounds can coexist in a women's movement, the issue of power imbalances and agency, which are integral to class relations, are not overcome by simply labelling class differences as 'heterogeneity' (*ibid.*). According to Moser (2004) social movements, in general, are passing through difficult times as they are facing different challenges that require a platform for action to bring social change amidst inequality and social injustice. The same challenge confronts the Palestinian women's movement, which requires further conceptualization and contextualization in order to understand the real conditions that put the sustainability of the movement at risk if it does not address social injustice within the society. Although plurality reflects a level of democratic space and representation of different points of view, it can develop into internal conflict that threatens the strength of the movement and causes a loss of its vitality, especially in a context of political fragmentation and national oppression. Moreover, the claim to unity and homogeneity within national liberation struggles is sometimes shallow and idealistic, in a way that masks the different levels of conflict a women's movement may experience. Power relations among women's organizations, and class and ideological differences, can surface and fragment social movements. Here one needs to consider not only the way the women's leadership may impose a particular feminist approach, but also how this influences grassroots women, their discourses, resource mobilization, organization, programmes and activities.

Inside versus outside leadership: new political culture

A mixed political culture resulted from the merging of opposing or dissonant political cultures – the 'inside leadership' in the OPT, that maintained its militancy against the occupation and formed the informal national leadership, and the 'outside leadership' which was established in exile and became the new

PA post–Oslo. This mixed culture in turn affected the level of collective solidarity among the women's leadership, as power relations changed, and weakened the value of resistance, limiting women's capacity to contribute to nation building and political transformation.

The local Palestinian community, particularly the activists from the historical revolutionary cadres, were exposed to a new culture of bureaucratic governance that estranged and interrupted their culture of resistance and confused women's capacity to view the new context critically. Women had played an active role in the struggle and their work with the grassroots had been effective in mobilizing and organizing women to campaign on different national and social issues (Hiltermann 1991; Taraki 1991), ensuring the sustainability and continuity of the struggle. The new culture of governance of the 'outside' leadership undermined resistance as an everyday way of life, and expanded the public sector to become the service provider and the large employer of the young fighters. This has resulted in the political co-option of these activists and their adoption of new consumption patterns and lifestyles, causing a shift in attitudes in regard to the value of steadfastness and resistance. A new type of leadership that was accountable to the donor community was created, adopting neo-liberal policies and weakening self-reliance, public legitimacy and accountability.

This process created new social groups, namely technocrats and bureaucrats, who became more powerful than the earlier activists, whose legitimacy and accountability were derived from the masses. This period marked a critical transition in the political process, as the PA was transformed into a technical and professional administration rather than a representative body accountable to people and their aspirations for independence (Jamal 2001). At the same time, it broadened the gap between the political leadership and the constituency. One consequence was the creation of an unvoiced class conflict that was also profoundly gendered and liable to play a deeply fragmenting role in the future – if undemocratic and unrepresentative governance continues, and social injustice becomes more entrenched. Women's voice had been shattered and transformed, from being a powerful collective voice that represented women's interests, to individual voices of professionals who represented global agendas and narrow professional and bureaucratic interests, promoting the benefits of the few.

Shifting contexts: professionalization and institutionalization of women's activism

The Palestinian women's movement, one of the most organized and dynamic of the social movements, reorganized and shifted its discourse to adapt to the new reality and engage in lobbying for a greater involvement and representation of women in decision making after the peace accord (Jamal 2001). Consequently, when the PA came to power, different technical committees were formed to prepare the ground for establishing the PA's political infrastructure. Women activists (both independents and Fateh cadres) who were outside the state-building process initiated their own technical committee to position themselves on the new political map and take their rightful space.

The Women's Technical Committee was established in 1993 as a quasi-governmental structure to address women's issues. It managed to get some external grants to help create its own mandate and programme. Although it was a brave move by women to announce their existence within the new reality, it raised a controversy with the opposition parties who were against the peace process and the formation of technical committees, which were considered to be a creation of the Oslo Agreement. This initiated a debate on the concept of 'state feminism', and the value of autonomy in the women's movement, which resulted in the formation two years later of an independent umbrella organization – the Women's Affairs Technical Committee (WATC), to integrate all the different women's committees, including the opposition parties and professional institutions, to advocate collectively for women's rights and gender equality in the Palestinian context.

It was at this juncture that some of us from the Institute of Women Studies at Birzeit University exposed the shortcomings of state feminism in a conference held in Ramallah in 1994 and critiqued the women's agenda, which was overloaded with depoliticized women issues. We set out to build an agenda that addresses national issues in a gender perspective, and to represent the concerns of all women rather than only those that stand out for the elite (Hammami and Kuttab 1998).

Representation versus exclusion

While the WATC co-ordinated women's programmes and activities to empower women at the grassroots, the General Union of Palestinian Women (GUPW), being the historic women's representative body, has transformed itself to adapt to the new political phase. It was started by Palestinian women in the diaspora and later opened a branch in the Occupied Territories with a structure adapted to the security conditions of the Israeli occupation, which had banned it. GUPW in the West Bank worked through charitable women's organizations, which at different stages of the struggle had been harassed or shut down by the Israeli forces, which placed some women leaders under house arrest (Jad 2010). Post-Oslo, GUPW, which represented different political parties and women's charitable organizations, has been revived by women leaders from the diaspora who returned and tried to direct the union to work within the parameters of the Oslo Agreement, and under their control. This created a conflict with the local 'inside' leadership, mainly the women's committees. One major conflict was the issue of GUPW's autonomy. Although it was formally announced as independent of the PA, real practice suggested otherwise: its staff were paid by the PA, and their agenda was controlled by it. This broadened the conflict between women's committees and the GUPW, who saw themselves as an extension of the PA to ensure their power and political affiliation (Jad 2010; Kuttab 1999). This deepened the fragmentation of the women's movement and caused further deterioration in its effectiveness.

Unique experience and diverse voice

The Palestinian women's movement has emerged through a unique experience in confronting a settler-colonial occupation, and its different voices have been heard even at the national level. How this heterogeneity of the unique Palestinian movement was voiced politically, and reflected gender concerns, is a complicated topic because women have been mobilized at different levels: as an occupied population and women oppressed by colonialism and patriarchy; as 'citizens', albeit with no rights; and as workers, peasants, mothers and wives, discriminated against by ascribed gender roles. Hence gender identity integrates the national, social and class identities reflecting the different feminisms, voices and streams of thought that make this a heterogeneous women's movement. For instance, the GUPW, as a political body representative of all women living in the OPT, has been a platform for women in the political parties that represent the Palestinian Liberation Organization (PLO), the sole representative of the Palestinian people, excluding Hamas. This structure, only elected once since 1967, represents Fateh, the ruling class, and the different democratic secular political forces. While some of them have maintained their Marxist-Leninist ideology, others adopted more social democratic or liberal approaches, reflecting the pluralistic nature of the left.

How the GUPW voiced women's concerns was problematic, as they did not have the same authority on women's issues, nor were they agreed on women's priorities. The question of whose voice was being represented within this body was of concern, when observing relations of voice and power as well as how the women's agenda reveals the different schools of thought – including neo-liberal, radical and Islamic. Even when secular women elected the Islamic movement to power to condemn the ruling party, others saw them as rescuers and protectors of national issues, particularly due to their militancy and their critical voice on corruption and alienation. Others criticized the opportunistic nature of the Islamic movement, using religion for political goals.

The nature of the women's agenda was also a subject for

disagreement. It represented a post-conflict agenda for some whereas it was still a conflict agenda for others, reflecting different voices and concerns. In the post-conflict agenda, gender issues were reflected in a narrow framework representing the interests of the elite within a neo-liberal rationale. The conflict agenda represented the voices and issues of the radicals and the poor which, although more relevant and legitimate, could not be as effectively pursued within the constraints of their limited resources.

The diversity of women's voice has been produced and reproduced at different stages reflecting the priorities of the political stage and the nature of the ideological and practical commitment the women's committees had towards class- and gender-specific concerns. This diversity cannot produce unity within the women's movement. But, as with other social movements, it stands on common ground in relation to a range of national and gender issues, each of which must be addressed at a strategic time. We also had different political positions and voices in regard to such matters as the peace process, future political solutions, future visions of the state, or the tools and dynamics of resistance. For instance, the issue of armed struggle as one of the legitimate tools for resistance has also been a dividing factor in the new political context and in view of the PA approach to political resolution.

In a seminar organized by the Institute of Women Studies at Birzeit University on 20 March 1995, four major women's committees representing the PLO reflected their views on critical political and gender issues, after the peace agreement was signed. Issues addressed included the institutionalization and professionalization of women's activism; the relationship of feminism and nationalism; attitudes and positions towards the PA and the peace agreement; their view of the post-Oslo stage, and their position on resistance and its role within the national movement. The positions of the committees varied and reflected their different political views. For instance, regarding the relation between nationalism and feminism, the secular opposition parties Popular Front for Liberation of Palestine (PFLP) and the

Democratic Front for Liberation of Palestine (DFLP) – Marxist-Leninist parties who opposed the Oslo Agreement – insisted that the peace agreement did not solve the conflict situation, and that the national liberation struggle should continue, especially since core issues remained such as self-determination, right of return of refugees, and the achievement of a sovereign independent state. The other women's streams of Fateh and Fida (originally a leftist party which split from DFLP) and the People's Party (the erstwhile Communist Party) accepted that the Oslo Agreement was critical but were more pragmatic, claiming that they had entered a state-building stage requiring integration to maintain effectiveness and influence for the sake of women's interests in the future state.

With regard to women's representation in political parties or the PA, the women's committees explicitly exposed the patriarchal nature of the PLO and PA, which continuously undermined women and excluded them from the decision-making process. This became a priority issue and a future task for all, hence imposing on the opposition a kind of engagement with the new reality to assure movement towards gender equality. Some saw it as entering a reconciliation stage, arguing that the Oslo Agreement should not be a dividing factor but could be viewed as an opportunity for political empowerment and more coordination. Although this argument is legitimate, it was clear that their pragmatic position delinked and depoliticized women's issues, especially since the PA emphasized state building or developing its political and legal infrastructure, rather than nation building or the empowerment of people through participation and resistance.

It has become clear, however, that women's opposition has been unable to achieve much progress in advocating women's issues, including representation and resistance. Neither opposition nor mainstream campaigners were able to promote gender issues forcefully or effectively within the Palestinian national agenda.

In relation to the issue of institutionalization and professionalization of women's activism, the women's committees also held divergent positions. Women in the opposition insisted that the post-Oslo stage is still a national liberation stage – and hence the work at the decentralized grassroots, sustaining resistance and maintaining relevance and responsiveness to the masses, is still legitimate. Other committees felt that the institutionalization of the PA could be countered by a parallel institutionalization of women's activism, which could develop women's issues further through a more technical and specialized approach. This would enable women to present their issues effectively within the international arena and achieve autonomy from the parties to create and expand a more tranformative space. The trend of institutionalization that the women's movement underwent – registering as societies based on the PA's requirement; limiting their work to the PA's agenda (dictated by major donors like the World Bank and the UN) – alienated women activists, depoliticized their issues, and disrupted the development of grassroots democratic work (Hammami and Kuttab 1999; Jamal 2001).

Finally, the issue of defining the post-Oslo stage was discussed in the light of the different positions of the mainstream and opposition parties. The mainstream identified it as a state-building stage, adopting a new agenda and programme relevant to the political phase. For the opposition it remained a national liberation phase, requiring strategies of resistance – although the hegemony of the global agenda limits the ability of the opposition to reflect their position.

This diversity of the women's movement did not prevent activists from coordinating or unifying their positions on some critical national and gender issues, exemplified in the formation of the Higher Council of Palestinian Women – a coordinating body of the different women's committees formed in 1988 during the *Intifada* to ensure collective planning and coordination of activities. Yet, although there was unity on the ground, diversity and internal disharmony with regard to the inclusion of independent women (not party-affiliated) within the decision-making structure created difference. However, coordination across the different women's committees had always been strong and continuous compared to other social movements, reflecting the urgent needs of the struggle and women's commitment to bring change.

Conclusions

In contextualizing the tension between the radical grassroots movement and the new more liberal movement, it is necessary to focus on internal and external factors, and on the forces that manipulated the cultural and political heritage of women's organizations.

First, one must consider the issue of 'associational linkages' (Molyneux 2001) or relationships between the women's movement and the national movement within a colonial context. Palestinian women face three levels of oppression and subjugation:

- the *national level* – due to the colonial occupation that structurally transformed state structural violence to other forms of public and domestic violence within the society.
- the *social level* – representing the patriarchal system and institutions which manifested in different forms within the hierarchical, patriarchal Palestinian family and society, including the informal and formal political system, the political parties, and the PA.
- the *class level* – affecting both genders due to the exploitative colonial economy and neo-liberal economic practice. However, from a gender perspective, class oppression can be seen through limited resources and economic opportunities, and the exploitation of women within the market economy.

Thus a gender perspective that combines all levels of oppression – including national oppression, political marginalization and social and economic exclusion caused by the Israeli policies and the PA's development paradigm – is needed to expose all levels of gender discrimination, particularly for poor women. It is important to emphasize here that the notion of gender has been actively deployed in anti-colonial struggles, as shown by different experiences, such as in Algeria, when women's interests were left to become separate and subsidiary to national interests, and were subsequently excluded from the benefits of independence (Gallagher 2002).

Another level of complexity expressed in the women's movement was the rise of religious nationalism, or the Islamic movement (Hamas) in 1987, which represented a liberation movement and a populist reaction to neo-liberal policies and what was perceived as Western domination. The PA's weak political and administrative performance (one reason why it was defeated in the 2006 Legislative Council election) has promoted Hamas's success, indicating the failure of the nationalist project (including the left parties) which could not cater for the poor and lower-middle classes, whose support later fuelled the fundamentalist movements. How the rise of religious fundamentalism and the gradual growth of Islamic feminism will affect the women's movement further is still to be seen. Yet some argue that, when compared to other Arab countries such as Egypt for example (Ray 1999; Badran 1994), the rise of Islamism in Palestine has generated a new brand of pragmatic gender activism practised by both secular and Islamist feminists, which advocates for a public role for women (Ray 1999).

In Palestine, there are calls from some feminists who argue that there is a common thread between secular feminism and Islamic feminism that should be explored and used as a stepping stone for collective mobilization and the realization of women's rights. Hamas, which is undergoing changes to accommodate itself within the global parameters, has also claimed that Islamists should change, anticipate Islamic reform, and take the lead in promoting women's rights which they see as competitive with other more secular parties. In addition, they have taken a stand regarding liberation of women by women, which enhances the role of women in public life. Like the leftist secular parties, the Islamists have questioned the legitimacy of the women's rights discourse that in their view is individualistic and Western, and does not reflect the national context (Jad 2005). Hence, in the absence of a coherent and clear gender discourse of the secular parties, or a clear agenda by the women's movement, the Islamists, with their discipline and commitment, will be able to subvert the 'complementarity' attributed to women in Islam and portray it as total equality (Jad 2005).

At the same time, there are other voices which have not yet articulated their argument, but view the scenario of coordinating and emphasizing commonalities as risky, and perhaps an incompatible and conflict-prone alliance for feminism in general, and the Palestinian women's movement in particular. Although there are similar and common *national* anxieties and concerns over which secular groups and Islamists can work together, there is still a threshold regarding the *social* issues that secular groups would like to cross in order to explore these issues further.

Considering the current political and economic conditions of the region and the country in general, as well as the weakness of the secular left parties, it could be argued that such an approach may not be appropriate. It could dissolve the identity of secular feminism and put it at high risk, especially as it is more closely correlated with Western feminism and non-traditional, cosmopolitan culture. In an effort to endorse a Palestinian legislation that guarantees equality and human rights, the experience of the Model Parliament (which was launched by the Women's Center for Legal Aid and Counselling in 1988) shows that the stage was not ready for negotiating power between secular activists and Islamists. The Islamists attacked the project as they saw it as donor-driven and set against Shari'a law for Muslims. They also saw women as intruders who had no legitimacy to talk about issues on which the clergy has the sole agency to rule (Jad 2010; Hammami and Johnson 1999). The secular groups were alienated within the process and were bitter, disappointed and distrustful as the objective had changed from legislative reform to freedom of expression (Jad 2010). This experience made some secular groups believe that there could be no way of negotiating power between them and the Islamists, or having a functional relationship. However, this remains to be tested within the current conditions flowing from the Arab Spring.

How one views the future of Palestine and what it means to be committed to a democratic secular state where people coexist under a framework that offers equal representation based on equal citizenship, and not on sect or religion, is still a strategic choice that we as women have to make and for which we continue to struggle. Any kind of fundamentalism can be a threat and an obstacle towards realizing such a vision. At the same time, secular feminism is not homogeneous. There is a more radical stream of secularists who believe that a common ground between Islamism and secularism is not possible as the issue is not only national liberation, which has united classes and genders together, but also the social, class and future vision of the state and society. Other secularists still see the social vision as part of the national identity that needs to be realized.

It may also be possible to combine national and social struggles by integrating women's interests as part of the national struggle (counter to the Islamist view) in order to ensure women's rights after independence. All these issues should be taken into consideration when the women's movement and women's voice are discussed in undertaking future reorganization and mobilization.

Palestine is facing an acute and risky transition, with the new politics of recognition of the Palestinian state as a member in the United Nations, and with the escalating violence of the colonial occupation in response to that. The national movement, including the women's movement, has to regain its power of organization and mobilization to face the future threats that the new political era will generate. This could be another opportunity for the women's movement to reorganize and re-mobilize its forces.

Acknowledgements

I am grateful to Professor Rema Hammami and also to participants at the 2009 Bellagio conference on feminist voice for comments on the draft.

Notes

1 The peace talks between PLO members and Israeli officials began in Oslo in 1993, when the path of bilateral negotiations to bring about a permanent solution to the Palestinian-Israeli conflict was outlined.
2 A study conducted by the Institute of Women Studies at Birzeit University for the World Bank has investigated the impact of restrictions of mobility caused by the Israeli occupation policies on gender relations and violence, and exposed the gendered impact of political violence on gender roles and women's conditions, particularly increasing women's social isolation and vulnerability in terms of early marriage, school drop-outs, and education in general.
3 The uprising (*Intifada*) erupted on 9 December 1987 in Gaza, when four Palestinians were killed as an Israeli truck collided with two vans carrying Palestinian workers; clashes ensued which spread rapidly to the rest of the OPT.

References

Abdel Hadi, R. (1998) 'The Palestinian Women's Autonomous Movement: Emergence, Dynamics, and Challenges', *Gender and Society*, Vol. 12, No. 6 (Special Issue: Gender and Social Movements, Part 1), pp. 649–73.

Alvarez, S., E. Dagnino and A. Escobar (eds) (1988) *Culture of Politics, Politics of Cultures: Re-visioning Latin American Social Movements*, Westview Press, Boulder, CO.

Badran, M. (1994) 'Gender Activism: Feminists and Islamists in Egypt', in V. Moghadam (ed.), *Identity Politics and Women*, Westview Press, Boulder, CO.

Basu, A. (1995) 'Introduction', in A. Basu (ed.), *The Challenge of Local Feminisms: Women's Movements in Global Perspective*, Westview Press, Boulder, CO.

—— (ed.) (2010) *Women's Movement in the Global Era: The Power of Local Feminism*, Westview Press, Boulder, CO.

Bisan (1991) *Some Social Issues in Social Liberation Struggle*, Bisan Center for Research and Development, Ramallah, West Bank.

Davis, Y. (1997) *Gender and Nation*, Sage Publications, London.

Fleischmann, E. (2003) *The Nation and Its New Women: The Palestinian Women's Movement 1920–1948*, University of California Press, Berkeley, CA.

Gallagher, N. (2002) 'Learning Lessons from the Algerian War of Independence', *Middle East Report*, No. 225, pp. 44–9.

Hammami, R. (1990) 'Women the Hijab and the Intifada', *Middle East Report*, Nos. 164/165, May–August.

——— (2001) 'An Uprising at the Crossroads', *Middle East Report*, No. 219, Summer (with Jamil Hilal).

Hammami, R. and P. Johnson (1999) 'Equality with a Difference: Gender and Citizenship in Transitional Palestine', *Social Politics: International Studies in Gender, State and Society*, No. 6, pp. 314–43.

Hammami, R. and E. Kuttab (1998) 'Towards New Strategies for the Women's Movement Democratic Transformation and Independence', in *After the Crisis: The Structural Changes in the Palestinian Political Life*, Muwaten (The Palestinian Institute for Democracy) (in Arabic), Ramallah.

——— (1999) 'The Palestinian Women's Movement: Strategies towards Freedom and Democracy', *News from Within*, Vol. 15, No. 4.

Hilal, J. and M. H. Khan (2004) 'State Formation under the PNA: Potential Outcomes and Their Viability' in M. H. Khan (ed.), *State Formation in Palestine*, Routledge Curzon, London.

Hiltermann, J. (1991) 'The Women's Movement during the Uprising', *Journal of Palestine Studies*, Vol. 20, No. 3, pp. 48–57.

Jad, I. (2000) *Women and Politics: Palestinian Women in Current Situation*, Institute of Women Studies, Birzeit University.

——— (2003) 'The NGO-ization of Arab Women's Movements', *Al-Raida*, Vol 20, No. 100.

——— (2005) 'Islamist Women of Hamas: A New Women's Movement?' in F. Nouraie-Simone (ed.), *On Shifting Ground: Muslim Women in a Global Era*, Feminist Press, New York, NY.

——— (2010) 'The Demobilization of the Palestinian Women's Movement', in A. Basu (ed.), *Women's Movement in the Global Era: The Power of Local Feminism*, Westview Press, Boulder, CO.

Jamal, A. (2001) 'Engendering State Building: The Women's Movement and Gender-Regime in Palestine', *Middle East Journal*, Vol. 55, No. 2, pp. 256–76.

Jayawardena, K. (1986) *Feminism and Nationalism in the Third World*, Zed Books, London.

Johnson, P. and E. Kuttab (2001) 'Where Have All the Women (and Men) Gone? Reflections on Gender and the Second Palestinian *Intifada*', *Feminist Review*, No. 69, pp. 21–43.

Kuttab, E. (1988) 'Community Development under Occupation: An Alternative Strategy', *Journal of Refugee Studies*, Vol. 2, No. 1.

——— (1990) 'Women's Participation in the Intifada: The Inevitable Element of National Liberation Struggle', in *Intifada : A Popular Initiative*, Jerusalem.

—— (1993) 'Palestinian Women in the *Intifada*: Liberation within Liberation', *Arab Studies Quarterly*, Vol. 15, No. 2.

—— (1996) 'Women's Movement in Palestine', *Arab Women Facing New Era*, Arab Women Publishing House (NOUR).

—— (1999) 'Feminism and Nationalism: The Palestinian Case', in *The Palestinian Women's Movement: Problems of Democratic Transformation and Future Strategies*, Muwaten (The Palestinian Institute for Democracy), Ramallah.

—— (2006) 'New Challenges for the Palestinian Women's Movement', in *This Week in Palestine*, No. 95.

—— (2008) 'Palestinian Women's Organizations: Global Cooption and Local Contradiction', *Cultural Dynamics*, Vol. 20, No. 2, pp. 99–117.

Malley R. (1996) *The Call from Algeria: Third World Revolution and the Turn to Islam*, University of California Press, Berkeley, CA.

Mohanty, C. T. (1991) 'Under Western Eyes: Feminist Scholarship and Colonial Discourses', in C. T. Mohanty, A. Russo and L. Torres (eds), *Third World Women and the Politics of Feminism*, Indianapolis University Press, Bloomington, IN.

Molyneux, M. (2001) 'Women's Movements in International Perspective: Latin America and Beyond', Institute of Latin American Studies, University of London.

Moser, C. (2004) 'Happy Heterogeneity? Feminism, Development and Grassroots Women's Movements in Peru', *Feminist Studies,* Vol. 31, No. 1, p. 211.

Ray, R. (1999) *Fields of Protest: Women's Movements in India*, University of Minnesota Press, Minneapolis, MN.

Ray, R. and A. C. Korteweg (1999) 'Women's Movements in the Third World: Identity, Mobilization, and Autonomy', *Annual Review of Sociology*, Vol. 25, pp. 47–71.

Sayigh, R. (1988) *Palestinian Peasants to Revolutionaries: A People's History Recorded by Rosemary Sayigh from Interviews with Camp Palestinians in Lebanon*, Zed Books, London.

Taraki, L. (1991) 'The Development of Political Consciousness among Palestinians in the Occupied Territories, 1967–1987', in J. Nassar and R. Heacock (eds), *Intifada: Palestine at the Crossroads*, Praeger Publishers, New York, NY.

World Bank (2010) 'Checkpoints and Barriers: Searching for Livelihoods in the West Bank and Gaza, Gender Dimensions of Economic Collapse', Report No. 49699-GZ, World Bank, Washington DC.

About the Contributors

• •

Ana Alice Alcantara Costa is coordinator of the masters and PhD programmes on interdisciplinary studies on women, gender and feminism at the Nucleus of Interdisciplinary Studies on Women (NEIM) at the Federal University of Bahia, where she teaches on gender and power and on gender and history. She was one of the founders of NEIM, acting as its director from 1999 to 2004. Costa has worked in the area of gender and public policies in Brazil, both as practitioner and researcher, for over twenty years, publishing several articles and books on feminist studies in Brazil and abroad. She has been active in the Brazilian and Mexican feminist movements since the late 1970s and a member of the UFBA's faculty of philosophy and human sciences since 1982.

Gertrude Fester is professor of transitional justice and gender equality at the Center for Gender, Culture and Development at the Institute of Education, University of Kigali. Her research and activism explore the root causes of violence against women and citizenship for vulnerable groups, focusing on the influences of culture and religion, and she is currently working on a manuscript featuring young Rwandans' writings on transitional justice and mainstreaming gender. In 2001 she was the Wynona Lipman chair for women political leaders at the Centre for American Women and Politics, Rutgers University, and distinguished visiting professor at the African and Afro-American Studies

Department at Washington University in St Louis. Gertrude was a member of South Africa's ANC-led parliament until 1999 and a commissioner on gender equality for five years. She has published both fiction and non-fiction, focusing mostly on women's lives, and has performed her play, *The Spirit Shall Not Be Caged*, in various countries. Fester received the Hammet–Hellman Human Rights Prize for Writers in 1997.

Eileen Kuttab is a tenured assistant professor in sociology at the Institute of Women Studies in Birzeit University. A founding member and director of the institute from 1998 until 2008, she is also a founding member (since 2006) of the Arab Council for Social Sciences, based in Beirut, and a core member of the Arab Families Working Group, a collaborative group of researchers working on Arab families in the region. She has been involved with grassroots women organizations, and served on boards of trustees of human rights and development research centres. Eileen was the first elected woman in Palestine to head the Teachers and Employees Union at Birzeit University (from 2011 to 2013). Her main publications focus on feminism and nationalism, social movements (particularly women's movements), gender and development, youth and political participation. Currently, she is working on youth groups in the Arab uprisings.

Rabéa Naciri has taught at the University of Rabat in Morocco for nearly twenty-two years. She is the executive director of DEMOS Consulting, a research working group and think tank on gender and democratic development. A life-long activist, she has founded and worked in prominent domestic, regional and international women's rights and human rights organizations. She actively participated in the major coalitions and movements leading to reform of the Moroccan personal status code, and resulting in the Family Code (2004). She has served as president of Association Démocratique des Femmes du Maroc and chaired the Collectif 95 Maghreb Egalité for ten years, and she continues to be actively involved with both organizations. Naciri has conducted extensive research on women's rights, including studies on CEDAW, democratic development in Morocco, the women's movement in Morocco and the Maghreb, and questions of gender-based violence.

Alexandra Pittman runs a consulting business specializing in monitoring and evaluation and research on women's rights and movements. She has worked with a diverse set of donors and international non-profit organizations since 2005, including Women's Learning Partnership, Association for Women's Rights in Development (AWID), FRIDA – The Young Feminist Fund, Mama Cash, Open Society Foundations (NYC Office and Armenia Foundation), Oxfam International, Oxfam Great Britain and UN Women. She also held a senior research fellowship at the Hauser Center for Nonprofits at Harvard University in 2010–11, working on the role of brand in international non-profit and philanthropical organizations. Pittman's publications span professional and policy spheres, and she is the creator of the AWID's M&E Wiki.

Cecilia M. B. Sardenberg is a Brazilian feminist activist and since 1982 has been a member of the faculty of philosophy and human sciences of the Federal University of Bahia (UFBA). She was one of the founders of UFBA's Nucleus of Interdisciplinary Studies on Women (NEIM), where she teaches feminist theory and where she helped create the masters and PhD programmes on interdisciplinary studies on women, gender and feminism. She has worked in the area of gender and development in Brazil, both as a practitioner and researcher, and has published several articles in Brazil and abroad on feminist and gender studies. She is the convener of the Latin American Hub in the Pathways of Women's Empowerment Research Program Consortium, and national coordinator for OBSERVE – the Observatory for the Application of Maria da Penha Law, the new domestic violence legislation in Brazil.

Mariz Tadros is a research fellow at the Institute of Development Studies. She was formerly a professor of political science at the American University in Cairo and worked for almost ten years as a journalist for the *Al-Ahram Weekly* newspaper. Her most recent publications are *Copts at the Crossroads: The Struggle for Inclusive Democracy in Egypt* (2013) and *The Muslim Brotherhood in Contemporary Egypt: Democracy Redefined or Confined?* (2012). She works on democratization in the Middle East, religion and development, the politics of gender and development, and Islamist political movements in the Middle East. Her work has featured in the *Guardian*, openDemocracy and *Middle East Report*.

Afiya Shehrbano Zia is an independent feminist scholar, researcher and activist, based in Karachi. She is the author of *Sex Crime in the Islamic Context* and *Watching Them Watching Us* and is currently working on a new book, *Faith and Feminism in Pakistan*. She has also edited a series of books on women's issues and has authored several essays published in *Feminist Review*, *Journal of International Women's Studies*, *Economic and Political Weekly*, *Global Social Policy*, openDemocracy, and the University of Cambridge's Occasional Paper Series. Zia is an active member of Women's Action Forum in Pakistan and an advisory board member of the Centre for Secular Space in the UK.

Index